Cybercrime

Cybercrime

The Transformation of Crime in the Information Age

David S. Wall

polity

First published in 2007 by Polity Press

Polity Press
65 Bridge Street
Cambridge CB2 1UR, UK

Polity Press
350 Main Street
Malden, MA 02148, USA

ISBN-10: 0-7456-2735-8
ISBN-13: 978-0-7456-2735-9
ISBN-10: 0-7456-2736-6 (pb)
ISBN-13: 978-0-7456-2736-6 (pb)

A catalogue record for this book is available from the British Library.

Typeset in 10.5 on 12 pt Plantin
by Servis Filmsetting Ltd, Manchester
Printed and bound in India by Replika Press Pvt Ltd

For further information on Polity, visit our website: www.polity.co.uk

Contents

Figures and Tables

Figures

Tables

Preface and Acknowledgements

When I was young, there was a programme on British TV called *Tomorrow's World* which presented new technologies and inventions. It symbolized the 'White Heat of Technology' of the 1960s and made the viewer privy to an exciting world of whirring and clicking computers administered by people in white coats. This was a world of hovercrafts, jet packs, cures for this, that and the other – James Bond stuff for real. The show was inherently optimistic in tone and promoted technologies either as benign or in terms of the ways they could advance the human cause. Unfortunately, the youthful optimism it bred in me was later shattered by my academic study which made me realize that the chilling reality of the real *Tomorrow's World* was quite different because the technologies are by no means benign. Yes, they may do good, interesting and useful things and I still retain some optimism to this effect, but they can also put people out of work, victimize individuals, and potentially threaten our liberties. Moreover, technologies are now becoming more pervasive, especially when they converge, and they are beginning to frame our lives in ways that are both good and bad. It is therefore from this perspective of critical optimism that I approach the subject of this book.

With the benefit of 20:20 hindsight, this was not an easy book to write because the subject matter changed so rapidly. Indeed, it was the very nature of this change that subsequently became an important part of the narrative. Because of this, the book possibly tries to achieve too much. Furthermore, it is also a snapshot of the state of play in 2006, so by the time of its publication in 2007, new events may have either confirmed the predictions or even superseded them. Such is the risk in writing about the internet. Then why bother? The answer is simple; the account within this book is a thematic history of cybercrime's present. Epistemologically, without an historical awareness of the behaviour we call cybercrime how can we understand what it is and in what direction it is developing?

This book is intended for upper-level undergraduates and graduates. It contains a monograph style narrative that can be read in its entirety, but also contains much specific information that can be accessed via the index to search out particular issues, or through the list of cases and references to follow up any reference streams.

It will be apparent from my institutional affiliation that I live and work in the UK. However, where possible, I have sought to provide cross-jurisdictional information and examples. Since one of the book's central arguments is that the internet is a global information and networked medium, it is no surprise that the broader findings show thematic similarities across jurisdictions.

In writing this book there are many people I need to thank. Some have been directly involved, others indirectly. So, the first group to thank are the funders. The School of Law at the University of Leeds gave me research leave during which I brought together many of the ideas that had been informed by prior research projects funded by the bodies I list in the introduction. An AHRC award then provided additional funding to extend my period of research (Award APN18143).

I must then thank my immediate colleagues at the University of Leeds, especially Yaman Akdeniz, Adam Crawford, Paul Taylor, Clive Walker, but also Anthea Hucklesby, Sam Lewis, Stuart Lister, Norma Martin Clement, Emma Wincup and the others in the School of Law and Centre for Criminal Justice Studies. In the broader academy I have to thank for their friendship, help, or just inspiration (in alphabetical order): Richard Ericson, Peter Grabosky, Kevin Haggerty, Yvonne Jukes, Tony Krone, Mike Levi, David Lyon, Peter Manning, Sam McQuade III, Soumyo Moitra, Hedi Nasheri, April Pattavina, Ken Pease, Ernesto Savonna, Jackie Schneider, Clifford Shearing (Clifford and Jennifer Wood gave particularly insightful comments on an earlier draft of chapter 8), Russell Smith, Mike Sutton, Matt Williams, Maggi Wykes, Majid Yar. And, of course there are the providers of information about events that is so important to the narrative, such as the staff at *The Register* and *Wired*, and the various columnists at the *BBC News Online* site.

Moving on to others, I am indebted to Emma Longstaff, commissioning editor at Polity for her forbearance and very useful editorial input; Ann Bone (desk editor) and Anne Dunbar-Nobes (copy editor); plus, of course, the anonymous reviewers whose comments were invaluable.

Finally, I thank Helen, Harrison, Sophie and James for their support and for being there for me. Sophie (aka Bubble-Pop Electric) and Harri enlightened me as to how central the internet is to the world of teenagers. Unfortunately, in so doing, they also showed me just how hard it is to remove malicious software in the form of trojans, viruses and worms from their computer – kids eh!

But, contrary to tradition, I do not dedicate this book to them, or to my colleagues, funders, friends, helpers or inspiration. Instead, I would like to dedicate this book to the 7.06 am and 6.55 pm trains between York and Leeds which gave me that much needed hour or so of solitude each day to have a cup of coffee and ponder on the text.

David S. Wall

Acronyms

APACS	Association for Payment Clearing Services
APWG	Anti-Phishing Working Group (UK)
BBS	bulletin board services
BCS	British Crime Survey
BPI	British Phonographic Industry
CAUCE	Coalition Against Unsolicited Commercial Email
CERT	Computer Emergency Response Team
CNSA	Contact Network of Spam Authorities
CPS	Crown Prosecution Service (UK)
CSI	Computer Studies Institute
CVC	card validation code
DCC	Distributed Checksum Clearinghouse
DDOS	distributed denial of service
DHS	Department of Homeland Security (US)
DNS	domain name servers
DTI	Department of Trade and Industry (UK)
ENISA	European Network and Information Security Agency
FBI	Federal Bureau of Investigation
FTC	Federal Trade Commission (US)
GATS	General Agreement on Trade in Services
GUI	graphics user interface
HTCC	High-Tech Crime Consortium
ICANN	Internet Corporation for Assigned Names and Numbers
IP	internet protocol
IPR	intellectual property rights
IPTS	Institute for Prospective Technological Studies
IRC	internet relay chat
ISIPP	Institute for Spam and Internet Public Policy (UK)

ISP	internet service provider
IWF	Internet Watch Foundation
LAN	local area network
MPAA	Motion Picture Association of America
NCIS	National Criminal Intelligence Service (UK)
NFIC	National Fraud Information Center
NHTCU	National Hi-Tech Crime Unit
NIM	National Intelligence Model (UK)
NIPC	National Infrastructure Protection Center (US)
NISCC	National Infrastructure Security Co-ordination Centre
OCJS	Offending, Crime and Justice Survey
P2P	peer-to-peer
PDA	personal digital assistant
PITO	Police Information Technology Organization (UK)
POLCYB	Society for the Policing of Cyberspace
RAT	remote administration trojans
RIAA	Recording Industry Association of America
SDR	software defined radio
SOCA	Serious Organized Crime Agency (UK)
TCP	transmission control protocol
TIA	terrorism information awareness
VoIP	voice over internet protocol
WTO	World Trade Organization

1

Introduction

How easy it is to jump to conclusions. A young woman sits alone with
her laptop in the corner of her favourite internet café. She has just
pressed the send button and is looking over her shoulder. But why?
Who is she, what is she doing, what has she done? She looks vulnerable, nervous, possibly a little worried. Perhaps she has just become
the victim of a cyber-stalker, or is she replying to a blackmailer?
Perhaps, she has unwittingly just given her personal information to an
identity thief? On the other hand, she could be a major fraudster, a
cyber-terrorist, a notorious hacker or a mass spammer. With that one
click she may have just caused a cybercrime wave that will simultaneously victimize tens of thousands of people all over the planet and
cause untold misery.

   Actually, it is not clear at all who she is or what she is doing because
the internet distorts conventional reference points and forces us to

challenge our previously held assumptions, particularly about crime
and the internet. This book is an exploration of a new era of criminal
activity – cybercrime – so-called because it is being rapidly transformed by networked technologies that expand the reach of individuals who have access to networked computers. This technological
transformation of crime is an ongoing process – indeed, while this
book was being written a step-change occurred that takes us towards
an entirely new generation of automated cybercrime, which, although
still in its early stages, I have tried to capture here.

A simple reading of history shows that the relationship between
crime and technology is by no means new and that the potential for
creating harm never seems to be far away from any apparently beneficial technological development. Although the hardware used to
implement technological ideas may change across the span of time,
many of the basic crime ideas remain familiar, particularly those
which exploit chains of trust supported by technology. Some of the
nineteenth-century wire frauds perpetrated by tapping into the early
electric telegraph systems, for example, bear an uncanny resemblance
to modern day hacks. This long standing, though 'uneasy', relationship between crime and technology also extends to ideas about crime
prevention and security – the architects of the pyramids, for example,
employed sophisticated security technologies to thwart tomb raiders –
a few wrong or unexpected moves and . . . slam! . . . the tomb entrance
was sealed forever – not so different in principle to the automated surveillant technologies installed at airports to detect potential terrorist
actions by identifying abnormal patterns of movement. And on the
subject of the electric telegraph, no sooner had it been invented than it
was being used to catch criminals, as murderer John Tawell reflected
upon in the moments before his execution in 1845. After murdering his
mistress and fleeing to London by train, Tawell's description was tele-
graphed forward by the police and he was arrested upon his arrival
(Standage, 1998: 51).

Today the technological cat-and-mouse game between offender
and investigator remains much the same as in the past. Offenders still
exploit new technologies while the investigators catch up quickly and
then use those same technologies for investigation, apprehension and
prevention. What has changed significantly in late modern times,
however, has been the increase in personal computing power within a
globalized communications network. The time frame during which
harmful behaviour occurs and changes substantively is now much
shorter in this era of networking. It is also particularly worrying that
the length of time for a cybercrime opportunity to turn into a cyber-

crime wave is now measured in hours and minutes rather than months and years. As a consequence, networked technology has become more than simply a 'force multiplier' – not only are ideas about committing crime, its investigation and prevention being shared on a global scale, but high levels of computing power also enable these ideas to be put into practice across the global networks. So fast has been the rate of change that this book has already been revised considerably during the course of writing, living proof of Moore's calculation that one internet year is approximately equal to three months or less in real-time (based upon Moore, 1965: 114).

Drawing upon empirical research findings and a diverse range of contemporary multidisciplinary sources this book explores the above transformations. Although it tends to focus upon the high end of cybercrimes (those which are solely the product of networked technologies), the book seeks to explain the broad range of behaviour currently referred to as cybercrime as well as addressing the various legal, academic, expert and popular constructions of cybercrime and the disparities between them. It is argued that not only have networked technologies changed the criminal process to create a new generation of hackers and crackers, fraudsters and pornographers and the like, but these have themselves now been superseded. A third generation of cybercrimes (the first being computer crimes and the second being hacking) is emerging which is almost completely caused by networked technologies that are themselves converging with others. It can now be argued, for example, that earlier concerns about 'hacking' have become sidelined because 'botnets' of many thousands of 'zombie' computers infected by remote administration trojans can now automate the hacking process and also the process by which offenders engage with their victims. These are explained in more detail later.

Individually, cybercrimes may not be particularly serious and surveys of individual victimizations, police actions and prosecutions show the figures to be quite low, despite expectations to the contrary. However, these local statistics tend not to grasp the global picture as their true seriousness lies in their aggregate impact. We have now entered the world of low-impact, multiple victim crimes where bank robbers no longer have to plan meticulously thefts of millions of dollars; new technological capabilities mean that one person can now commit millions of robberies of $1 each. This 'de minimism' creates a number of important challenges for law enforcement and the policing of offenders. On the one hand, criminal justice systems are not geared up to deal with such offences. On the other hand, the realism, indeed digital realism, of cybercrime is such that the more a behaviour is mediated by new technology, the more it can be governed by that same technology. So, in addition to the prospect of being faced with 'ubiquitous' and automated victimization, we also – simultaneously – face the prospect of being exposed to ubiquitous law enforcement and prevention and the potential problems it creates, such as a potential 'pre-crime' agenda.

The book's aim and thesis

The primary aim of this book is to contribute to our knowledge and understanding of cybercrimes. It is not a manual of computer crimes and the methods by which to resolve them; others do that far better. Rather, it is a critical exploration of the transformations that have taken place in criminal activity and its regulation as a result of networked technologies. Central to the arguments put forward in the forthcoming chapters is a 'transformation thesis' which views cybercrimes as criminal or harmful activities that are informational, global and networked. They are the product of networked technologies that have transformed the division of criminal labour to provide entirely new opportunities for, and indeed, new forms of crime which typically involve the acquisition or manipulation of information and its value across global networks. This notion of transformation is important because it offers the prospect of reconciling seemingly different accounts of cybercrime by representing them as different phases in the process of change. The transformation concept is also important because its flip-side, as indicated above, is that the same technologies which create cybercrimes also provide unique opportunities for their regulation and policing. However, while this may provide a solution, it also stimulates an important debate about the framework for maintaining order and law enforcement on the internet.

Intended audience and methodological orientation

The book's main academic reference point is the intersection between law and criminology, particularly as it relates to the 'law in action'. This is because many of the harmful internet behaviours that raise public concern do not necessarily fall neatly within the criminal or civil codes. Furthermore, how they are currently resolved is framed increasingly by the broader discourse over public safety as well as specific law enforcement debates. Although the narrative is driven by a progressing thesis, it also maps out and contextualizes the range of cybercrimes, and in so doing the book contributes to ongoing academic debates. The book's intended audiences are advanced undergraduates and graduate students as well as the professional communities involved in cybercrime-related policy-making or practice. This book contains a discussion about cybercrimes and complements some of the very good texts that have recently emerged on the subject; see, for example, Sam McQuade's (2006b) scholarly and very informative overview of cybercrime and the management issues it raises, and Majid Yar's (2006) sociological treatise on cybercrime and society.

The narrative is constructed from a grounded analysis of events and draws upon a range of different sources. This is because the distributed as opposed to centralized organization of the internet creates multiple flows of often conflicting information about cybercrime offending and victimization. Networked information has the tendency to flow quite freely in all directions and so evade the editorial verification and control of dissemination which characterized previous media ages. Some of these information sources are the product of impartial and reliable news reporting, others are not. The latter may be the product of vested (usually commercial) interests, or the results of academic research, or surveys conducted by the many governmental and non-governmental agencies that have an interest in most things 'cyber'.

Wherever possible, original and independent sources of information have been sought to ensure the reliability of information in order either to confirm a particular trend in two or more independent datasets or to record the occurrence of an event. Adopting such an approach has helped to counter polemical accounts. Particular care was taken to avoid following purely sensationalized news streams, where one article reporting a sensational news event tends to spawn a chain of others. The resulting analysis therefore takes a multidisciplinary approach to respect the many voices of crime (Garland and Sparks, 2000). The digital realist perspective adopted here is not, however, to be confused with the artistic theory of pseudo-realism which carries the same name (see Surman, 2003: 11) or indeed debates about left-realism (Young, 1997). Rather, it originates in the work of Lessig (1998a, 1998b, 1999) and Greenleaf (1998) has been adapted here to contextualize cybercrime. It is essentially a multiple discourse approach which recognizes that cybercrime, like ordinary crime, is a form of behaviour that is mediated by technology but also by social and legal values and economic drivers. The interrelation between these four influences not only shapes the digital architecture of criminal opportunity but also provides some directions for resolving the same harms.

What follows, then, is a systematic enquiry based upon available knowledge, literature and research findings, much of which is outlined in the next chapter. It is also informed by my own research projects into crime, criminal justice and the internet conducted between 1999 and 2005 for the Home Office, Department of Trade and Industry (Foresight Initiative), European Commission, and Arts and Humanities Research Council (Wall, 1997, 1998, 1999, 2000, 2001a, 2002a, 2002b, 2003, 2004, 2005a, 2005b, 2006, 2007).

Principal research questions and chapter structure

In pursuing the central aim of exploring the transformation of crime in the information age, this book seeks to answer six research questions that frame the discussion in each of the forthcoming chapters.

What are cybercrimes and what do we know about them? Chapter 2 looks at the origins of the term, at the various discourses that give meaning to it, before exploring critically the tensions that exist between various ways in which knowledge about cybercrimes is produced.

How have networked technologies changed opportunities for criminal activity? Chapter 3 discusses the emergence of the networked society and networked technology, and then explores the ways in which their distinctive characteristics have transformed criminal behaviour and created new conduits for criminal activity.

How has criminal activity changed in the information age? Chapter 4 outlines specifically the various challenges to the integrity of computing systems, for example through hacking, to gain access to established boundaries in spaces over which ownership and control has already been established. Chapter 5 discusses computer assisted (or related) crime. Much of the discussion here focuses upon the various permutations of cyber-theft – deceptive and acquisitive behaviour in cyberspace. Chapter 6 considers content-related cybercrimes in the context of three key broad areas of concern: pornography, violence and offensive communications.

How is criminal activity continuing to change in the information age? Chapter 7 looks at how technology is now automating victimization and creating an entirely new generation of cybercrime. It also contemplates some of the informational problematics that arise with regard to identifying offenders and their victims. In some contexts, the concepts of offender and victim are challenged. Both of which are central to the understanding of law and criminology.

How is cyberspace policed and by whom? Chapter 8 maps out the compliance framework that currently shapes behaviour online to illustrate how order and law is currently maintained on the internet. It then identifies the challenges posed by Cybercrimes for criminal and civil justice processes before positioning the 'public police' as gatekeepers to the criminal justice system, within that structure.

How are cybercrimes to be regulated and prevented? Chapter 9 looks at the regulatory challenges by focusing upon the processes that govern online behaviour and the roles played by law, technology and other influences in the regulation of cyberspace.

Chapter 10 summarizes the findings of the preceding chapters and concludes the book.

2
Understanding Crime in the Information Age

What are cybercrimes and what do we know about them?

Chapter at a glance

- **Why call it 'cybercrime'?**
- **From where does our knowledge about cybercrimes originate?**
- **What are the tensions in the production of knowledge about cybercrimes?**
  The media construction of cybercrime imagery and its consumption
  The reliability of statistical claims and constructions
  Under-reporting and a lack of knowledge about victims
  Inadequate knowledge about offenders and their motivations
  The ongoing power struggle for control over cyberspace
  Competing expert claims
  Conflicts and confusions between public and private sector interests
  The danger of confusing the rhetoric with reality
- **Conclusions**

Although few would deny that the internet has had a major impact upon criminal behaviour, there is much less consensus as to what that impact has been. Even when nations agree that cybercrimes are a problem there appears to be no overall consensus about how to deal with them collectively (Goodman and Brenner, 2002: 89). All too often claims about the prevalence of cybercrimes lack clarification as to what it is that is particularly 'cyber' about them. Indeed, when so-called cases of cybercrime come to court they often have the familiar ring of the 'traditional' rather than the 'cyber' about them. These offences typically comprise hacking, fraud, pornography, paedophilia, etc., which are already part of existing criminal justice regimes. Perhaps more confusing is the contrast between the many hundreds of thousands of incidents that are supposedly reported each year and the relatively small number of known prosecutions. Is this a case of the absence of evidence not being evidence of its absence, to paraphrase former US Secretary of State, Donald Rumsfeld (Barone, 2004). Or, should we be asking if there are actually such things as cybercrimes? (Brenner, 2001: para. 1). Other authors have questioned whether cybercrimes are actually categories of crime in need of new theory, or whether they are understood better by existing theories (Jones, 2003: 98).

These contrasting viewpoints expose a large gap in our understanding of cybercrimes and beg a number of important questions about the quality of the production of information about cybercrimes. They fall into two groups. The first relate to the reliability and partiality of the informational sources that mould opinion. Has, for example, the cybercrime problem simply been blown up out of all proportion? If so, how has this happened? Has, for example, the media news gathering process effectively fabricated an apparent crime wave out of a few novel and dramatic events? Alternatively, are we experiencing a calculated attempt to peddle 'Fear, Uncertainty and Doubt' by the cyber-security industry – which has been described as a 'self-dramatizing and fear-mongering world of security pundits' (Schneier, 2003) with a stake in sensationalizing cybercrimes. 'FUDmongering', as this process has become known, claims Green (1999), 'is a tactic often used by vendors within a monopoly market in order to propagate their monopoly'. The second group of questions relates to the conceptual basis upon which information is gathered and assumptions are made. Could it be the case that the criminal justice processes are just woefully inefficient at bringing wrongdoers to justice? Indeed, can we realistically expect criminal justice processes designed to counter the social effects of urban migration to respond to an entirely new set of globalized 'virtual' problems? There again, could it be that we are perhaps simply failing to understand the epistemological differences between the various legal, academic, expert and popular (lay) constructions of cybercrime.

There is not enough room in this book to answer all of these questions conclusively, if indeed they are mutually exclusive, but there is clearly the need here to 'separate the air that chokes from the air upon which wings beat' (Barlow, 1996). To this end, this chapter seeks out a critical understanding about what cybercrimes are, how we understand them and, importantly, the nature of the problems and tensions that arise from the competing viewpoints that constitute the production of knowledge about them. The first part, therefore, looks at the origins of the term 'cybercrime'. The second part outlines the various sources of knowledge that inform our understanding of crime in the information age, in particular the various 'voices' present within the literature. The third part identifies the various tensions and competing views in the production of knowledge about cybercrimes.

Why call it 'cybercrime'?

First coined by William Gibson (1982) and then popularized in his 1984 novel *Neuromancer*, the term 'cyberspace' became a popular descriptor of the mentally constructed virtual environment within which networked computer activity takes place. 'Cybercrime' broadly describes the crimes that take place within that space and the term has come to symbolize insecurity and risk online. By itself, cybercrime is fairly meaningless because it tends to be used metaphorically and emotively rather than scientifically or legally, usually to signify the occurrence of harmful behaviour that is somehow related to the misuse of a networked computer system (Wall, 1997; NCIS, 1999). Largely an invention of the media, 'cybercrime' originally had no specific reference point in law in the UK or US[1] and the offending that did become associated with the term was a rather narrow legal construction based upon concerns about hacking. In fact, many of the so-called cybercrimes that have caused concern over the past decade are not necessarily crimes in criminal law. If we could turn the clock back in time then perhaps the term 'cyberspace crime' would have been a more precise and accurate descriptor. However, regardless of its merits and demerits, the term 'cybercrime' has entered the public parlance and we are stuck with it (Wall, 2005a). It is argued here and elsewhere in this book that the term has a greater meaning if we construct it in terms of the transformation of criminal or harmful behaviour by networked technology, rather than simply the behaviour itself. As stated earlier, cybercrimes are understood here to be criminal or harmful activities that involve the acquisition or manipulation of information for gain.

Not only has the term 'cybercrime' acquired considerable linguistic agency, but over the past decade 'cybercrimes' have become firmly embedded in public crime agendas as something that must be governed. This is an interesting happenstance within the context of the transformation thesis, because although the contemporary meaning of 'cyber' is firmly linked to technological innovation, its origins lie in the Greek *kubernetes*, or steersman, which is also the root of the word 'govern'. See, for example, the French usage of the term 'cybernétique' – the art of governing (*Oxford English Dictionary*). The word 'cyber' entered the English language in 'cybernetics', which is the study of systems of control and communications (linked with computers). More by coincidence than design, the words cyber and crime actually sit well together linguistically. This linkage becomes more significant if we understand cybercrimes as crimes which are mediated (governed if you like) by networked technology and not just computer.

From where does our knowledge about cybercrimes originate?

The internet is only about a decade old. Before it emerged, bodies of computer law already existed, as did a number of very relevant discourses within the academic literature that inform our understanding of the impacts of technology upon society and the way they relate to crimes. Indeed, Castells (2000a) explicitly observes that contemporary networked society, often attributed to the internet, predated the internet by a number of decades. Most notable of the academic discourses about the social impact of technology were the long-standing concerns expressed in the volumes on industrial sociology from Karl Marx through to Braverman (1976) and the Frankfurt School through to today. Technology's function in this literature, with some caveats, was perceived primarily as a means of rationalizing the power of capital by specializing the division of labour to reduce the cost of the production process. Building upon this tradition is an equally long-standing debate over the technologies of social control, which ranges from Bentham and Foucault through to Gary Marx (2001) and others. Attending these concerns are socio-legal discourses of freedom of expression, privacy and human rights (Balkin, 2004; Kerr, 2003; Kozlovski, 2004; Lessig, 1999; Rotenberg, 2001), often informed by the various theories of information society (Bell, 2001; Castells, 1997b, 2000b, 2000c; Webster, 2002). As a meta-narrative to these are a range of broader discourses about late, high or post-modernity (Bauman, 1998; Giddens, 1990), but also governance and risk (Miller and Rose, 1990; Rhodes, 1996;

O'Malley, 1999). A key driver of each discourse is the need to identify what is normal, as opposed to abnormal, behaviour in a rapidly technologizing society to identify the step-change. Moving closer to cybercrimes are various debates over deviance and society; deviance and its governance (see Braithwaite, 1992; Crawford, 2003; Garland, 2001; Furedi, 2002; Shearing, 2004; Stenson and Edwards, 2003); theories of crime science and prevention (Hughes et al., 2001; Clarke and Felson, 1993; Felson, 2000; Yar, 2005b: 407); policing society (Crawford and Lister, 2004; Loader and Walker, 2001; Jones and Newburn, 2002; Reiner, 2000; Shearing, 2004; Stenning, 2000), and policing the risk society (Ericson and Haggerty, 1997; Beck, 1992, 1999).

Focusing the lens upon the network technology and crime axis reveals specific discourses about the governance of online behaviour. Some authors address the physics of digital law (Geer, 2004) while others address the architecture created by the codes that constitute the internet (Lessig, 1998b, 1999; Post, 2000; Katyal, 2001, 2003). Accompanying these debates are texts which outline and debate the intricacies of specific computer crime legislation (Akdeniz et al., 2000; Akdeniz, 1996, 1997; Carr, 2004; Lastowka and Hunter, 2005; Reed and Angel, 2003; Walden, 2003, 2007; Wasik, 2000). Finally, there is the literature that addresses the issue of cybercrimes more generally (Barrett, 2004; Brenner, 2001, 2002; Broadhurst and Grabosky, 2005; Denning, 2000; Grabosky and Smith, 1998; Grabosky et al., 2001; Smith et al., 2004; Loader and Thomas, 2000; Jewkes, 2003; McQuade, 2006a, 2006b; Moitra, 2003; Morris, 2004; Newman and Clarke, 2003; Pattavina, 2005; Wall, 2001b, 2003, 2004, 2005a; Yar, 2005a, 2005b, 2006). Other literature deals with the more specific aspects of cybercrime, such as policing and law enforcement (Barrett, 2004; Brenner, 2001; Britz, 2003; Goodman, 1997; Jewkes and Andrews, 2005; McQuade, 2006a; Shinder and Tittel, 2002; Sommer, 2004; Wall, 2002a). The more topic-specific cybercrime literature is discussed in later chapters.

The rich vein of literature identified above tends to fall into four main discourses which, collectively, exhibit a wealth of knowledge about the content of cybercrime and its attendant issues (see box 2.1). The *legislative/administrative* discourse about cybercrimes defines or debates the rules that set the boundaries of acceptable and unacceptable behaviour as its primary concern. The *academic discourse*, on the other hand, seeks out criminological, socio-legal, sociological, computer science, information management, economic and/or technological understandings of what has actually happened. The *expert*

Box 2.1 Key discourses about cybercrime

- legislative/administrative discourse
- academic discourse
- expert discourse
- popular, emotional or layperson's discourse

---

discourse explores and understands trends in cybercrimes in order to provide explanations and inform solutions. Finally, there is the *popular, emotional or layperson's discourse*, reflecting the person on the street's understanding of cybercrime, which also has a bearing on the market, social values, the security response and eventually the law. The claims made about the extent, breadth or number of cybercrimes, however, are often contradictory because of their respective epistemologies. But they are more often at odds with the public or lay discourse about cybercrimes as expressed in the popular media. Whereas the legal, academic and expert discourses are typically driven by rational considerations, the latter are predominantly emotive in construction. This dissonance does not assist the acquisition of a broader understanding of the nature of the problem(s) and the subsequent formation of good public policy. So, how do we judge which of the available information is reliable? Is, for example, our understanding of cybercrime based upon verifiable 'reliable data' or are we forced into 'condensing facts from the vapour of nuance' (Stephenson, 1992: 56). We need reliable information about criminal trends not only to make sense of 'the problem', but also to act as a key driver of (criminal justice) policy reform and resource allocation within relevant agencies.

What are the tensions in the production of knowledge about cybercrimes?

There is no simple answer to the question of how to judge the quality of information sources, online or otherwise, because, as Mike Levi has opined: 'the normal disciplines by which we evaluate the plausibility of threat levels are absent' (Levi, 2001: 50). It is a situation, he states, which is also found in the risk assessments of other non-traditional types of crime. It is therefore important to take a critical view of the production of knowledge about crime in the information age in order to understand the many tensions which researchers, policy-makers and interested parties must eventually reconcile.

The media construction of cybercrime imagery and its consumption

Perhaps the conflicting viewpoints about cybercrime are simply indicative of the way in which we now 'consume crime' as just another sensationalized news item in contemporary consumer society. Baudrillard argued back in 1970 that: '[w]hat characterises consumer society is the universality of the news item [*le fait divers*] in mass communication. All political, historical and cultural information is received in the same – at once anodyne and miraculous – form of the news item' (1998: 33). In this respect, little has since changed. Far more than ever, the news item nowadays is reduced to its signs, the symbols to which individuals emotionally react. After being spectacularly dramatized, the news is then consumed by readers or viewers who may not have any personal experience of the issue. Baudrillard's point is that mass communications do not give us reality; rather they give us what he calls 'the dizzying whirl of reality [*le vertige de la realité*]' (1998: 34). Most cases of crime reporting are now so distanced from the consumer that only the fact that the crime event has taken place has any meaning. This observation adds weight to Garland's 'crime complex' argument (mentioned earlier) whereby public anxiety about crime has become the norm and now frames our everyday lives.

Currently, the internet is so newsworthy that a single dramatic incident of cybercrime has the power to shape public opinion and fuel public anxiety, frequently resulting in (political) demands for 'instant' and simple solutions to extremely complex situations. This situation reflects a broader shift in the reorganization of news dissemination in the information age. The news business was initially built upon its singular ability to control the distribution of news information, but this power has been weakened by the internet because unlimited information can now be made available on a range of different devices and from a multitude of sources. Sambrook (2006) has argued that '[t]hanks to the internet, the role of media gatekeeper has gone. Information has broken free and top-down control is slipping inexorably away.' Sambrook further argues that the news business no longer controls what the public know and that the internet has led to 'a major restructuring of the relationship between public and media . . . Public discourse is becoming unmediated.' This disintermediation of news is affecting politics and policy because the public can now access the politicians and the political process directly, or they can address, even mobilise, other members of the public with similar views (Sambrook, 2006). Once voiced, demands for governmental and agency responses cannot simply be ignored, precisely because of the fear of the political consequences of not responding.

Yet, this disintermediation of the news process runs counter to the construction of the imagery surrounding cybercrime, which originates in the days prior to the internet when the mass media was organized more centrally. Before news media became transformed by contemporary networked technology, understandings of crime were mediated at source by state agencies associated with the criminal justice processes, for example through UK Home Office crime statistics. They were therefore shaped by the more traditional (Peelian) notion of dangerousness and of the need to protect the public at large (Reiner, 2000: ch. 2; Wall, 1998: 23). Indeed, media accounts of cybercrimes still frequently invoke the dramatic imagery of a vulnerable society being brought to its knees by forces beyond its control such as an 'Electronic Pearl Harbor' (Smith, 1998; Taylor, 2001: 69) or a 'Cyber-Tsunami' (Wall, 2001: 2). In some ways, this is hardly surprising because early thinking about the application of networked technologies was closely entwined with science fiction media. The now defunct *Omni Magazine*, which was published between 1978 and 1998, was one of a range of contemporary publications that combined articles on science fact with short works of science fiction to form popular technology-related narratives. It was, coincidentally, in the pages of *Omni Magazine*, that William Gibson first coined the word 'cyberspace' (1982).

The construction of contemporary imagery specifically linking computers to crime originates in a series of popular films dating back to the 1960s, which exploited the prevailing 'white heat of technology' theme. The films include the *Billion Dollar Brain*, 1967; *The Italian Job*, 1969; *Superman III*, 1983; *Bellman and True*, 1988; *Die Hard*, 1988. These first generation computer crime films were followed by a more distinct genre of hacker-themed movies during the 1980s in which the role of the hacker – rather than the hack – was more central to the plot. They typically identified the hacker as a young genius, usually a misunderstood male teenager, who used technology to put wrongs right and usually have some have fun while doing so. The early second-generation hacker films (*War Games*, 1983; *Electric Dreams*, 1984; *Real Genius*, 1985; *Weird Science*, 1985; *Ferris Bueller's Day Off*, 1986; *Sneakers*, 1992; *Independence Day*, 1996) highlighted the dangers to be found in computer systems that were interconnected mainly by modems and, in so doing, confirmed the stereotype of hackers which endures to this day. The later hacker films (still mainly second generation) were a little more sophisticated in that the hackers they depicted tended to use the internet, or an imaginative sci-fi equivalent (*Goldeneye*, 1995; *Hackers*, 1995; *The Net*, 1995; *Johnny Mnemonic*, 1995; *Enemy of the State*, 1998; *Takedown*, 2000; *AntiTrust*, 2001; *Swordfish*, 2001; *The Italian Job* (remake), 2003). Although hackers were still being depicted as young people, they were now less gender specific and much less likely to adopt the moral high ground than in the earlier films. Furthermore, the later second-generation cybercrime films also began to portray the hacker as 'a dark antihero capable of causing serious destruction. Sometimes thrust into the world of hacking against their will, at other times eager participants, the fictional movie hacker began to reshape the general public's view of the underground community alternatively as dark conspirators and sympathetic protagonists' (Brandt, 2001). A third generation of hacker movies (e.g. *Tron*, 1982; *The Matrix*, 1999) differs from the second generation in that most of the action takes place within virtual environments. This generational differentiation has significance in the next chapter.

Contemporary movie and media imagery subconsciously orders the line between fact and fiction (Furedi, 2006) and has crystallized 'the hacker' offender stereotype as the archetypal 'cybercriminal'. It was, and still is, a powerful image characterized by introverted youth utilizing technological might to ubiquitously subordinate 'the system' and indiscriminately victimize its subjects. It is an image which invokes in its audience a 'Future Shock' of helplessness or anomie, which not only contributes to the propagation of a culture of fear (Furedi, 2002) but also serves to heighten levels of public anxiety while also moulding public expectations about desirable legal and regulatory responses. Ironically, these same anxieties enhance the apparent dangerousness of the cybercriminal and provide regulatory bodies with an implied mandate for taking action to protect the public. Moreover, a pervasive 'culture of fear' (Furedi, 2006) assumes that individuals are naturally fearful of the absence of any broadly recognized measure of the actual risk of cybercrimes – the 'unknown unknowns'. Therefore, public anxiety becomes intensified by the tendency of journalists, pressure groups and policy-makers – and also some academics – to fail to differentiate between the 'potential' and 'actual' harms. Once risk assessments are confused with reality then the only perceivable way to satisfy heightened public anxiety about cybercrime is to introduce additional legislation and stringent technological countermeasures. This 'ideology of regulation' shifts the debate towards the needs of the state and corporate interests, and away from important principles such as liberty and freedom of expression. The main way to counter the effects of ideology, and indeed erroneous media constructions, is through the presentation of reliable empirical data.

The reliability of statistical claims and constructions

The most conventionally accepted 'reliable' data are metrics expressed as statistics; however, the distributed environment in which cyber-crime thrives undermines conventional methodologies for collecting data. This is because information about reported victimization does not flow through a single portal such as the police in the same way as does the reporting of street and related crime. In this, cybercrime is little different to other invisible or hidden crimes such as white-collar or organized crime (see Davies et al., 1999). There exist many reports and surveys that purport to estimate the extent of cybercrime, typically covering network abuse and commercial crime (see Ryan and Jefferson, 2003), but very few 'official' sources. This point was raised by the UK All Party Internet Group in May 2004 when it reviewed the Computer Misuse Act 1990:

> One problem is that, officially, the government is not aware of exactly how big a problem cybercrime is, since figures are not audited by the National Audit Office – and this means there is no political pressure to deal with the issue. 'The first thing we have to do is find out the extent of the problem. We won't win the battle of resourcing the police if we don't get the crimes recorded.' (APIG chairman Derek Wyatt, cited by Broersma, 2004)

But, even if there did exist the possibility to collate 'official' statis-tics, there remains the additional problem of applying standardized conceptualizations of 'crime' to systematic reporting or recording methodologies, with the consequence that they are hard, if not impos-sible, to replicate. Frequently cited for many years as a source of infor-mation about cybercrimes were the intrusion statistics published online by the Computer Emergency Response Team (CERT) at Carnegie Mellon University. Reports rose from six in 1988 to 137, 529 in 2003, and these statistics were initially accepted as a barome-ter of cybercrime activity. However, because confusion arose from these being mainly low-level and often automated reports of intru-sions with few representing actual crimes, CERT discontinued the 'Incidents reported' data stream in 2003 with the following statement:

> [g]iven the widespread use of automated attack tools, attacks against Internet-connected systems have become so commonplace that counts of

the number of incidents reported provide little information with regard to assessing the scope and impact of attacks. Therefore, as of 2004, we will no longer publish the number of incidents reported . . . (CERT/CC Statistics 1988–2005, at www.cert.org/stats/cert_stats. html)

An indication of the inexact science of cybercrime estimation was given in October 2005 when John Leyden, a journalist from *The Register*, deconstructed claims by an anti-spyware firm about the level of infections caused by spyware (Leyden, 2005j). The data upon which the statistics were based were collected by Webroot's *Phileas* automatic web crawler, which proactively sought out data about active spyware (Webroot, 2005: 13).[2] The findings were dramatic and revealed high levels of spurious infections. However, Leyden subsequently found that the methods used to calculate the statistics clumped together benign 'cookies' with much more malicious spyware such as trojans and keylogger programs. Once the cookies were removed from the calculation the average number of spyware infections on each PC fell from 18 to 4.5 (Leyden, 2005j). While still relatively high, the revised calculations radically change the meaning of the statistics and any conclusions that can be drawn from them. This example highlights graphically the need to understand first the methodological assumptions underlying the compilation of statistics.

In addition to the 'incidents reported' lists are a number of self-reporting victimization surveys run by organizations such as the US National White-Collar Crime Center and the National Fraud Information Center. Most focus specifically upon the business and financial sector. Currently one of the most frequently cited sources of data is the Computer Studies Institute/Federal Bureau of Investigation (CSI/FBI, 2005, 2006) annual computer security survey which questions US businesses about their experience of victimization. Similarly, companies such as Experian, KPMG and others produce occasional (rigorous) surveys. In the UK, similar surveys have been conducted by the Department of Trade and Industry (DTI, 2004), also the National Hi-Tech Crime Unit (NHTCUb, 2002) and the National Criminal Intelligence Service (NCIS, 2003). The survey results tend to find high rates of victimization, but it is important to note that most businesses are more likely to become victims of crime simply because of the risks they are exposed to in the course of their day-to-day operations, both online and off. So problems of data interpretation arise when survey data collected for quite specific purposes or specific corporate or client bodies are used to support general observations about the impact of the internet, or its impact on individuals. Such generalizations can fuel sensational news stories which subsequently depict the internet as ungovernable and criminogenic, when in fact, information such as that related to online frauds suggests that the internet is very secure for personal online transactions and that the main risk lies in the vulnerability of input and output procedures (APACS, 2005b; Wall, 2002b) (discussed further in chapter 5).

The most effective way that statistics about patterns of individual victimization can be reliably captured is through surveys of individuals. To this end there are some encouraging signs, because the main victimization surveys in the UK and US have either recently incorporated, or are currently in the process of incorporating, questions about online victimization. In the UK in 2002–3, the British Crime Survey (BCS) incorporated a small number of questions about individual internet victimizations. The BCS canvasses a sample of about 37,000 people (75 per cent response rate) about their experience of victimization (Allen et al., 2005: 3; Wilson et al., 2006). Complementing the BCS is the Offending, Crime and Justice Survey (OCJS), which asks a smaller sample of 12,000 about their experience of offending. The results of the BCS of 2002–3 and the first OCJS survey in 2003 were made available in mid-2005 and did not show the high levels of prevalence previously anticipated by the reported incident data (Allen et al., 2005). Only 2 per cent of respondents reported that they had been the victim of a hack during the previous year; 21 per cent reported receiving an offensive email. Interestingly, levels of internet card fraud were found to be lower than other forms of card fraud (Allen et al., 2005: vi). These early findings, replicated by the BCS 2003–4 findings (Wilson et al., 2006: 7) lend weight to the argument established in this book that cybercrimes may not be individually as serious as many of the statistics claim, but their seriousness lies in their globalized aggregate volume. This observation brings into question whether cybercrimes can be quantified by traditional local and national recording methods, or whether they should be considered within a much larger global context. If cybercrimes are indeed, minor in nature but large in aggregate, this may affect the way that we construct victim profiles.

Under-reporting and a lack of knowledge about victims

Until victimization survey findings begin to build up a cumulative picture of victims of cybercrime, confusion will remain as to who they are, the manner of their victimization, and the amount of policing resources that should be allocated to the problem. Even then there are a number of factors that will continue to vex the construction of victim profiles, because not only can they vary from individuals to social groups, but also the harms done to them can range from the actual to the perceived. In types of offending, such as cyber-stalking, the theft of cyber-cash or fraud, the victimization is nearly always focused upon the individual. However, in other patterns of offending, such as cyber-piracy or cyber-spying/terrorism, the impact of victimization is usually directed towards corporate or governmental bodies. Similarly, the focus of hate crimes tends to be upon minority groups. Moreover, as found with the reporting of white-collar crimes, it is likely that many primary or secondary victims of cybercrimes, individuals and organizations may be unwilling to acknowledge that they have been victimized, or at least it may take some time for them to realize it.

At the individual level, reluctance to report offences may arise because of embarrassment, ignorance of what to do, or just simply 'putting it down to experience'. Alternatively, where victimization has been implied by a third party upon the basis of an ideological, political, moral or commercial assessment of risk, the victim or victim group may simply be unaware, or may not believe, that they have been victimized, as is the case in some of the debates over pornography on the internet. At the corporate level victims are disincentivized from reporting their victimizations because of the fear of damage to reputation and loss of consumer confidence from adverse publicity. Corporate victims are particularly fearful that publicizing corporate vulnerabilities might encourage attackers, damage the business and compound workforce concerns about their job security (Cashell et al., 2004: 13). Both sets of factors greatly reduce corporate willingness to report their victimization to the police. Evidence of the impacts of reporting disincentives can be illustrated by comparing fraud victimization survey findings with the relatively low incidence of internet-related frauds reported by the public to the police (Wall, 2003: 132). Low levels of reporting, for whatever reason, lead to low levels of police action, fewer prosecutions and fewer statistics, reducing the amount of available knowledge about offenders and ultimately hampering the development of a criminology of virtual offenders.

Inadequate knowledge about offenders and their motivations

The small amount of factual knowledge currently available about virtual offenders comes from the findings of a few research projects, such as Smith et al. (2004), and also reported cases and offender surveys, such as the UK-based OCJS (Allen et al., 2005; Wilson et al., 2006). These sources suggest that offender profiles are like those of most offenders – young and male – but they possess rather different, if not opposing, personal characteristics found in criminologies of street criminals. They are more likely to be introverted and more likely to share a much broader range of social characteristics. Perhaps more significant is that their use of the internet enables them to commit crimes at a distance and also crimes that would previously have been beyond their means. Consequently, when combined with the offenders' relative isolation from others, these characteristics reduce the amount of available criminal intelligence about them and makes the law enforcement job harder.

The generalizability of the above observations will, of course, vary further according to the types of crime involved and the available opportunities to offend. Such is the view of the situational crime prevention theorists (see Newman and Clarke, 2003). However, while this may easily explain computer mediated thefts, it sits less comfortably with computer integrity and computer content crimes. McQuade (2006b: 113–35) gives a very useful overview of offender profiles, but acknowledges the problems in so doing because: '[i]n reality, cybercriminals carry out different types and combinations of illicit actions in the course of committing abuse, attacks and/or crimes, thus underscoring the difficulty and limitations of categorising offenders' (p. 133).

If the construction of offender profiles is problematic, so too is the ability to isolate offender motivations. Normally in criminology we may turn to the more complex theories of criminalization for some guidance here. McQuade (2006b: 179), for example, applied six criminological theories to cybercrimes, which each outline different motivational factors. They are *classical choice theories*, based upon rational decision-making; *trait theories*, which focus upon psychological imperfections in the individual; *social process theories*, which explore how individuals learn criminal behaviour; *social structure theories*, which consider the individual's social and economic position in society; *conflict theories*, based upon non-consensual, pluralistic and conflict views of social organization. He also observed a sixth, *integrated theories*, which combine aspects of the previous five. The problem McQuade identifies is that criminologists have long tended not to consider the impacts of technology in the commission of crime. Furthermore, the field of study is currently unfolding – especially where an act of cybercrime involves a number of forms of offending behaviour.

One powerful theory of motivation that begins to explain the transformative impacts of the internet (see chapter 3) is based upon social structure/alienation theory, but also integrates themes from other criminological theories. Presdee's 'carnival of crime' thesis expresses a broader concern about the criminalization of everyday life in which: 'everyday responses to modern, highly commodified society become themselves defined as criminal' (Presdee, 2000: 15). He argues that much of the crime occurring in society, especially that relating to social disorder, is a product of the fact the existing relationships of production encourage us to live two lives. Our 'first life' is our official life characterized by work and imposed order, which sustains our physical existence. In contrast, our 'second life' is where we live out our fantasies and obtain emotional fulfilment (not to be confused with the website of the same name). It runs counter to the alienation caused by the 'rhythms of production' in the 'first life', by working to restore some meaning to our lives and control over our existence (Presdee, 2000: 62). During the course of living out this 'second life', which Presdee calls our 'carnival of leisure', the boundaries of order are frequently crossed. We, in effect, consume crime, not just through our diet of entertainment, but also when the 'commodification of excitement' that characterizes much of our leisure is taken that one step further.

Presdee's main concern is that the 'bulk of crime is created, through the criminalisation and policing of social behaviour as against dishonest behaviour and that it is a crime to be many things including poor, young, disadvantaged, to fail and even at times to be creative' (Presdee, 2000: 162). This explanation of second-life fulfilment can go a long way to explaining much of the internet's broader popularity but also offending and victimization. In Presdee's view, the internet has become a ' "safe site" of the second life of the people' (Presdee, 2000: 54) and it certainly does provide an environment 'where we can enjoy in private immoral acts and emotions' (Presdee, 2000: 64). But, he is also right when he states that the days when the consumption of crime, as he puts it, has become 'a blissful state of "non-responsibility", a sort of never-ending "moral holiday", are long gone, if they ever existed, especially on the internet'.

The ongoing power struggle for control over cyberspace

The increasing political and commercial power of the internet is forging new power relationships that are gradually shaping and reshaping what is and what is not a cybercrime. This political economy of information capital is marked by an ongoing power play, or 'intellectual land grab', for market control and protection (see Boyle, 1996). Consequently, definitions of acceptable and deviant cyber-behaviour are being shaped by the interests of the 'new' powerful – those who gain a commercial and legal hold on the upper ground. The rising intolerance of the new powerful towards 'risk groups' they perceive as a threat to their own interests is causing concern, especially when 'the problem', as it becomes regarded, is reconstructed within a criminal, rather than civil, law discourse that contrasts competing interests in an adversarial good guys/bad guys binary. See, for example, the debates over MP3 and MP4s and also the threats of prosecution (typically 'letters before action') and actual prosecutions brought by the Recording Industry Association of America (RIAA) and British Phonographic Industry (BPI) (see Carey and Wall, 2001: 36; Marshall, 2002: 1) and the Motion Picture Associations. Alternatively, see the technological and legal tactics employed to control spammers that are outlined in chapter 9.

It would be wrong, however, simply to assume that the construction of deviance is one-sided. Even if definitions of crime and deviance are originated by the social activity of elites or powerful groups, they have to be embedded in the lives and understandings of ordinary members of society as well as offenders themselves for them to translate into social action. On this, Melossi has observed that 'the struggle around the definition of crime and deviance is located within the field of action that is constituted by plural and even conflicting efforts at producing control' (1994: 205). The key issue here is therefore about whether reliable information flows freely to form reliable viewpoints.

Competing expert claims

Very influential in the production of knowledge about cybercrimes and in shaping public and governmental opinion are the claims of 'experts'. Without reliable knowledge, especially recognized metrics, it is not only hard to validate expert claims, especially when they compete, but it is also difficult to counter inaccurate claims with factual information. The cyber-security industry, which comprises security consultants and aspects of private and public law enforcement agencies, has an economic interest in cybercrime that can shape the focus of any claims made. While claims may be grounded in good information, industry members will tend to present views that favour

their own particular interests. There has, for example, been a historical tendency to overestimate the extent of crime on the internet by
inflating the importance of low-level automated intrusion statistics.

Levi argues that this is systemic and that the potential impacts of
cybercrime may simply be 'talked up' by 'experts', who may deliberately or paranoically inflate the threat, conflating 'experience of with
theoretical risk from computer crime' (Levi, 2001: 50) for their own
gain, particularly when competing for government resources. Levi has
argued that the conflation of experience with theoretical risk is part of
the broader 'intelligence threat-assessment mental set' that is perpetuated by 'the self-serving PR of security consultants whose income
depends on shocking . . . or . . . "creating awareness among" . . .
senior executives and government agencies who complacently fail to
spend "enough" money on security' (Levi, 2001: 50). The same PR
also feeds the media's current lust for internet-related news and subsequently shapes public knowledge about, and attitudes towards, the
internet and drives the resulting debate over crime, providing the regulatory bodies with a mandate for taking action (Wall, 2002a: 190). It
is alleged, for example, that the hacking exploits of Richard Pryce and
Matthew Bevan (aka Datastream Cowboy and Kuji) were overblown
by experts in order to secure funding for government agencies. During
the course of a Congress hearing Pryce and Bevan were purportedly
described as 'possibly the single biggest threat to world peace since
Adolf Hitler' (Power, 2000: ch. 6; Bevan, 2001). Yet, not only were
both very young, but Pryce was still at school (Ungoed-Thomas,
1998: 1) and despite the claims against them, the case against Bevan
was dropped because there was no evidence and, as Bevan himself
explains, the 'Crown Prosecution Service (CPS) held that it was not
in the public interest to prosecute me' (Bevan, 2001). Pryce was fined
£1200. While Bevan openly states that he was a hacker, he feels with
the benefit of hindsight that he became part of a larger agenda.

> Looking back, I now believe that my case was not about hacking, but an
> exercise in propaganda. In the same year that a handful of hackers
> were caught, there was an estimated 250,000 attacks on computers in
> the US, Department of Defence. It was a prime target. I believe it was
> no coincidence that when the Senate was being asked for money to fund
> protection against Information Warfare, a case study appearing to prove
> their point fell in their laps. (Bevan, 2001).

This is a view also held by journalist Duncan Campbell (1997: 2):
'The collapse of Bevan's trial has exposed the US infowarriors. On the

back of overblown rhetoric and oversold threats, they have won lavish funding from Congress for new military and intelligence infowar units, and recently sold their security services to private corporations.'

The irony here is that Bevan is now an expert himself.

Echoes of the Datastream Cowboy and Kuji affair were heard a decade later in the case of Gary McKinnon, the 'Pentagon Hacker'. Accused of being a threat to US national security following what is maintained to be 'the biggest military computer hack of all time', McKinnon faced extradition to the US from the UK in 2006 to face charges that could lead to up to 70 years in prison (BBC, 2006k). McKinnon claimed to have explored the Pentagon website out of curiosity, looking for evidence of the existence of extraterrestrial technology, but finding, instead, unsecured areas containing highly confidential information. His supporters argue that the prosecution was purely politically motivated rather than to prevent crime and that he has actually exposed expert failings that caused 'the shortcomings of security policies on US military networks' (McKinnon's defence: BBC, 2006l, 2006k).

The point of this section is not to denigrate the value of the expert, indeed most expert claims are well informed, but to emphasize that expert sources are not 'value' free and to highlight that an objective view must incorporate a range of perspectives, not one. This observation also applies to the claims of another expert group, the hackers themselves who have a tendency to overexaggerate claims of their technical prowess and proficiency. Hackers, more usually, crackers (who are driven by less ethical motivations), may 'fake' the methodology of their crime to hide the fact that they actually used social engineering, or deception, to trick people into giving out personal information such as passwords to secure systems by exploiting their weaknesses, rather than using technological skills to obtain key access information. This fact was revealed by the notorious hacker Kevin Mitnick, himself now an 'expert' (see Mitnick and Simon, 2002).

Conflicts and confusions between public and private sector interests

A recurring theme of this discussion is the tension between the public and private sectors in seeking forms of justice that represent their different interests. The relatively low levels of prosecutions for breaches of computer security and low levels of recorded internet-related fraud are poignant examples of this tension (see chapter 4). They suggest that most breaches of security tend to be dealt with by victims rather than the police, highlighting the preference of corporate victims to seek private justice solutions instead of invoking the public criminal justice process that might expose their weaknesses to commercial competitors (Wall, 2001b: 174). The model of criminal justice offered to corporate victims by the police and other public law enforcement agencies is not generally conducive to their business interests (Goodman, 1997: 486). They prefer to sort out their own problems by using their own resources in ways that are more likely to meet their own instrumental ends. Even where there is a clear case for prosecuting an offender, corporate bodies will usually tend to favour civil recoveries rather than criminal prosecutions. This is partly because a lesser burden of proof is required, but also because they feel they can maintain a greater control over the justice process. In other cases, they may take no actual action and simply pass on the costs of victimization directly to their customers, or claim for losses through insurance. With regard to the latter, however, Cashell et al. (2004) found that many businesses do not tend to include cyber-attacks in their insurance policies.

The danger of confusing the rhetoric with reality

What this chapter has illustrated is that cybercrime is not a given, incontrovertible fact. Our understandings of it have been constructed over the past two decades from various countervailing discourses and their attendant epistemologies. Some are concerned with risk assessment (what ought), others with reality (what is). In acknowledging the respective strengths and weaknesses of these discourses we increase our understanding of cybercrimes. To ignore their origins lays us open to confusing risk assessment with reality and its accompanying dangers, particularly the way that it can 'corrupt systems' by creating mindsets in which the only way to combat cyber-crimes is thought to be an increase in resources for the enforcement of law and/or to introduce stringent technological countermeasures. This confusion can be further compounded by the over-reliance by the media on contestable statistical 'guesstimates' produced by the cyber-security industry (see above, Leyden, 2005j) and the media's dependence upon so-called 'experts' for confirmation. This sometimes results in what Rosenberger (2003) has termed 'false authority syndrome'. On top of all this, the internet allows both good and bad ideas to proliferate quickly and so is a fertile ground for myths (Rosenberger, 2003) and conspiracy theories: '[m]ore than anything, the Web encourages viewers to make links and trace the hidden connections . . . so conspiracy theory on the Web provides surfers with a substitute sense of empowerment of being an active participant in the process of discovery and detection (Knight, 2000: 211).

Together, these self-confirming sources can quickly create panic and prejudice rational solutions and explanations, but they can also become self-fulfilling by announcing system flaws and potential opportunities for offending. At the time of writing, for example, 'hotspot paranoia', brought about when individuals use free public wi-fi hotspots to communicate or do business on the internet, was one of the concerns *du jour* along with pharming and phlooding (see below, and Glossary), with no clear evidence of any large-scale occurrence. The expressed concern was that 'evil twin' sites might be set up to spoof established sites to harvest usernames, passwords and any other useful information that could subsequently be used in criminal activity. As Kewney (2005) argues, this is perfectly feasible:

> yes I could sit down at a public hotspot, give my PC the ability to act as a hotspot . . . properly done . . . I could even make the logon screen look exactly like a Starbucks logon screen, which is where most T-Mobile hotspots are. And if you logged on with your credit card, I could get your details. And if you logged into your bank to do some financial work, I might get your password.

However, he argues that the flaw in the 'evil twin' argument against wi-fi hotspots is why go to the trouble when broadband internet-based exploits are a much easier and effective means of obtaining passwords and accompanying information. Therefore, while there is a risk, the chance of victimization is likely to be small. 'So, yes: there will be hackers setting up "evil twin" access points, but your chance of meeting one is pretty slim – they'll be students trying to prove they could do it. They'll have useful careers ahead of them, and middle-class aspirations, and after a couple of experiments, they'll either get caught or, get bored' (Kewney, 2005).

Another concern at the time of writing was 'pharming' or 'cache poisoning', which is a more automated version of 'phishing' (fraudulently obtaining personal information) that does not rely upon social engineering to trick the recipient into clicking onto a bogus site because it automatically redirects them to it (Jackson, 2005; Leyden, 2005a; Lemos, 2005a). At the time of writing, examples of pharming related mainly to drug sales and redirection to online pharmacies – hence 'pharming' – but redirections to banking sites were increasing in number (Jackson, 2005). In this case, the headlines acted as the 'determining agent of reality' and preceded the offending, thereby creating the danger of the 'self-fulfilling prophecy . . . the coming to pass of the myth' (Baudrillard, 1998: 128).

Conclusions

Reliable information about cybercrime informs policy, practice and the public. It helps to prevent information sources over-representing their own interests and it reconciles the needs of the state and corporate interests, rather than dividing them. It also upholds important principles such as liberty and freedom of expression. But just as important as the constitutional need is the requirement to obtain reliable information in order to shape public expectations more realistically. This helps to mitigate the existing tensions within the production of knowledge about cybercrimes between the actual shock of the 'Future Shock' and also the expectation that we will be shocked by the 'Future Shock'. This needs a little further explanation. 'Future Shock', is what Toffler (1970) describes as the anxiety, stress and disorientation that arises from too much change in too short a time. But Standage argues that because of the '[t]he hype, scepticism and bewilderment associated with the Internet – concerns about new forms of crime, adjustments in social mores, and redefinition of business practices', the 'shock' is 'only to be expected [as] the direct consequences of human nature, rather than technology' (Standage, 1998: 199). We find here a strong resonance with Garland's 'crime complex' (2000: 367), which he describes as a symptom of late modernity where order is 'brittle' and public anxiety towards crime has not only become the norm, but also expected. In a nutshell, we are shocked by cybercrime, but also expect to be shocked by it because we expect it to be there, but – confusingly – we appear to be shocked if we are not shocked (if we don't find it)! So, if information about cybercrime distorts public expectations generally, then it is all the more important that the information should be reliable.

But how feasible is it to create reliable data streams in distributed systems where the activities are so heterogeneous? Indeed, is it possible to create such data in the same way as we do for non-cybercrime? For a number of practical reasons it may not be possible to gain an overall picture of the prevalence of cybercrime; however, it is still important to know why this may not be achievable and whether the information, statistics and data that are currently available have value. Do they display common trends? The distributed nature of information flows means that, at best, one can do little more than draw together many sources to build up a composite picture of cyber-crime as social action. To maximize use of these resources it is essential to understand the range of dynamics outlined above that shape the production of criminological knowledge about cybercrimes.

3

Cyberspace and the Transformation of Criminal Activity

How have networked technologies changed opportunities for criminal activity?

Chapter at a glance

- **The internet and the information society**
- **The transformative impacts of cyberspace upon criminal activity**
  Networking and the convergence of technologies
  Informational transfer and value
  Globalization
- **Changes in the organization of crime and the division of criminal labour**
  Greater control over the criminal process by the individual
  New forms of criminal organization through collaborations between different skill-sets
  Deskilling and reskilling criminal labour
- **Changes in the scope of criminal opportunity online**
  The first generation of cybercrime: crimes using computers (to assist traditional offending)
  The second generation of cybercrime: opportunities for crimes across a global span of networks
  The third generation of cybercrime: true cybercrimes wholly mediated by technology
- **Three criminologies of cybercrime: impacts upon substantive areas of criminal behaviour**
  Computer integrity crimes
  Computer assisted (or related) crimes
  Computer content crimes
- **Conclusions**

The origins of the internet and its associated information technologies are well documented from its military origins through to educational, commercial and, later, social use (Castells, 1997b, 2000a; Jordan, 1999; Bell, 2001; Webster, 2002; Rheingold, 1994). From this literature comes the clear message that the internet has radically changed aspects of our lives, but how much? Some commentators argue that it has only had a marginal effect, while others, mostly the post-modernists, believe that the information society has contributed to the rupturing of traditional links across time and space and has caused the demise of modernity. Yet, authors such as Castells (1997b: 7) and Giddens (1999) have steadfastly maintained that the shift towards post, late or high modernity (depending upon author) was already occurring well before the popularization of the internet in the early 1990s. Indeed, Standage (1998) has ambitiously traced the internet's historical links back to the nineteenth-century 'Victorian internet', which, he argues, was comprised of information networks created by the electric telegraph.

This chapter looks at how the internet has created new opportunities for criminal activity. It starts by exploring the emergence of the information society before attempting to identify its transformative impacts upon criminal behaviour. It then goes on to explore the ways in which those impacts have helped to create new conduits for criminal activity. By drawing upon the above characteristics this chapter examines what is distinctive about cybercrime in terms of criminal opportunity and substantive areas of criminal behaviour.

The internet and the information society

A simple keyword search on Amazon.com confirms that there are many academic commentaries on the subject of the 'information age'. However, the most prominent thinker in this field is Manuel Castells whose influential trilogy of work was published under the series title *The Information Age: Economy, Society and Culture* (Castells, 1997b, 2000a, 2000b, 2000c). Castells claims that the information age has transformed the relationships of production/consumption, power and experience (2000c: 5). He specifically argues that one of the hallmarks of the information age, the network society, was the product of the historical convergence of three independent processes during the late twentieth century: the constitution of the information technology revolution in the 1970s; the restructuring of capitalism and of statism in the 1980s aimed at replacing their contradictions with sharply different outcomes; and the cultural social movements of the 1960s and their 1970s aftermath, particularly feminism and ecologism, (1997a: 7). Consequently, Castells believes that although the information technology revolution did not create the network society, the latter would not exist in its present form without it. Although Castells's explanation is much contested (see, for example, Van Dijk, 1999), he does nevertheless explain why some characteristics associated with the internet pre-date it, such as globalization. He also shows that the internet has accelerated change and accentuated the qualities which have come to characterize late modernity, particularly the 'discontinuities' highlighted by Giddens (1990: 6) that separate modern and traditional social orders. The social orders which bind time and space have become *disembedded* and *distanciated*; 'lifted out of local contexts of interaction and restructured across indefinite spans of time-space' (Giddens, 1990: 14; Bottoms and Wiles, 1996).

Castells goes on to observe that a new information economy has emerged which possesses three distinct characteristics (2000c: 10) which together provide a conceptual starting point for analysing changes in crime. First, the information economy is based upon *informational* productivity that has 'the capacity of generating knowledge and processing/managing information'. Secondly, it is *global*. Its 'core, strategic activities, have the capacity to work as a unit on a planetary scale in real time or chosen time'. Thirdly, it is *networked*. These three characteristics have created a new era of economic organization in the form of networked enterprises that comprises networks of organizations or parts of organizations. Therefore, the main unit of production has shifted from the organizational unit to the 'project'. Castells contends that while the organization remains the legal unit of capital accumulation, it is nevertheless just one node in a global network of financial flows (Castells, 2000c: 10; see also the discussion in Mendelson and Pillai, 1999). Cyberspace is a virtual environment in which economic value is attached to ideas and their virtual expression rather than physical property (Barlow, 1994). In short, the information age argument is based upon a shift in values from more tangible to less tangible forms of wealth; from things to ideas expressed in informational sources. If the organization remains the legal unit of capital accumulation, as Castells predicts, then the global networked informational economy and its valuable content will become attractive to criminals.

The full social and economic impact of cyberspace upon the individual is only just beginning to be understood. In principle, individuals are freer than probably at any time in history to develop social relations commensurate with their own interests and lifestyles – relations which are potentially more meaningful than they could otherwise be (see Rheingold, 1994). Some individuals can, for example, now work outside the traditional workplace, doing office work at a distance without the office politics. They can work where their abilities can be best utilized and their pay and conditions maximized, thus reducing many of the alienating aspects of work. They can also maintain essential personal and familial connections whilst experiencing a broader personal fulfilment through participation in internet-based activities (see the 'second life' theory, in chapter 2). The realities are, however, more pragmatic, being much less ideological or romantic in outlook.

The internet is arguably not a substitute for face-to-face interactions. But in a society where 'the personality' transcends politics (Sennett, 1992: 238), individuals are no longer accustomed to doing things together or performing public roles and are therefore unable to find community and the intimacy it gives. Community, in its satisfying and organic form, is not to be found, so culturally reinforced expectations of community, often embedded in policy, result in what Sennett calls *destructive gemeinschaft* (Sennett, 1992: 238). The virtual relationships within online communities contain neither the full panoply of social relationships nor the cohesive or organic expectations of gemeinschaft (community relationships), an argument also to be found in Presdee's (2000) 'Carnival of Leisure' critique. Instead, they find a form of gesellschaft-based community, which encourages the social deskilling[1] of the individual through the specialization and compartmentalization of interactions. It can certainly be argued that the internet has been successful in supporting the subsequent growth of new social networks which Licklider and Taylor described in their ground-breaking 1968 paper as the 'network of networks' (1990[1968]: 38). And yes, individuals can lock into networks that give the illusion of satisfying emotional or informational needs, but these networks are nevertheless restricted experiences and despite expectations to the contrary, networked individuals do not experience holistic community experience.

As access to the internet becomes more widely available through falling network charges, hardware costs and public access policies, major divisions in society will be the result more of inequalities in access to information than conventional socio-economic inequalities. Those individuals who do not engage with the technological revolution face informational exclusion. Consequently, a new order is emerging in the information society as described by Castells (2000a, 2000c) and others. One visible expression of this new order has been an increase in the overall numbers of registrations for trademarks and patents, combined with a new aggression in the application of intellectual property laws to protect properties and the expression of ideas. This suggests that information, some of which was previously in the public domain, is routinely becoming commodified as intellectual property. This encourages not only the growth of a new political economy of information capital and new power relationships (see Boyle, 1996; Wall, 2004), but also new forms of deviant behaviour in a bid to appropriate the value of informational content. In this way, cyberspace today not only challenges our conventional understanding of ownership and control, but it also blurs the traditional boundaries between criminal and civil activities along with some of the principles upon which our conventional understandings of criminal harm and justice are based. A good example here is the reduced ability of prosecutors to prove an offender's intention to permanently deprive another person of their digital informational property (as would be required under section 1 of the UK Theft Act 1968). Consequently, important questions emerge as to what cybercrimes are and to what extent they differ from other activities that we currently recognize as crime.

The transformative impacts of cyberspace upon criminal activity

Because the defining characteristic of cybercrime is its mediation by networked technologies, the test of a cybercrime must focus upon what is left if those same networked technologies are removed from the equation. This *transformation test*[2] is not intended to be scientific, rather it is a heuristic device, a rule of thumb. It simply enables us to understand further how the internet has become a conduit for criminal activity. The particular transformations that affect the digital architecture of criminal opportunity are, after Castells (2000c: 10), the growth in *networking* through the convergence of technologies, the importance of *informational* transfer and brokering (acquisition of information but also dataveillance through data mining), and *globalization*. These transformations are not simply the product of technology, nor are they necessarily mutually exclusive; rather, they signify broader processes and provide useful focal points for further discussion.

Networking and the convergence of technologies

Reduced to its basic form, the internet is essentially a set of agreed informational protocols that enable personal computers to communicate with each other across networks. It represents the successful convergence of computing and communications technologies into a consumable and easy to use product. The process of convergence is therefore an important key to understanding how criminal opportunity began to change in the information age, and can be defined in simple terms as the ability of different (networked) technology platforms, such as consumer devices (telephone, television and personal computers), to deliver similar kinds of services (European Commission, 1997: 1). A decade on from the early debates over digital convergence, the definition has not really changed, but the extent of convergence may now surprise the early commentators. We can, for example, now make phone calls (Voice over Internet Protocol – VoIP) from computers to mobile phones, we can send text messages to mobile phones, we can send emails to computers from mobile phones and then use those same phones to change the interactive TV channel (TVs that we have purchased using our computers) to be played on our phones or computers – (computers we may also have bought using other computers). Interfunctionality, new permutations and function creep caused by convergence are increasing, particularly since the advent of (wireless) ambient (AMI) technologies, identification (biometric) technologies and technologies of location through affordable satellite linkage (IPTS, 2003). Although still unproven, Software Defined Radio (SDR) (BBC, 2006o) could be a particularly significant convergence development in years to come. Sometimes known as 'Tower of Babel' technology because of its ability to read and understand different kinds of radio waves, SDR has the ability to link a range of different technologies and communications systems thus creating many new opportunities for linking individuals to each other, and also their homes and workplaces – assuming that the two will remain separate in the years to come.

The significance of convergence is that it creates a new value-added – the information network – which had not been envisaged when each individual technology was invented, being outside their individual capabilities. The subsequent convergence of newer communications technologies to make them interfunctional has refined and extended our ability to construct new social networks across a global, social and cultural span. Perhaps the most graphic illustration of the growing sophistication of networks has been the emergence of distributed and decentralized peer-to-peer (P2P) networks, or grid technologies,[3] that rely upon user participation and generate new forms of decentralized commercial and informational relationships between individuals. Other examples are networks that have grown up in virtual worlds, virtual environments in which participants are represented by avatars, or visual representations of users as they would like to be seen; or through discussion groups and blogsites (see below). The relationships that emerge can enhance citizenship and democratic participation, while also facilitating e-commerce and improving the overall quality of life. But, as illustrated earlier, there are some limits to the claims that can be made about these.

Informational transfer and value

If the internet is little more than a set of agreed informational protocols then at its heart is the process of information transfer to trade access protocols or content. Simply switching on a networked computer begins a process of information brokering, but once computers have exchanged their network protocols, the procedure for gaining access to a particular network is invoked. During this procedure an individual's access codes (personal information) are compared with data already held by the computer system to verify his or her access rights and identity. This *data doubling* is an act of surveillance that all computer users experience. Once access to a particular network has been obtained, informational content can be exchanged, usually at a price, as we shall see below.

Value in cyberspace is attached mainly to the expression of informational ideas rather than things. The focus of cybercrime, therefore, is to acquire information in order to extract its value. Activities that we understand as cybercrime include the illegal acquisition of access codes to closed systems, access to sources of finance, the manipulation or destruction of intellectual property in the form of copyrighted, trademarked materials, information and data. They also include new aspects of pornography in the form of distributed extreme sexual materials and video nasties, information warfare, economic espionage and many other activities.

Interestingly, the ability of networked technologies to create and retain informational data records of all internet transactions, usually for billing, advertising or even explicitly for law enforcement purposes, means that the intensity of informational surveillance increases to the point that it is now becoming impossible to escape from the electronic gaze. These data, or 'mouse droppings' as they are sometimes known, are primarily designed to make the system work by ensuring security and assisting the user. A subsequent analysis of the data trail (dataveillance) can also assist law enforcement. Data records can be recalled either to prove or disprove that a user had undertaken a transaction, or they can be monitored in real time to identify abnormal patterns of behaviour that may be criminal in much the same way that financial institutions currently monitor transactions to identify money laundering, payment card fraud and other areas of illegal activity (Levi and Maguire, 2004: 397). We begin to experience what Haggerty and Ericson have described as the 'disappearance of disappearance' (Haggerty and Ericson, 2000: 619). This, of course, poses a potential threat to the maintenance of privacy and human rights and has engendered a further debate that is touched upon later.

Globalization

The internet, as an information network, has contributed to the acceleration of globalization by collapsing traditional geographies of distance to the point that 'in the networked world, no island is an island' (McConnell International, 2000: 8; Goodman, and Brenner, 2002: 83). It is, for example, as quick to communicate by email half way across the planet as it is within a locality. While 'equidistance' can have immense benefits in terms of information dispersal, democratic participation in society and commerce, it can also bring risk that much closer. Within the specific context of crime, globalization has created informational crime opportunities across cultures and jurisdictions by extending the reach of criminals globally. Dan Geer has rather dramatically observed that everyone moves that little bit nearer on the internet with the consequence that 'every sociopath in your neighbourhood is now living next to you, and there are no good neighbourhoods' (Geer, 2004).

But globalization should not simply be interpreted as an extension of technological reach; rather, it is a social process that configures and reconfigures 'relationships between multiple entities – from individuals to international agencies – which are widely distributed in space' (Cain, 2002). These relationships are neither innocent nor power free because they are based upon the exchange of informational value, and not always a fair exchange. Swift has argued that globalization 'is the product of a kind of turbo-capitalism that utilizes technologies to project itself through trade, investment and speculation at ever-faster speeds to ever-farther horizons' (2002). As a consequence globalized information flows have broadened the imagination of criminals beyond traditional cultures and geographical boundaries, and disparities between the local and the global have created new criminogenic scenarios. Cybercrime is, then, more than a globalized phenomenon that can be committed anywhere on the internet, from anywhere, at any time, but it is built on ideas that transcend cultural and geographical boundaries. Theoretically, at least, changes in one place should also be found in another.

At some point, however, the 'local' enters into the equation, first via the offender, because the crime has to be committed somewhere, and secondly, via the victim, because they are victimized somewhere. A third intrusion of the 'local' comes via the investigation, which has to take place somewhere, usually, though not necessarily, where the offending or victimization took place. It is important to note here that this is a different 'local' than that found in the analysis of street crime because it is a 'local' that is transformed by the global. Bauman (1998) conceptualizes this 'glocalization' as an intrinsic linkage between global and local processes and which he points out, are not 'trans', or 'inter'-national, rather they are 'glocalized'. The internet may, for example, introduce entirely new types of victimization into a locality. So, from a law enforcement point of view, globalization not only impacts upon local criminal practices, but it also changes the relationship between the global and the local (Robertson, 1995; Findlay, 1999), thus shaping local enforcement and policing cultures. Of course, the local can also shape the global in that local events can generate broader criminal opportunities, for example the prohibition or excessive taxation of goods in one jurisdiction may immediately create criminal business opportunities elsewhere and the internet provides the global links through which those opportunities can be exploited.

Although concepts like 'globalization' and 'glocalization' are highly contestable, they nevertheless provide a language for understanding change. One certainty is that cybercrimes will proliferate and become increasingly more global. Visible examples of this trend are already to be found in the criminal opportunities that exploit the convergence of different information technologies, for example email spams and viruses, or the convergence of communications technologies with linked databases that contain very private information about ourselves or our patterns of consumption and lifestyles. The upshot of the transformations in networking, informational transfer and globalization is that networked information technology creates quite dissimilar and novel information flows that join participants together in different ways and in different time frames. Information of interest can flow by word of 'mouse' (email) very quickly and the information flows can be almost viral in the way that they are distributed, travelling quickly from node to node across networks (see discussion about videos in Geist, 2006). This use of the term 'viral' is not to be confused with malicious software, although there is an indirect link in terms of the escalation of distribution. Rather, it is about the way that relationships are organized across the internet along which information can flow, particularly following the rise in popularity of the virtual social spaces created by the interaction of email, webmail, social networking websites, blogging sites, chat rooms and instant messenger services. These viral information flows create the possibility of asymmetric gesellschaft or transactional relationships with other individuals in place of symmetric face-to-face relationships. Just as one individual can be in touch with many others simultaneously during the course of routine communications, the same technology can also engender asymmetric relationships between offender and victim with the result that one individual can simultaneously victimize a number of individuals, either synchronously in real-time, or asynchronously in chosen-time (Morris and Ogan, 1996: 42–3). The latter condition can mean that the victimization can take place in real-time or some time after the initial communication. A useful example of asymmetry and asynchronicity in viral information flows is found in the computer-mediated offender–victim relationship caused by malicious spams (discussed in greater detail in chapter 7). Together these transformations in networking, informational transfer and globalization have contributed to radical changes in the organization of crime and the division of criminal labour, and to changes in the scope of criminal opportunity.

Changes in the organization of crime and the division of criminal labour

Each of the above three transformations now gives individuals greater control over the criminal process across a global span and facilitates new forms of criminal organization.

Greater control over the criminal process by the individual

Perhaps the most profound transformation has been the power that the internet places in the hands of a single person, often referred to as the 'empowered single or small agent' (see Rathmell 1998: 2;

Pease 2001: 22; Artosi, 2002). These are lone offenders who exploit networked technology to carry out incredibly complex and far-reaching tasks that can be repeated countless times globally. Tempered only by technological limitations such as bandwidth and language, they are now able to commit crimes previously beyond their financial and organizational means. The changes in the dynamics of the return on investment now make offending more cost-effective and represent a significant step-change in criminality. On the one hand, offenders can commit smaller-impact, bulk victimizations across a broad geographical span, while, on the other hand, they do not have to have many successes before they break even. Furthermore, because they tend to work alone and remotely, their chances of getting caught are reduced by the fact that there is little criminal intelligence circulating about them (in comparison, to, say, a bank robbery, the organization of which involves a comparatively large number of individuals). The knock-on effects of this change in the organization of criminal activity for the justice process are considerable. This is particularly true where the principle of *de minimis non curat lex* (the law does not concern itself with trifles) begins to apply: the problem of small or low-impact multiple victimizations distributed across many jurisdictions collectively constitutes a significant criminal activity yet individually does not justify the expenditure of resources in investigation or prosecution (see chapter 8).

New forms of criminal organization through collaborations between different skill-sets

The second most profound effect of the transformations is the new genre of collaborations between different offending groups: hackers, virus writers and spammers. Initial concerns about the transfer of organized crime to the internet were largely dispelled by Brenner. She predicted that organized criminal activity would likely manifest itself online in 'transient, lateral and fluid' forms, as networks of criminals (2002: 1) rather than replicate the two principal models of organized criminal activity found in the 'real world': the 'gang' model and the hierarchical American 'Mafia'. This is mainly because they evolved largely in response to real world opportunities and constraints that are largely absent in cyberspace. Brenner anticipates that 'online criminal activity will almost certainly emphasize lateral relationships, networks instead of hierarchies . . . [a] "swarming" model, in which individuals coalesce for a limited period of time in order to conduct a specifically defined task or set of tasks and, having succeeded, go their separate ways' (Brenner, 2002: 50). Instead, individuals with different skill-sets are more likely to join in ephemeral relationships to commit a common act, or to reproduce their skills and knowledge. These predictions are largely borne out by contemporary evidence – see, for example, Mann and Sutton's research into the operation of cracker news groups (1998) and Wall (2000). The important questions here are why should this be the case and will the pattern continue?

Although an entire (cyber) criminal process can be perpetrated by very few people, the division of labour has become very specialized and an array of specialized components needs to be drawn together to make it work. While virus writing, for example, can be part-automated, the higher specifications of sophisticated malicious software today require increasingly specialist skills in their construction, as the later discussion about botnets and zombie computers illustrates. But to give a brief illustration, in 2004, German Magazine *C'T* found that virus writers had been selling the internet protocol (IP) addresses of computers infected with their remote administration Trojans to spammers (*C'T*, 2004). Not only do these infected computers, or 'zombies', enable spammers to use the infected systems to illegally distribute spams without the knowledge of the computer owners, but the 'botnet' network of installed trojans (see Glossary) forms a powerful tool which the distributors of the viruses can use, among other things, to launch distributed denial of service (DDOS) attacks (McQuade, 2006b: 99; BBC, 2003d, *C'T*, 2004; Libbenga, 2004 – see chs 4 and 7).

Behind this collaboration of skills sets and the rise in trojan attacks from botnets are concerns that 'organized crime' interests are now exploiting this 'third generation' of cybercrime. In June 2005, the NISCC (National Infrastructure Security Co-ordination Centre) warned of the practices of 'a highly sophisticated high-tech gang' reputed to be located in the Far East using various means to infect sensitive computer systems in order to steal government and business secrets (Warren, 2005; NISCC, 2005). The warning provides details of forms of criminal organization that are not only unique, but also depart from traditional thinking on organized crime, although it is thought that high-level organized crime may be involved. The attacks 'demonstrate a high level of expertise . . . coupled with the use of . . . social engineering to obtain email addresses and names of targets' (Warren, 2005). The warning confirmed the suspicions of security analysts who stated that they believed the attacks, about three per day, had been launched over a period of up to a year (see Naraine, 2005).

The attacks described above were distinctive for a number of reasons. The first was that they did not demonstrate the patterns of behaviour that hackers have traditionally displayed and they did not 'appear to have the incentives that organized crime is after in terms of a fast financial return' (Warren, 2005). What was more certain, according to Warren, was that those involved were 'one of a number of organized groups that are spreading around the world in a high tech crime wave'. The second reason was that the pattern of the attack was more like a phishing expedition than a premeditated assault on one or more organizations. The gang was believed to be composed of a dozen or so individuals who attacked systems using information that had been returned randomly from infected computers within the network. For example, it was not simply targeted at corporations, because governmental organizations and agencies were also found to have been caught out (Leyden, 2005f). The third reason was that the information returned would then be used to identify quickly key individuals in the target organization about whom further information would be sought, often with a turn-around of as little as two hours. The 'personal' information contained in subsequent emails sent out in a subsequent targeted attack would 'engineer' the individual to open an attachment. In so doing, their computer would become infected by sophisticated trojans, which have the ability to regularly change themselves to evade detection by anti-virus and spyware software. The trojans would then seek out and return to the gang corporate and personal information that may be passed on to a competitor or be used to compromise the target organization (Warren, 2005; Leyden, 2005f; Lueck, 2005). Only time will tell if these 'gangs' come to constitute a 'new internet mafia' (Berinato, 2006).

Deskilling and reskilling criminal labour

A useful way of understanding the impacts of networked technology is to explore them in terms of the 'deskilling effect' (Braverman, 1976). The deskilling hypothesis draws upon Marxist theory to argue that the main rationale behind the development and utilization of technology is to increase the efficiency of human labour and actions to maximize investment in capital. Central to this operation is the process of rationalizing and 'degrading' labour by breaking it down into essential tasks and then automating each of those tasks to make them more efficient and economical to carry out. Examples can be found in most occupations, notably in the factory where legions of manual assembly-line workers have now been replaced by machines. The deskilling effect is by no means restricted to the production process; for example, in most clerical and managerial occupations, typing is now a generic skill along with using computers, whereas not too long ago both typing and computing were carried out by specialists. While the critics of technology have been quick to highlight the negative effects of the deskilling effect upon labour (e.g. unemployment), they have largely ignored the inevitable and simultaneous reskilling process that also occurs when workers (albeit fewer of them) take control of more complete, but automated, production processes.

These deskilling and reskilling arguments can equally be applied to the organization of the labour of crime – as can be seen, for example, in the increasing use of networked computers to automate offending. At a basic level, computers were, and still are, a sophisticated tool that can be used to commit offences, such as the 'hack', the theft, etc. Originally performed manually by hackers trained as programmers, hacking subsequently became enhanced by the use of 'scripts' – as in the first and second generations of cybercrimes (described below). It was, however, the automation of the process, using web-based 'point and click' tools that enabled malicious software and code to be more easily and effectively compiled *en masse* (BBC, 2005h). Some interesting evidence of the deskilling and reskilling of online criminal labour is found in the demise of the once popular hacking magazine *Phrack*. For over two decades *Phrack* 'spanned the evolution of hacking from the days of bulletin boards to 3G mobiles with a knowledgeable, politically aware and frequently controversial take on information security' (Leyden, 2005i). Its last editor (Ollie) complained that 'the basic skill level hackers need to build up was rising all the time. It's much harder to get to a point where you can actually do stuff . . . [y]ou have to learn much more and read many more books. The entry-level of skills has been raised' (Ward, 2005a).

The internet clearly provides a new conduit for criminal and harmful behaviour. The transformative impacts change the traditional spatial and temporal relationships between offender, victim and the state by creating entirely new opportunities for harmful or criminal behaviours, for example by widening the offender's reach of opportunity globally, enabling offenders to engage victims in new ways and providing new means for the organization of criminal behaviours. So, although the fundamental nature of the victimization may be familiar, for example deception or theft, when the behaviour has been transformed by the internet, it is referred to as a cybercrime. But, what actually is a cybercrime? Without a systematic clarification of the nature of cybercrimes, dystopian and often inapt concerns about them can result in misplaced or exaggerated public demands for policy responses from criminal justice and other agencies.

Changes in the scope of criminal opportunity online

The origins of cybercrime can be traced back to the interception of semaphore signals in the eighteenth century, or the wire tap in the nineteenth and early twentieth centuries (Standage, 1998). In both cases, valuable information was intercepted as it was being transmitted across hitherto unparalleled spans of time and space and then sold. However, the true genesis of cybercrimes originates in early computer crimes prior to their subsequent transformation by networking over two further generations. It is useful to explore these milestones, because although the notion of 'generation' invokes the passage of time, each generation is distinctive and the conceptual differences between them can be used to explain contemporary differences currently present in the scope of criminal opportunity.

The first generation of cybercrime: crimes using computers (to assist traditional offending)

The first generation of cybercrime took place *within* discrete computing systems and was mainly characterized by the criminal exploitation of mainframe computers and their discrete operating systems. Usually related to the acquisition of money or the destruction or appropriation of restricted information, this first generation marked a departure from conventional criminal opportunity. See, for example, the 'Salami fraud' (Singleton, 2002: 39; Kabay, 2002) committed by Gus Gorman in the film *Superman III* where he corralled the surplus half cents from banking transactions into his monthly pay cheque. The opportunity was created by inconsistencies in the computing system relating to 'rounding up' fractions less than the lowest denomination of money. In this way, even though the crime appeared to be completely mediated by technology, the offending was localized by the limitations of the mainframe computing system. Although this first generation of cybercrime involved, and still involves, the use of computers, networked or otherwise, the behaviours, frequently referred to as cybercrimes, are in fact 'traditional' (Wall, 2001) or 'ordinary' (McQuade, 2006a, 2006b). They are low end cybercrimes, a distinction borrowed from Brodeur's (1983) work on policing, where computers are used mainly during the preparation stage of a crime, either as a tool of communication or to gather preparatory information (for example, how to kill someone or how to manufacture drugs or weapons).

Here, existing patterns of harmful activity are sustained by networked technologies, but remove them, and the activities will still persist by other means. Drug dealers, for example, will use whatever form of communications and information technology are available, convenient and less risky. It is similarly the case with information about weapons and other harms, even manuals on how to commit crimes, which existed before the internet. Radical book retailer Loompanics, for example, has long specialized in selling books that describe the technologies and techniques involved in potentially harmful actions and are therefore illegal in many jurisdictions outside the US. Thinking back to *Superman III*, even Gus Gorman's 'Salami Fraud' could still have been committed by a subtle misuse of the internal banking orders.

The second generation of cybercrime: opportunities for crimes across a global span of networks

The second generation of cybercrimes are those committed *across networks*, such as hacking and cracking. They were originally the product of a marriage between the skills of the early computer operators and the communications skills of the phone phreakers who imaginatively 'cracked' telephone systems to make free telephone calls. The phone phreaker was epitomized by the legendary exploits of Cap'n Crunch (aka John Draper), so named because he used a toy whistle obtained from a box of Cap'n Crunch cereal to access AT&T's phone system by whistling its long distance dial tone. The marriage gave birth to 'hackers', who were driven by a combination of the phreakers' ethical belief in their moral right to hack into systems and the post-Vietnam culture of the 1970s with its youthful promotion of civil liberties and suspicion of government and large corporations. Hackers would use their knowledge of telephone systems in conjunction with their computing and 'social engineering' skills to 'talk' information out of the owner and access discrete but linked computing systems. For the uninitiated, hackers claim to be driven by ethical principles, whereas crackers are not. The term 'cracker' was originally adopted to avoid the misuse of the word 'hacker' by the media. Useful histories of cybercrime can be found in Shinder and Tittle (2002: 49–92), Britz (2003) and McQuade (2006b).

When the first personal computers became available in the 1970s and 1980s they could be connected by phone-in Local Area Networks (LANs). The early hackers tested systems and shared their philosophies and knowledge of 'hacks' on bulletin board services (BBS). Those same BBS systems developed into early virtual trading posts from where information services and goods were sold, thus creating opportunities for theft and the acquisition of goods and services. This second generation of cybercrime was given a boost when the internet was opened up for general commercial use and TCP/IP (Transmission Control Protocol/Internet Protocol) was accepted as the standard. Until the mid-1980s the internet had been the preserve of the military who originally conceived it as an attack-proof communications system. It was subsequently released for governmental and academic purposes before being opened up for general usage. The internet's massive potential for good and bad was realized following the development and commercial popularity of the graphics user interface (GUI) in the early 1990s.

The second generation of cybercrimes are mostly 'hybrid' (Wall, 2001) or 'adaptive' (McQuade, 2006a, 2006b). They are effectively 'traditional' crimes for which entirely new globalized opportunities have arisen. For them, the internet has created a transnational environment with entirely new opportunities for harmful activities that are currently the subject of existing criminal or civil law. Examples of these activities include trading in sexually explicit materials, including child pornography, through interactive hardcore websites, and fraud (see Grabosky et al., 2001: 30; Levi, 2001: 44). The increasing prevalence of deception through internet auctions, for example, is a vivid example of this level of opportunity (see Newman and Clarke, 2003: 94).

Networked environments also contribute to the circulation of criminal ideas. Newsgroups and websites circulate information about 'chipping' – how to bypass the security devices in mobile telephones or digital television decoders (Mann and Sutton, 1998; Wall, 2000). They also provide information on how to manufacture and distribute synthetic drugs (Schneider, 2003: 374). Take away the internet and the offending behaviour remains, but the new opportunities for offending disappear and the behaviour continues by other means, though not in such great numbers or across such a wide span. Consequently, hybrid cybercrimes are examples of the 'modernization of modernity' (Beck, 1992; Finnemann, 2002: 36). Furthermore, there is a common understanding and an institutional view as to which agencies are responsible for offending behaviours falling under these first two levels of opportunity. Indeed, their subject matters are not only covered by law and the public policing mandates of most countries (in so far as there tends to be clear public support for policing agencies to intervene) but any problems that arise tend to relate to matters of trans-jurisdictional procedure rather than substantive law. This contrasts with the third level where the responsibilities are not so clearly cut.

The third generation of cybercrime: true cybercrimes wholly mediated by technology

The third generation of cybercrime is characterized by its *distributed and automated* nature, and was ushered in by the wholesale replacement of dial-in modem access with broadband at the turn of the twenty-first century. Originally, online offender–victim engagement took place via spammed emails which encouraged recipients to respond directly or to click onto websites. More recently, spam email has converged with virus attachments to further automate cybercrime. A particularly potent example of the latter is the multifunctionality of the 'blended threat', which submits control of the infected computer to the infector via a botnet while also gathering and passing on personal information from the same computer. The two actions were previously considered parallel threats, but they now have one source. They are almost wholly mediated by networked technologies in that they rely less and less on social engineering. Most importantly, they illustrate a step-change in the transformation of cybercrime that is beginning to make the traditional hackers and crackers 'by and large, an amusing diversion and [no longer] an opportunity to dust down 20-year old clichés about teenage geniuses' (Sommer, 2004: 10). This is not of course, to imply that the seriousness of 'hacking' has in anyway diminished – see, for example, the Ohio children's hospital hack which exposed 230,000 files to identity thieves (Leyden, 2006g). Rather, it suggests not only that the cybercrime agenda has changed, but also that the culture of fear that once surrounded hacking has transferred to botnets.

The true cybercrimes exist at the high end of the continuum. They are the spawn of the internet and therefore embody all of its transformative characteristics. True cybercrimes break the temporality of

the geo-social relationship between time and space by distanci-
ating (distancing and estranging) it across a global span. Since they
are solely the product of opportunities created by the internet, they can
only be perpetrated within its cyberspace and are therefore *sui
generis* (of their own kind). At the far extreme of this third category
are the more controversial harms, particularly the appropriation of
intellectual properties which fall outside the jurisdiction and
experience of the criminal justice process. See, for example 'cyber-
rape' (MacKinnon, 1997) or the 'virtual vandalism' of virtual
worlds (Williams, 2003), and also the ongoing battle between the
music and movie industry and downloaders (Carey and Wall, 2001;
Marshall, 2002: 1). Spamming is a particularly good example of a true
or pure cybercrime because it is now an illegal behaviour in its own
right in US and EU law and many other jurisdictions. It also facilitates
secondary offending by enabling offenders to engage with potential
victims. Take away the internet and spamming and the other true
cybercrimes vanish.

Although not discussed here in detail because the technologies are
still in the development phase, it is anticipated that a fourth generation of cybercrimes will eventually emerge from criminal opportunities generated by the *ambient* intelligent networks being created by
the convergence of wireless, including Software Defined Radio, and
networked technologies (briefly mentioned earlier) (IPTS, 2003).
Although ambient technologies are still in their infancy, research is
already being conducted into predicting the legal, regulatory and
technological safeguards that will be required in a world of ambient
intelligence (see further Friedewald et al., 2006).

By placing cybercrimes within a framework of time rather than
space we can understand them as successive generations defined by
different states of technological development with each transforming
criminal opportunity. This approach also helps us to identify quickly
the core issues and then position the subject area within criminology
and its associated discourses, avoiding the confusion caused by applying the term to all crimes involving computers. For example, where
digital evidence is involved, or even where computers and their components are stolen, '[t]his is misleading at best, and self-serving, at
worst' (Britz, 2003: 4). More specifically, the 'transformation test'
proves useful in categorizing the different types of online offending
behaviour currently being referred to as cybercrime, for example in
distinguishing between those which have a familiar ring to them and
those which appear to jump straight out of the pages of a science
fiction novel.

Three criminologies of cybercrime: impacts upon substantive areas of criminal behaviour

Online offending tends to fall into one of three basic groups that each invokes different bodies of law and requires individual legal and criminological understandings. These groups are: offending relating to the integrity of the computer system, offending assisted by computers, and offending which focuses upon the content of computers. Each also illustrates specific discourses of public debate and experiences within the criminal justice processes.[4] The three criminologies serve as the basis for the next three chapters, although it is admittedly becoming harder to disaggregate the three in practice within the new generation of automated cybercrime. In practice, there will be some blurring across boundaries because the true cybercrimes will appear to involve combinations of two or more. Phishing, is a good example of this 'blending' of crime because offenders engage their victims through spam (integrity), steal their personal information (computer assisted) by deceiving victims into logging on to a bogus website (content) which they think belongs to their bank. Phishers then assault the integrity of the victim's own financial system to perpetrate a fraud. However, in all cases, only one of the three, the principal *modus operandi*, to steal money, will tend to be the primary driver behind the crime. Hence, some of these newer mediated forms of offending will appear across a number of chapters in different guises, and (unfortunately) with a degree of repetition.

Computer integrity crimes

Computer integrity crimes assault the security of network access mechanisms. They include hacking and cracking, vandalism, spying, denial of service, the planting and use of viruses and Trojans (see further Gordon and Chess, 1999). Many jurisdictions now have legislation, such as the UK's Computer Misuse Act 1990, to protect them against unauthorized access to computer material, unauthorized access with intent to commit further offences, and unauthorized modification of computer material. Computer integrity crimes can also pave the way for more serious forms of offending, as in the case of phishing. Crackers, for example, may use trojan viruses to install 'back doors' that are later used to facilitate other crimes, possibly by spammers who have bought lists of the infected addresses.

Computer-assisted (or related) crimes

Computer-assisted crimes use networked computers to commit crimes, usually to acquire money, goods or services dishonestly. In addition to internet frauds there are socially engineered variants such as the aforementioned 'phishing', '419' advanced-fee frauds (see Glossary), and the manipulation of new online sales environments, particularly auction sites. Most jurisdictions now have thefts acts and legal procedures for the recovery of lost assets, along with intellectual property laws to protect citizens against the illicit acquisition of the expression of ideas.

Computer content crimes

Computer content crimes are related to the illegal content on net-worked computer systems and include the trade and distribution of pornographic materials as well as the dissemination of hate crime materials. Most jurisdictions have variants of obscenity laws and laws which prohibit incitement, although their legislative strength can vary where internet content is also protected by legislation that guarantees freedoms of speech and expression.

The above not only illustrate the development and diversity of cybercrimes, but they also provide practical demarcations for analysis. They can, for example, be used to identify the different resourcing implications for investigation and enforcement, or for choosing methodologies when designing research to further our knowledge of cybercrime.

Conclusions

In his analysis of the Victorian electric telegraph, Standage observed broadly that '[g]iven a new invention, there will always be some people who see only its potential to do good, while others see new opportunities to commit crime or make money. We can expect exactly the same reactions to whatever new inventions appear in the twenty-first century' (Standage, 1998: 199). The above analysis shows that the particular characteristics of the internet – informational activity, networking and globalization – have transformed criminal behaviour by creating new opportunities for old crimes and, importantly, also new opportunities for new crimes. It also explains how the present cybercrime debate often confuses traditional patterns of offending using computers with the forms of cybercrime that are solely the product of the internet. The next three chapters look in greater detail at the transformations taking place within substantive areas of criminal activity.

4

Computer Integrity Crime: Hacking, Cracking and Denial of Service

How has criminal activity changed in the information age?
Part 1

Chapter at a glance

- **Hacking and cracking/hackers and crackers**
  The ethical hackers
  The unethical hackers (crackers)
  Cyber-terrorists and information warfare
- **Hacker tactics to compromise the integrity of networked computers**
  Social engineering
  Using spyware and surveillance software
  Using malicious software and code
- **Cyber-barrage: distributed denial of service attack (DDOS)**
- **Motivations for offending and reproducing criminal knowledge online**
  Self-satisfaction
  The need for peer respect
  To impress potential employers
  Criminal gain or commercial advantage
  Revenge
  Distance from victim
  Politically motivated protest
- **Reproducing 'hacking' skills online**
- **Conclusions**

Without trust in the integrity of a computer system everything that it represents becomes compromised. A major problem, therefore, in assessing the impact of a trespass or hack is to be able to ascertain accurately whether or not it is an end in its own right, or whether it is a precursor to other crimes – which is a useful principle for distinguishing between different types of hackers. With this important distinction in mind, this chapter will focus upon attacks on the integrity of the networked computer, at the point where the access system of networked computers is the object of criminal attention. The first section will look at the variations of hacking; the second discusses the tactics employed to breach the integrity of systems, while the third identifies a relatively different type of assault on network integrity, the barrage or denial of service attack, which illegitimately prevent users from gaining legitimate access to systems.

Hacking and cracking

Hacking generally describes deliberate unauthorized access to spaces over which rights of ownership or access have already been established. The primary aim of hacking is to breach the security of a networked computer system by assaulting its integrity. The term 'trespass' would probably be more descriptive of the broader range of attacks upon system integrity because it does not carry the emotional and ideological baggage that comes with the term 'hacking'. However, the use of the terms 'hacking' and 'hackers', like cybercrime, is now embedded in everyday language.

It is no great surprise that hacking has generated public and corporate concerns. For many years surveys from both sides of the Atlantic have consistently indicated high numbers of security breaches. The UK Department of Trade and Industry's (DTI) *Information Security Breaches Survey 2002* found that '44% of UK businesses have suffered at least one malicious security breach in the past year, nearly twice as many as in the 2000 survey' (DTI, 2002: 1). Such a high level of victimization also reflects the experience in the US. During 2002, the Computer Emergency Response Team (CERT) at Carnegie Mellon University recorded about 100,000 incidents of security breaches. Another US source, the CSI/FBI survey found in its *2002 Computer Crime and Security Survey* that '[n]inety percent of respondents (primarily large corporations and government agencies) detected computer security breaches within the last twelve months' (FBI/CSI, 2002: 4). The common theme running through these sources (and others) is the consistently high level of victimization and therefore offending. However, as noted above, these fairly high levels of victimization contrast sharply with the remarkably low prosecution figures and also the results of the surveys of individual victimization (see the BCS Survey, Allen et al., 2005; Wilson et al., 2006). In England and Wales, these security breaches fall under the Computer Misuse Act 1990 which protects victims against unauthorized access to computer material (s.1); unauthorized access with intent to commit or facilitate commission of further offences (s.2); and unauthorized modification of computer material (s.3). During the first decade following its introduction (1991–2000), 53 offenders were cautioned under the Act and a further 88 prosecuted. Of the latter, 68 (77 per cent) were convicted: 15 under section 1, 11 under section 2 and 42 under section 3 (*Hansard*, 26 March 2002: column WA35; Wall, 2003: 131). It is very possible that since security breaches are usually precursors to further offences, some might have been prosecuted under the more substantive offence or under the Telecommunications Act. However, like the reporting statistics, even if the true figure was ten or even a hundred times the number prosecuted, then a shortfall would still appear to exist. Is this a failure of law and of the police, or is it a problem relating to the nature of integrity offences? The former two questions drive much of the enquiry in the later part of this book, especially chapters 8 and 9. In this chapter, however, the focus is upon outlining the nature of computer integrity crime.

Hackers and crackers

The hackers were initially regarded as a celebration of the genius of youth and the pioneering spirit of America, but they have subsequently become demonized (see Chandler, 1996: 229; Duff and Gardiner, 1996; Ross, 1990: para. 4; Sterling, 1994; Taylor, 1999). Today, there is a clear distinction between 'white hat hackers', who celebrate the original ethical hacking traditions, and 'black hat crackers', who are driven by unethical motivations such as financial gain or revenge. Although there remains some regard for the public service/civil liberties ethics of the hacker, their skills and beliefs have become co-mingled with those of the 'cracker' and both are now outlawed by most computer misuse laws as being a major threat to the public interest. More specifically, hacking has developed far beyond the original first generation system hacks to reveal a broad array of activities and motivations. Under close scrutiny this range of behaviours are found to represent a spectrum of qualitatively different types of trespass, from intellectually motivated acts at one end to politically or criminally motivated trespass at the other.

In its least invasive form, hacking is considered, mainly by the hackers themselves, to be an intellectual challenge resulting in a fairly harmless trespass intended to test security systems, release information or to advertise the intruder's hacking abilities, rather than to purposefully cause any serious and lasting damage. Hacking can even help to improve security procedures and processes through penetration testing. At its worst, it can cause considerable damage to the infrastructure and also to information, leading to financial and possibly physical losses, plus there is also the damage caused by secondary impacts in the form of loss of trust, loss of business, and reduced participation in networks. Since 'hacking' is now largely the accepted term, it is appropriate to talk of the distinction between hackers and crackers in terms of ethical and unethical hackers.

The ethical hackers

The ethical hacker possesses a high level of specialized knowledge combined with a belief in the ethics of freedom of access to public information. From the early days, the hackers played a crucial role in the development of the internet (see Chandler, 1996; Duff and Gardiner, 1996; Ross, 1990: para 4; Sterling, 1994). They tested systems and forced code writers to achieve higher standards of quality, while also lending their skills and imagination to shape the internet. Written in 1986 and published in the now defunct *Phrack* magazine, these ethical values are encapsulated in the Hacker's Manifesto: 'Yes, I am a criminal. My crime is that of curiosity. My crime is that of judging people by what they say and think, not what they look like. My crime is that of outsmarting you, something that you will never forgive me for' (The Mentor, 1986). There are three basic levels of ethical hacker, the 'Gurus', who are experts, and 'Wizards', who are renowned for their knowledge. Both espouse the hacker ethic that sharing information is a positive activity that contributes towards the good of society. The 'Samurai', in contrast, hire themselves out to undertake legal 'cracking' tasks, legitimate or justified surveillance, such as in corporate disputes, assist lawyers working on privacy-rights and First Amendment cases, and to assist any other 'parties that have legitimate reasons to need an electronic locksmith'.

The unethical hackers (crackers)

The unethical hackers fall somewhere between white and black hat, depending upon the level of maliciousness and harm inflicted. Crackers are driven by a range of motivations and different *modus operandi*. Young (1995: 10) distinguished between *utopians* who naively believe that they are contributing to society by demonstrating its vulnerabilities, a self-justification rather than a conviction, and *cyberpunks* who are aggressively anti-establishment and intentionally cause harm to targets which offend them. Both, of course, tend to create disruption through their unauthorized presence at a particular site. It is often fairly hard to discern between the two in practice and further distinctions may be made in terms of experience. 'Script kiddies', according to *Wordspy*, are inexperienced and unskilled hackers 'who attempt to infiltrate or disrupt computer systems by running pre-fabricated scripts designed to crack those systems' (wordspy.com). Since their primary motivation is to command peer respect for their skills or their sheer audacity, script kiddie achievements (evidence of audacious hacks) are often displayed on one or more of a number of sites. One such site, *2600: The Hacker Quarterly*, has an archive of 'hacked' sites (www.2600.com). Once they become experienced, script kiddies usually graduate into 'black hat' hackers or 'dark-side' crackers.

Whereas the script kiddies and many hackers and crackers want to be noticed, cyber-spies, in contrast, do not. They want to enter and exit sites discreetly, avoiding detection[1] in order to obtain restricted information such as trade secrets, which might, for example, enable the possessor to gain a market-place advantage over their competitors. The internet can assist the act of cyber-espionage in a number of distinct ways. The first is that it enables disgruntled insiders, who are a prime source of information, to seek revenge or gain by abusing their access system rights to obtain information electronically and send it outside the organizational boundaries. The second way is for insiders to provide outsiders with unauthorized access to closed systems to obtain information. This may be by getting an insider to install spyware or back doors into a system to allow remote access, or by 'socially engineering' an insider to reveal the access codes (see Mitnick and Simon, 2002). The third way is to discretely probe a system looking for default system usernames and passwords (e.g. 'guest' and 'guest'). The fourth way is much less dramatic and not necessarily illegal. The surveillant capacity of the internet enables outsiders to observe the intelligence radiated by organizations via their own websites. By pulling together many minor pieces of information, a fairly complete picture of the organization's structure, ambitions and plans can often be assembled.

Cyber-terrorists and information warfare

Although concerns about cyber-terrorism predate September 11, 2001 (see Denning, 2000), it has since become a very emotive topic. This is partly because of the real threat to infrastructure, but also because of the dramatic imagery that it invokes. The purpose of cyber-terrorism is to use computers to attack the physical infrastructure to generate mass fear and anxiety and, in theory, manipulate the political agenda. Writing in the early 1990s, Sterling warned that 'hackers in Amtrak computers or in air-traffic controller computers, will kill somebody someday' (Sterling, 1994: 185). In February 1998, the vulnerability of the US military computers was exposed when it was discovered that hackers had entered the Pentagon's system via a way-station computer in the United Arab Emirates. The implications of the attack were played down by the Pentagon, which, in contrast to its previous experience of intrusion, suggested that the break-ins were the result of a contest perpetrated by a small group of amateurs (Dolinar, 1998: A03). In this case what is not known is whether the hackers left themselves trap doors: 'the digital equivalent of the key under the welcome mat to use next time' (Dolinar, 1998: A03).

The main weakness with the concept of cyber-terrorism is that its risk assessment is hard to disaggregate from its reality. It is certainly possible that key public computer systems, networks, services and utilities could be disrupted or disabled through malicious intrusion. However, since most key state and corporate critical infrastructures have been protected since September 11, and many before that date, by protection and enforcement policies supported by the necessary financial and human resources, the likelihood of a successful cyber-terrorist attack will have been considerably reduced. Indeed, without understating the potential threat, this strength may well explain why the earlier doomsday predictions about cyber-terrorism have yet to materialize.

More likely to occur is a variant of what is commonly referred to as *information warfare* (Szafranski, 1995: 56), though whether or not it is correct to call it warfare depends upon the circumstances. Interestingly, the older accounts of information warfare define it as the military use of information as a tool of warfare against national information systems. Information warfare has long been used to weaken the resistance of 'the enemy' and examples can be found centuries before the internet came into being. It can take the form of using propaganda to persuade the enemy to surrender, or of feeding disinformation or propaganda to one's own population to persuade them to rally to the cause. As old as information warfare may be, networked technologies provide new possibilities for conducting it effectively and efficiently, and especially of undermining an enemy's data and information systems. So great is the concern within military circles about the potential for using networked technology for information warfare that military strategists regularly prepare counter information warfare strategies to be effected by formally constituted Information Warfare Units (Berger, 1996; Rathmell, 2001).

Contemporary definitions of information warfare tend to view it less militaristically and rather as the manipulation of information to obtain a competitive advantage over a corporate or other opponent. But it is important not to downplay the potential impact of information warfare just because the attack may use information or focus upon information systems. An attack on key government informational data, such as tax codes or social security numbers, could have serious long-term impacts on political and societal stability. It is important to note here that the main threats from information warfare are more likely to take the form of viral information flows, which are often of individual minor significance but which have a greater aggregate impact. Indeed, Berkowitz and Hahn (2003) and Francisco (2003) have concluded that the main threat from information warfare is not the economic damage resulting from a single large-scale attack, but the damage caused by a few small, well-publicized attacks that undermine public confidence in the systems being attacked.

Hacker tactics to compromise the integrity of networked computers

A common myth about hackers, perpetuated by hacker movies and fictional literature, is that they possess the superhuman ability to break into computer systems and map their way around them. The reality of hacking, as indicated earlier, is quite different because hackers tend to combine their expert computing skills with advanced knowledge about the communications systems and networks they are trying to penetrate, but also with key access information gained from the people working within the systems. There are essentially three ways in which this additional information can be obtained: through social engineering, by the use of spyware and surveillance software, and by using malicious software and codes.

Social engineering

Social engineering, or people hacking, is a technique to obtain access codes and information. It is both understated within, and runs counter to, the hacker mythology. Before being adopted by computer security managers, the term had a prior history in Skinnerian behavioural psychology. The expression was recently popularized by Kevin Mitnick in *The Art of Deception* (Mitnick and Simon, 2002) in which he explained that many of his hacks were achieved by exploiting the weakest link in the security chain, the people who have access to systems, rather than directly attacking the systems themselves. He described how the hackers' success lies in their ability to combine expert knowledge of communications and computing systems with their ability to build trust relationships with individuals who have access to systems, in order to 'socially engineer' passwords and pass codes out of them. The secret, according to Mitnick, lies in not making the target suspicious: '[t]he more a social engineer can make his contact seem like business as usual, the more he allays suspicion. When people don't have a reason to be suspicious, it's easy for a social engineer to gain their trust' (Mitnick and Simon, 2002: 41).

Social engineers use their knowledge of systems to make themselves appear credible to staff (usually administrative or secretarial) who have access to the system they are trying to enter. They will adopt the language of the organization, using first names, often referring to work colleagues using intimate terms. Once the 'engineer's' credibility has been established then access information will be sought from the victim. This activity does not usually take place in isolation. Other tactics may support or inform the practice of social engineering. If access information cannot be talked out of victims, then personal information may be sought from *discarded documents* retrieved from waste disposal. This personal information may be used to give the illusion of credibility in subsequent conversations with them. Of course, it may be that the operatives' paper waste could even directly provide the desired access information. Other more sophisticated techniques of social engineering, designed to trick individuals into parting with access information, may include *impersonating staff* by using credible documentation such as fake organizational identity cards. A further trick sometimes used is *reverse social engineering* where the hacker

causes a technical problem within a system and then positions himself
or herself to be commissioned to fix it, thereby gaining access (see
Mitnick and Simon, 2002: 60).

Using spyware and surveillance software

The second main 'hacking' tactic is to use clandestine spyware and
surveillance software to obtain access information. There are a
number of variants of spyware, each displaying different levels of
insidiousness. Moving from the seemingly inoffensive through to the
invasive, 'cookies' assist interactions between web browsers and
websites. They can also be used for low-level mass surveillance by
reporting back to a third party low-level information about the user's
browsing and purchasing preferences, for example, as used by advertising analysts such as DoubleClick (see *In re Doubleclick Inc.*, 2001).
Then there is password sniffing technology that can be used to
interrogate the access files of operating systems to identify passwords,
and a 'traffic movement logger' which records the communications
made by users but not the content, followed by the 'key-stroke logger'
which records what the users actually type. Finally, there is 'content
spyware' which conveys the entire actions of users on a specific
computer, including the content of any communications they may
send or receive.

Using malicious software and code

A third way of obtaining access information is by using *malicious software and code* (new generation hacking). During the past decade the
increasingly specialized division of criminal labour and growth in
strategic collaborations between hackers and virus writers and spammers, along with advances in hacking tools technology, has resulted
in the formation of a small industry around hacking. As a result,
hacking has quickly evolved into an asymmetrical activity through the
use of increasingly sophisticated malicious software (trojans) and
code (worms and viruses). Keylog programs, for example, are commonly included in rootkits and RATs (remote administration
trojans). These automate the hacking process by taking over computers, enabling them to be controlled remotely. The botnets facilitate a
new epoch in the organization of cyber-criminal activity, resulting in
a new generation of cybercrime in which 'old-style' hacking has, in
terms of prevalence, been displaced by its automated descendants
(the subject of chapter 7).

Cyber-barrage: distributed denial of service attack

Cyber-barrage is a fairly new but increasingly prevalent threat to network and computer integrity. In direct contrast to hacking, the primary goal of cyber-barrage is to prevent legitimate users from gaining access to networks and computer systems by bombarding access gateways with a barrage of data. It comes in the form of distributed denial of service (DDOS) attacks and its variants. DDOS attacks have a number of origins. They can be 'socially engineered' group actions in which large numbers of individuals gain access to a particular system within a short time period, usually assisted by scripted software, to overload its access gateways and achieve a political or ethically motivated objective. This fusion of ethical motivation and the use of computer technique is the basis of 'hacktivism' (Taylor, 2001: 59). In the 1990s, the Electronic Civil Disobedience Theatre successfully orchestrated high profile hacktivist attacks aided by Floodnet, a Java applet that reloads the target web page every few seconds to flood the host server with requests for access and eventually disrupts the operation of the targeted website. A less computer-intensive variant of this type of hacktivism has been the deliberate spreading of damaging rumours, for example about a system's insecurity or about the owner's ethical practices to discourage usage of a network or system.

In the future, it is likely that the motivations behind DDOS attacks will replicate those of hacking and shift from ethics or politics towards criminal gain. There already exist examples of such a shift with attacks being launched to demand the payment of a ransom (Wakefield, 2005). DDOS attacks are now being launched from botnets, often without the knowledge of the owner of the computer. The use of the botnet in this way introduces a completely new dimension in DDOS attacks: not only does the increased frequency of malicious automated DDOS attacks mark a strategic shift in approach when compared to the initial DDOS attacks, but the intensity and ruthlessness of the DDOS attacks create internet blizzards, storms and (spam) tsunamis which consume bandwidth and generally interfere with the running of the internet. In the British Parliamentary session of 2004–5, the Computer Misuse Act 1990 (Amendment) Bill (HC Bill, 2004–5, 102) sought to include DDOS under the legislation and comply with the European Convention on Cybercrime, but was prorogued by the General Election of that year. An attempt was made to revive it in the following session (HC Bill, 2005–6, 42) under the ten-minute rule, but on receiving its first hearing it was overtaken by the Police and

Justice Act 2006, which amends the Computer Misuse Act 1990 to include DDOS attacks (CL 40). It also increases the penalty for unauthorized access (CL 39) and makes illegal the making, supplying or obtaining of articles for use in computer misuse offences (CL 41) (HL Bill 104, 2005–6).

Motivations for offending and reproducing criminal knowledge online

Relatively little is known about offender motivations other than what can be gleaned from literature, known offences and the small amount of information that we have on the relatively few offenders who have been prosecuted. This is because of the tendency of victims to under-report instances of cybercrime, for all the reasons outlined in chapter 2.[2] Because relatively little is known about victims, relatively little is also known about the offenders beyond their offending (see Wall, 2001a: 8–9). Furthermore, as the focus shifts away from the public towards the private justice model of the corporate victims, the focus also shifts from the risk of criminal activity on society to the risk arising from the impacts of the crime on the interests of the organization. This penultimate part of the chapter pulls together some of these diverse sources to draw up a picture of motivations for offending. From what we do know, cybercrime offenders' motivations are not so far removed from traditional patterns of offending, particularly with regard to white-collar crimes (see Leyden, 2004b). However, the informational, networked and global qualities of the offending suggest some fundamental differences in the technological means that offenders use to broker information and culturally reproduce themselves online. Indeed, offending may not always be intentionally criminal or malicious; it could be innocent or even accidental. In other cases, it could be driven by an ethical belief that the behaviour can somehow be morally justified, or driven by recreational interests or intellectual curiosity. Drawing more generally from the literature, which covers the various generations of cybercrime, seven main groups of motivations for offending can be identified.

Self-satisfaction

Britz found that cyber-criminals were often in pursuit of 'an intellectual challenge' (2003: 65). Some, such as the 'informational voyeurs', were motivated either by curiosity or by boredom, or took part just for the thrill of it, the fun and enjoyment! Others involved in the more serious forms of offending, such as stalking and harassment, tended to be motivated by the need for sexual gratification (2003: 65). Weaver et al. (2003) observed that worm designers often 'express an experimental curiosity'.

The need for peer respect

Many accounts of hacking, cracking and virus/worm writing suggest that the offenders' behaviour is motivated by the need to obtain respect from peers by demonstrating their ability to show contempt for the system, or by displaying their ability and superior knowledge of how to inflict harm on others. If they are not looking to bolster self-pride they may feel a sense of empowerment from the respect they receive.

To impress potential employers

There exist a number of examples of past hackers being subsequently employed as security consultants. A fairly rare, but emerging, motivation of virus writers (VXers) in recent years has been to write viruses in order to prove their skills competencies to potential employers. One of the suspects in the 'Love Bug case', Michael Buen, created a macro virus and named it after himself (W97M/Michael-B) (Hayes, 2005). Buen designed his virus so that, if opened on a Friday after the 23rd of each month, it would interrupt any pending print jobs and print out Buen's own CV instead. The printed message allegedly ends with the following threat: '[i]f I don't get a safe job till the end of this month, i will send a third virus, that will delete every directory on the main HDD . . .'[3] In another example, the author of the MyDoom.V hid inside the worm's code in the message: 'We searching 4 work in AV industry' (Leyden, 2004h).

Criminal gain or commercial advantage

A popular motivation driving economic crimes is the lure of easy financial gain, if not directly through fraud, then through extortion or blackmail by threatening businesses with a DDOS attack unless a ransom demand is paid. Online bookmakers appear to be particularly vulnerable to DDOS threats. 'Criminals are pricing extortion rates at under the cost of preventing attacks. It's cheaper to pay up even if this encourages them [the crooks] even more' (Overton cited by Leyden, 2005m). In addition to the threat of DDOS attacks there are ransom viruses (Ransomware) that are designed to be neutralized by a code provided by the blackmailer once a ransom has been paid. An early example occurred in the late 1980s when organizations all over the world received sets of free floppy disks purporting to be AIDS training packages. When activated by installation, the program contained on the disks locked the target's system and could only be disabled by a code released to victims once they had sent a sum of money to a specified address in the US (Chandler, 1996: 241). Alternatively, the blackmailer may require credit card or restricted information (BBC, 2003h, 2003i, 2004c; Biever, 2004; Britz, 2003). During the first three months of 2006 Gostev et al. discovered an increase in cases of cyber-blackmail whereby data was illicitly encrypted and money extorted from its owners in exchange for the encryption key (Gostev, et al., 2006). In May 2006, a computer user fell foul of the Archiveus trojan and found that her files had been encrypted with complex passwords. She was instructed by the blackmailers not to contact the police but to buy some drugs from an online pharmacy where she would discover the password (Oates, 2006). The files were quickly unencrypted and the password was then published on the internet so that no other victims would have to pay up (BBC, 2006e).

Revenge

Revenge often motivates offending, especially with regard to disgruntled insiders in organizations (Britz, 2003). Revenge attack tactics vary, though offenders usually seek to redress some form of injustice felt to have been inflicted upon them by the organization or an individual within it. Where the intent is to cause damage, grievance worms or logic bombs are often used. They are set to go off at a specific time, usually after the employee has resigned from (or been fired from) the organization.

Distance from victim

Another motivating factor in cybercrime is the perception that the internet distances offenders from their victims. A convicted offender, interviewed for this book about conducting an internet fraud, claimed that it was the lack of direct contact with the victim that became the attraction for him: '[f]or me the internet made it, it was anonymous; you just tapped your details into the page.' When probed further, it became apparent that the real appeal was the anonymity afforded by the mechanized encounter that distanced the offender from the victim. The offender was quite clear that had the encounter been 'face to face, which is what the [credit card] transaction was designed for, then no way. It was a specific opportunity that arose.' In a twist to this distancing, online fraudsters are alleged to favour easy-to-set-up webmail accounts (website-based email) when conducting online frauds because they can hide, or obscure, their true identities and any trails they leave (Leyden, 2006e).

Politically motivated protest

Politically motivated protests aim to disrupt the political order and/or favourably influence the political process. Such protest can take the form of hacktivism or information warfare/information terrorism by targeting critical infrastructure.

Reproducing 'hacking' skills online

There is a regular tendency in the literature to depict the hacker as the criminal other and describe them in terms of their 'dangerousness'. But the evidence about known hackers would suggest that they do not follow these Peelian offender profiles. Rather they tend to be more reserved, often revelling in distancing themselves from their victims and shunning contact. Importantly, because of this need for social distance, they tend to be schooled online. Despite purges against such forums, there survive many chat groups devoted to brokering information about offending activities. Not only do they support criminal activity through information exchange, but they also reproduce skills sets and criminal cultures. The following discussion is an example of the ways that deviant hacking cultures can be reproduced online. The extract depicts the circulation of information about how best to breach the security of mobile phone and satellite TV processor security chips and it was drawn from a satellite television discussion list on 3 September 2000 (brand names have been changed). Although the technology and the main characters have since moved on, the lists still operate in much the same way. The example is included here to illustrate the dynamics of skill-set and sub-cultural reproduction. At the core of the network are the established hackers, the *gurus*, who provide the knowledge base; around them are the protégés (*cluebies*) who are learning the arts. On the periphery of this network are the *newbies* who, being new to the list, are not yet trusted by the members. They have yet to prove themselves. The excerpt in box 4.1 demonstrates how *ian*, a 'newbie', sought information to enable him to program a gold wafer card with the codes for 'Terrestrial Digital'. In the exchange, *hmmmmmmm* is the guru who guides *ian* through the process with the assistance of protégés (and cluebies)[4] *JOE* and *rainman*. Overseeing this exchange of information is senior guru *blackboy*, who gives his praise when the 'job' has been sorted.

Box 4.1 Digital hack discourse: the honing of hacking skills online

HEEEEELP!!!!!!!!! – September 03 2000 at 10:27 AM – ian

'can anyone out there tell me how to program a gold wafer card with the codes for [T] digital. i have a few gold wafers and also a card with a pic16f84 chip and 24c16 eeprom, i also have a card programmer which programs all the different cards and eeproms. i have tried different methods but without any luck. i would walk over broken glass if anyone could give me some step by step instructions.' – waiting in anticipation – ian

---

[T] *digital – September 03 2000 at 5:29 PM – JOE*

'i have programed a 24/eprom and picf84 with no problem, a gold card all you need is the loader software. if you still dont have any luck try and get an eprom+picf84 card they work with no hassel.'

[T] *DIGITAL – September 03 2000 at 5:34 PM – JOE*

'ITS EASY JUST PROGRAMME THE EPROM FIRST. THEN PROGRAMME THE PICF84. YOUR GOLD CARD SHOULD BE RESET WITH THE LOADER SOFTWARE. USE THE EPROM+CHIP CARD.THIS IS G, TEED TO WORK.'

[T] *dig – September 03 2000 at 6:04 PM – ian*

'thanks joe so is it, eeprom 1st, hex file 2nd, then loader also is it possible to just program a 16f84 chip without the eeprom for [T] dig' – thanks ian

---

wrong i think – September 04 2000 at 5:21 PM -=rainman=-

'loader – eeprom – pic thats the order to do them in.'

re – September 03 2000 at 9:10 PM hmmmmmmm

'the codes are held on the eeprom you need both files on ya card 16f84 and the eeprom files'

[T] *dig – September 03 2000 at 9:46 PM – ian*

'ok i have tried programming pic with loader, 24c16 with eeprom bin file then pick with 16f84 hex still won't work in [T] dig box just a blank screen and insert card message' – ian

----

re re – September 03 2000 at 10:02 PM hmmmmmmm

'when i did loadup kinks file to pip 02 the pwrt was set to off you will have to change this in your fuse menu to on you should then work m8'

[T] *dig – September 03 2000 at 10:18 PM ian*

'thanks hhhmmmmmmm – the contacts are facing downwards also there does not seem to be any way of setting the pwrt on my software. the software i am using is for programming goldcards with a multicard programmer. if it would help i will email you a copy of the gcard software i am using to see if it is any good for [T] dig' – ian

----

re – September 03 2000 at 10:40 PM hmmmmmmm

'its ok m8 i have shit loads of software i use winpheonix to do the eeproms or even a old dos proggy called cardem hope it worked for ya m8 if not, download pip 02 run the programme and loadup the 16f file use alt s, f to change the pwrt to on then re save the file then use the programme you have to programme the card BUT IF ITS WORKIN NEVER MIND HE HE HAPPY WATCHING M8'

[T] *dig – September 03 2000 at 10:51 PM – ian*

'still no luck with [T] dig have been told i can borrow a smart-mouse programmer but have no software can anyone tell me the best software to use with this, and also help with instructions' – ian

---

re – September 03 2000 at 11:29 PM – hmmmmmmm

'use win pheonix software'

---

to hmmmmmmm o/d September 03 2000 at 11:25 PM blackboy

'well sorted mate regards blackboy./'
[T] *digi – September 06 2000 at 12:13 PM ian*

'thanks to everyone who helped with my problems [T] digi now working, i could not have done it without your help/keep up the good work everyone' – ian

---

The practice of training newbies outlined above is similar to that documented by Mann and Sutton (1998) in their study of 'net crime', and the cyberworlds community observed by Williams (2003). Of course, online training such as this may become rarer as the entry-level skills for hacking rise (Ward, 2005a) or as key hacking procedures become scripted.

Conclusions

During the past decade or so the commercial popularity and mass usage of the internet has raised the financial stakes and introduced a generation of new players representing new entrepreneurial interests that they wish vigorously to protect. During this period, the once ethical art of hacking has become corrupted by less ethical motivations, simply because of the raised stakes. Also during this period, hacking has become automated and has also been deskilled through open source scripting and the use of malicious software in the form of blended threats. New generation hackers now use botnets to obtain illegal access (explored further in chapter 7). What this means is that the traditional, skilled and ethical hacker, as was, is now largely a historical artefact, and hacking, or cracking, has morphed into something quite different, presenting a range of new threats and exposing network users to a range of new risks.

5

Computer-Assisted Crime: Virtual Robberies, Scams and Thefts

How has criminal activity changed in the information age?
Part 2

Chapter at a glance

- **Virtual bank robbery: identity theft and exploiting financial and billing systems online**
  Input fraud (identity theft)
  Identity theft through trashing
  Identity theft through phishing
  Identity theft through DNS cache poisoning (pharming)
  Identity theft using spyware
  Fear of ID theft as a hindrance to commercial growth
- **The virtual sting 1: card-not-present payment frauds**
- **The virtual sting 2: arbitrage and other internet scams**
  Arbitrage/grey market exploitation
  Internet advertising frauds
  Premium line switching frauds
  'Short-firm' frauds: exploiting online auction reputation management systems
- **The virtual sting 3: using e-commerce as a means to deceive individuals**
  Pyramid selling online
  Direct investment scams
  Loans, credit options or the repair of credit ratings
  Deceptive advertisements for products and services
  Entrapment marketing scams
  Auction frauds
  419 (Nigerian) advanced fee frauds
  Drug sales/health cures/snake oil remedies

- **Virtual theft: cyber–piracy and 'stealing' informational intangibles**
  Informational services
  Intellectual property piracy and the internet
  Intellectual property piracy: music
  Intellectual property piracy: video (film and television)
  Intellectual property piracy: software
  The theft of virtual artefacts
- **Conclusions**

If 'Slick' Willie Sutton, the oft-quoted 1930s gentleman bank robber, was embarking on his criminal career today he would, likely as not, be contemplating using the internet to commit his robberies: '[b]ecause that's where the money [now] is!' The difference between then and now is that Willie would no longer be planning arduous and dangerous million-dollar bank robberies because networked technologies enable him to commit millions of $1 robberies with much less risk. Crime today, as in the past, still tends to follow opportunity (Grabosky and Smith, 1998: 1), but those opportunities have changed in scope. In 2004, '15 million adults used Internet banking, and 22 million adults purchased goods or services over the Internet' (APACS, 2005a: 28). All indications are that the numbers of users and the breadth of services offered will continue to rise. On the one hand this is great news for the financial services sector, but on the other hand it is quite bad news because of the rise in losses through frauds and deceptions. The 2005 YouGov poll of internet users estimated that as many as one in twenty UK internet users have lost money to some sort of online scam (Richardson, 2005b). These claims are also borne out by corporate internet fraud statistics which illustrate high levels of online victimization. Experian, one of many organizations conducting surveys of e-commerce, found that of 800 online retailers interviewed during August 2001 over two-thirds (70 per cent) felt that the internet was a 'risky route to market'. Over half (52 per cent) claimed that internet fraud was a problem for their organization (Experian, 2001). Similar trends were detected in cyber-crime surveys by KPMG (2001) and also the CBI (2001). Not surprisingly, because of the globalization effect, similar patterns were also found in the US, for example, by GartnerG2 (2001), CSI surveys (2001–6) and also in the Pacific Rim by the Confederation of Asian and Pacific Accountants (CAPA, 2001), though actual commercial victimization reporting rates do differ somewhat.

This chapter looks at the different ways that offenders use networked computers to assist them in performing deceptive and acquisitive harms upon individual or corporate victims for informational or pecuniary advantage. The types of digital malfeasance discussed here are not to be confused with those discussed in the previous chapter on computer integrity crime, or those in the next which focus upon informational content, although, as observed earlier, information and identity theft, and copyright piracy, are becoming major precursors to online economic crimes. Furthermore, the increasing sophistication of technology, particularly the blending of threats in one malicious software source, means that it is increasingly hard in practice to identify the boundaries between the three. As is the case elsewhere in this book, the object is to map out the range and variety of risk behaviour that fall under each specific theme.

Three distinct groups of computer-assisted crime activities are identified here and each forms a section of this chapter. The first explores *virtual bank robbery*, which exploits financial management systems online, mainly banking and billing. The second looks at the *virtual sting* and at the way the internet can be used to defraud individuals and commercial enterprises. The third outlines the *virtual theft* of intangibles in the form of informational or intellectual property. Central to each activity is the brokering of information which has an exchange value (Bates, 2001; O'Harrow, 2001: A01). As the importance of 'original data' declines in an age of digital simulacra, where valuable digital artefacts are wholly conceived and constructed in cyberspace, verification of rights and authority is becoming crucial in allowing access not only to virtual environments, but also to the exchange transactions that take place within them.

Virtual bank robbery: identity theft and exploiting financial and billing systems online

With the internet becoming a popular means of managing financial affairs, financial systems have become targets for criminal opportunity. Fraudsters have for some time used the internet to defraud banks, build up false identities, open accounts and run them 'as normal' to build up credit ratings to obtain personal loans that are subsequently defaulted upon. Electronic banking is also used to launder money and turn 'dirty money' into clean money by obscuring its origins through quick transfer from one bank to another and across jurisdictions. Although easy in principle, it is nevertheless quite hard in practice to deceive banking security checks and offenders will weigh up the risks associated with opportunities. Echoing the immortal words of 'Slick' Willie Sutton, the president of MasterCard Europe, Peter Hoch, stated that 'criminals will go to wherever the easiest target is' (Cards International, 2003). The fraudsters seek out the systems' weaknesses, which tend to lie at the input and output stages.

From the earliest days of e-commerce, online retailers have fallen victim to fraudsters who have obtained goods by deception, supplied false payment details or used a false address to which the goods can be sent. Initially, personal cheques and bank drafts, the preferred method of payment at the time, were the focus of online frauds, but they were quickly surpassed by credit cards when online credit card payment facilities became more popular and practical. Although third-party escrowed internet payment systems, such as PayPal and Mondex, have emerged as intermediaries, most payments are still made to them by credit or debit cards, though the former is usually favoured because of the issuing bank's guarantee. With offending patterns increasingly mediated by technology, payment fraud has gradually transformed from a hybrid cybercrime to a true cybercrime. Although not always easy to separate in practice, there are two distinct types of payment frauds: *input frauds*, in which fraudsters gain illegal access to credit facilities, in this case, typically credit cards, and *output frauds* whereby the access to credit is used fraudulently to obtain goods, services or money.

Input fraud (identity theft)

Input frauds involve the acquisition of credit facilities by fraudulent means, mainly by using information gained from identity theft.[1] Since the mid-1990s the term 'identity theft' has been routinely misused to describe the fraudulent use of stolen or falsely obtained credit card details to commit retail theft against online vendors. Bruce Schneier, a well-known security technologist, argues that the current emphasis upon identity theft 'is a misnomer which is hurting the fight against fraud', identity theft would be better conceptualized as 'fraud due to impersonation' (Leyden, 2005e). Here the discussion about identity theft is purely within the context of input fraud, which includes fraudulently obtaining information to apply for credit facilities, including making illicit credit card applications[2] or using the stolen personal information to take over the owner's accounts. Application frauds currently constitute a third of all UK losses from identity theft while account take-over constitutes three fifths,[3] but the proportion and amounts are likely to increase as identity theft becomes more prevalent through information-harvesting trojans. There are currently four main ways by which this personal financial information can be obtained: through trashing, phishing, pharming and use of spyware.

Identity theft through trashing

Personal information can often be obtained by *trashing* or 'dumpster diving', which is the practice of going through rubbish bags to obtain discarded documents and then using the information to apply for credit facilities. This is a labour-intensive and local activity and therefore fairly low yield.

Identity theft through phishing

Personal financial information collection is more effectively obtained through *phishing*, mentioned elsewhere in this book in various contexts because it marks a point of change in the automation of cybercrime. Phishing is the pursuit of personal financial information that is subsequently used to defraud the victim and relies upon the recipient's inability to distinguish a bogus email from a real one (see Toyne, 2003). The now traditional 'phishing expedition' is characterized by the indiscriminate mailing of millions of emails purporting to be from the recipient's bank, payment system or other regular form of financial transaction they use, such as eBay. The emails ask recipients, with a sense of urgency usually exaggerated by an alleged security breach, to log onto the URL given in the email and confirm their personal information details (Oates, 2004a). The following is a variant of the phishing expedition and is an example of what pundits are describing as 'spear phishing', a 'highly targeted and co-ordinated attack at a specific organisation or individual designed to extract critical data', in this case from participants of the eBay auction site (Leyden, 2006a).

The phishing email illustrated in box 5.1 had the look and feel of eBay, complete with appropriate logos, and, when read through quickly, it might appear plausible to the unsuspecting. As stated earlier, phishers 'socially engineer' their victims by relying upon their inability to distinguish the bogus email from a real one (see Toyne, 2003). Although the message means little to those who do not use eBay, it does to the millions who do use it, especially the phrase: '[p]lease Note – If you choose to ignore our request, you leave us no choice but to temporally suspend your account' (sic). However, closer examination reveals inaccuracies. The author's 'distinctive' misuse of

---

Box 5.1 A phishing expedition claiming to be from eBay

Dear eBay Member,

We recently noticed one or more log in attempts to your eBay account from a foreign IP address and we have reasons to believe that your account was used by a third party without your authorization If you recently accessed your account while travelling, the unusual login attempts may have been initiated by you.
The login attempt was made from:
IP address: 249.230.196.xxx
ISP Host: cache-66 proxy xxx com

By now, we used many techniques to verify the accuracy of the information our users provide us when they register on the Site However, because user verification on the Internet is difficult, eBay cannot and does not confirm each user's purported identity Theft, we have established an offline verification system to help you evaluate with who you are deal with.

click on the link below, fill the form and then submit as we will verify
http://ebay-xxxxpage.com/?eBaylSAPI.dll&VerifyRegistrationShow

Please save this fraud alert ID for your reference

Please Note – If you choose to ignore our request, you leave us no choice but to temporally suspend your account.

* Please do not respond to this e-mail as your reply will not be received Respectfully,
Trust and Safety Department
eBay Inc.

Received 20 May 2005 by the author and reproduced without formatting and logos. NB This is *not* from eBay and the fraudulent links have been changed here.

English grammar and syntax is not up to eBay's usual standards. Note, for example, the use of the word 'purported'; grammatical mistakes such as 'with who you are deal with' and 'fill the form and then submit as we will verify'; the misuse of the word 'temporally'. Finally, there is the rather strange placing of the (capitalized) word respectfully: '* Please do not respond to this e-mail as your reply will not be received Respectfully,' (sic). Ignoring the double negative, the fact that a carriage return has been omitted before 'Respectfully' achieves

---

Box 5.2   Bogus emailing purporting to come from a national UK bank

Dear Customer,

Recent fraudulent attempts to access our bank customers' accounts have forced us to introduce an additional authorization of our account holders.

The decision to implement a next-generation protection system launched by [Bank] Security Service was supported by our IT team which introduced a modernization concept, covering both data transfer protocols and transferred data encryption.

In accordance with the a.m. procedure please fill out the Additional Authorization Form below.

Click here to fill out the form!

These measures are introduced solely to protect the interests of our customers.

We highly appreciate your support.
Sincerely yours,
[Bank] Administration

Received 20 August 2005 by the author and reproduced without formatting and logos.

---

the opposite effect to that intended.[4] Other bank-related 'spear phishing' attacks have targeted online bank customers by offering them a cash reward for completing a bogus survey in which they disclose their critical personal information (Leyden, 2006b).

What is distinctive about phishing is the speed with which new variations on the theme emerge. One of the crucial advantages that offenders have over their victims is the, albeit narrowing, window of opportunity between the identification of a vulnerability in a system, the onset of an attack and the production of a technological fix to solve the problem. Therefore, as soon as the major financial institutions find ways to counter phishing attacks, the 'attackers' change their approach. One notable example of the adaptability of the phishers, following adverse publicity about their activities, has been their ability to deliberately play upon the recipient's concerns about phishing and provide reassurance (as the hook) to entrap them (see box 5.2).

In April 2005, the UK's pan-industrial Anti-Phishing Working Group (APWG)[5] reported a shift away from targeting banks (through their unsuspecting account holders) to smaller financial enterprises such as credit unions (APWG, 2005: 5; Lemos, 2005a). The rationale behind this shift was to increase the phisher's pool of potential victims and also to introduce novel twists that would increase the chances of ensnaring unsuspecting victims. In addition to applying versatility to their approach, there is evidence that phishers are reducing their own 'risk' of detection by employing 'middlemen', such as students and even children, to withdraw cash from banks using victims' access codes and then wiring the money to accounts controlled by the phishers. In a case exposed in early 2005, it was found that Australian gangs with links to Russian and Malaysian crime gangs established a network of young students 'to funnel money from compromised accounts overseas' of between A$200 and A$500 per day – large sums for those involved, but 'a small amount compared to the actual funds that have been obtained' (Leyden, 2005h).

In 2006, two interesting variants of phishing emerged which exploit the convergence of technologies: 'vishing' and 'smishing'. In vishing, the 'vishers' as they are called, use VoIP (Voice over Internet Protocol) to 'spam' recorded messages to telephone numbers rather than emails (Ward, 2006). The VoIP messages purport to be from banks, other financial institutions, online merchants such as Amazon or internet auction houses such as e-bay, and warn the recipient that their credit card has been used for fraudulent transactions. Those who respond to the call are requested to key into the phone their card and its three-digit security number. A fake caller number is usually identified and even included in the message to feign legitimacy. 'SMiShing' uses bulk text messaging facilities to target mobile devices such as phones or PDAs (personal digital assistants) (BBC, 2006n). Both are relevant examples of the ways that converged technologies can be adapted for criminal gain. One of the reasons why vishing and SMiShing can work where phishing now fails is because internet users have become very suspicious of emails from financial institutions, but not of personal – and seemingly plausible – phone calls (Ward, 2006) or text messages.

There are a number of contradictory opinions on the impact of phishing. Truste, non-profit promoters of online privacy, estimated that US phishing losses were around $500 million (Leyden, 2004e), whereas a subsequent survey by TowerGroup in 2004 found these losses to be overestimated and that global losses were more likely to be in the region of $137 million (Leyden, 2004f). Whether $500 million or $137 million, they still represent a considerable financial loss, but the later statistics do show a considerable increase in the impact of phishing since 2004, which suggests that the earlier larger estimates may now be being realized. The APACS 2006 card fraud statistics reported that direct fraud losses from online phishing scams in the UK almost doubled in 2005 to £23.2 million compared with £12.2 million in 2004 (APACS, 2006: 51). Similarly, the Symantec Internet Security Threat Report 2006 reported that the overall numbers of unique phishing messages detected increased by 81 per cent in the first six months of 2006 to 157,477 (Symantec, 2006: 22). Phishing incidents will continue to increase because the losses from the phishing variants will supplement the statistics.

Identity theft through DNS cache poisoning (pharming)

A development of phishing is *pharming*, which automatically directs recipients to the phisher's bogus website. Sometimes known as 'DNS poisoning', 'cache poisoning' or DNS spoofing, pharming uses malicious code embedded in the email to 'poison' or hijack domain name servers (DNS). It changes the stored records that the target computer uses to convert domain names into numerical addresses so that recipients are automatically redirected to fraudulent websites or proxy servers (see APWG, 2005; Jackson, 2005; Leyden, 2005a; Lemos, 2005a, 2005b). Unlike phishing, pharming does not rely upon 'social engineering' to trick the recipient into clicking on to a website. Instead, it tricks the DNS into automatically accepting incorrect, or forged, access data. Placed in the cache of a DNS, the incorrect data causes internet users to be signposted to internet sites different to those intended, or their email may be rerouted to mail servers not authorized to receive it. The effect of pharming is to increase the 'hit' rate at the spoof website, which has the look and feel of the victim's own bank site. As with phishing, the use of recognized symbols of trust 'socially engineer', or trick, the recipient into disclosing their financial information.

Identity theft using spyware

Illegally installed spyware can either keep a log of the victim's keystrokes (including passwords) or actively seek out key financial information stored on the hard-drive. In both cases the information is subsequently relayed back to the infector. The use of spyware to steal personal information has increased exponentially through the use of botnets and accompanying infecting tactics (described else-where). Once the specialist malicious software (see 'blended threats', Glossary) has infected a computer, it harvests information and returns it to the infector. The major shift brought about by spyware in input frauds is that it can obtain an individual's security information (account numbers, user ID, passwords and additional security information), clandestinely and remotely. Furthermore, this information provides direct access to the victim's bank account and therefore dispenses with the need to perpetrate an application fraud.

Fear of ID theft as a hindrance to commercial growth

Internet users' fears of falling victim to identity theft are proving to be a major hindrance to growth in e-commerce (Richards, 2005; BBC, 2005k; APACS, 2005a, 2005b) and also for plans to develop the information society. However, the messages here are mixed because while concerns over security are clearly deterring some people from using the internet, those who use it for commercial transactions are displaying high levels of satisfaction. Richards found that 'word of mouth [presumably including email] has played a more important role than corporate marketing in increasing awareness of websites and raising consumer confidence' (Richards, 2005: 16). It is hard to estimate the actual losses incurred from online identity theft because the financial system believes the transaction to be legit-imate – the fraud takes place outside it. In 2005, APACS estimated that identity theft constituted 7.3 per cent (£39.6 million) of all plastic card fraud losses (£504.8 million). However, this represents an increase of 24 per cent on the previous year (APACS, 2005c). These figures, shown in table 5.1, represent both online and offline losses.

The APACS statistics demonstrate that, with a few exceptions, losses occurring through identity theft in the ten years between 1996 and 2005 are increasing annually, but from a relatively low base in comparison to the overall losses. They consistently represent about 7 per cent, plus or minus 3 per cent, of the total losses due to card frauds, but it is important to note that this does not reflect the number of individuals concerned. CIPAS, the fraud prevention service, estab-lished that 16,077 individuals became victims of identity theft in the UK in the first three months of 2006, a sixth (17%) higher than in the previous quarter (Leyden, 2006i). Using self-reporting methods, the Federal Trade Commission in the US found in 2004

Table 5.1   Plastic card losses through ID theft, 1996–2005

Year	ID theft losses (£ million)	Change on previous year (%)	Total card losses (£ million)	ID theft as % of total card losses
1996	7.2	+300	97.1	7.4
1997	13.1	+82	122.0	10.7
1998	16.8	+28	135.0	12.4
1999	14.4	−14	188.4	7.6
2000	17.4	+21	317.0	5.5
2001	14.6	−16	411.5	3.5
2002	20.6	+41	424.6	4.9
2003	30.2	+47	420.4	7.2
2004	36.9	+22	504.8	7.3
2005	30.5	−17	439.4	6.9

Source: APACS, 2005e, 2006.

that 39 per cent (246,570) of the 635,173 complaints received concerned identity theft and 61 per cent (388,603) other types of fraud
(Richardson, 2005a). The average loss was $872 (total $548m). Since
there exists a range of reasons why both UK and US victimizations
might be under-reported, the losses outlined above may imply much
greater levels of actual loss. Businesses, including banks and individuals, will write off the minor losses because of the inconvenience of
reporting them, or in the case of the former, will not declare losses so
as to hide weaknesses; in both cases they carry the losses themselves
(Levi, 2001). For many years in the UK, regional police forces routinely referred credit card fraud victims to the issuing banks because
they bore the legal responsibility for the loss (Wall, 2002b). All indications are that input frauds will continue to rise, and because of this
a corresponding rise in output fraud is likely.

The virtual sting 1: card-not-present payment frauds

The internet's virtual shop window offers many opportunities for
payment or output fraud (i.e. obtaining goods or services by deception) using legitimate credit cards obtained fraudulently via identity
theft, account take-over, or fake cards obtained by counterfeiting or
cloning information.

Counterfeit card details can be generated by using software programs like CreditMaster 4.0, which is available over the internet. For

a number of years it and other similar programs were used to generate strings of valid credit card numbers for use in transactions, mainly for the purchase of mobile phone airtime (Kravetz, 2002). It is important to note here that while the counterfeit numbers were generated by downloaded programs obtained online, the internet was not usually the means by which the transaction took place. The counterfeit card transactions mainly took place using mobile phone systems which required only the card number. The introduction of card validation codes has reduced the value of card number generators.

If a card cannot be counterfeited then it could be cloned. The information needed to clone a credit card can be obtained either by 'skimming' the card (using an illicit card reader) during a legitimate transaction, or copying it from discarded credit card receipts. One of the offenders interviewed about internet frauds for a research project that has contributed to this book explained that his accomplice had a friend in a petrol station from whom receipts could be bought and the information from them used to make purchases from websites (Wall, 2002b). This pattern of information gathering was later confirmed by another respondent (a security manager at a bank) who said that the main sources of discarded receipts were 'petrol stations, taxi drivers and restaurants'.

The effectiveness of counterfeit or cloned credit cards has been greatly reduced by changes in transactional procedures such as the introduction of a further card validation code – the three-digit security number on the back of the credit card. Whilst this addition has reduced the incidence of minor card frauds, it has also increased the market value of cloned credit card information which includes the card validation code. At the time of writing, there are a number of illegal 'carding websites' such as 'carderplanet' and 'shadowcrew' (BBC, 2005e) where fraudsters can (or could) purchase cloned credit cards along with their validation codes. The message on one such website reads as follows: 'My name is Script, I'm a founder of forum.carderplanet.net and i can provide you with excellent credit cards with cvv2 code and without it . . . Minimum deal is a USD $200.00. . . . USD $200.00 – there are 300 credit cards without cvv2 code (visa + mc) – USA (included credit card number, exp. day. cardholder billing address, zip, state)'[6] ('Script' was subsequently arrested by the Ukrainian police; Mosnews, 2005).

From the fraudster's point of view, '[t]he actual process of putting the card details into the web site is something that anybody could do when you place the order'. The key to the payment fraud was to get 'an address that is not your own and then have someone who is there to receive the goods and sign for them'.[7] What distinguishes internet-related fraud in this respect is the fact that the fraudsters do not engage directly with their victims. When asked if he would have got into crime had the internet not been involved the respondent replied that he would not have done so: 'for me the Internet made it, it was anonymous; you just tapped your details into the web page'. This point was emphasized further when asked if he could have rung a vendor and ordered the same goods over the phone: 'no way, if it was face to face . . . then no way. It was a specific opportunity that arose.' This (criminal) opportunity was also accepted by his friends whose peer support helped to rationalize the act:

> I had some other friends who were into it and who had either done it themselves or they knew somebody who had done it. They told me that there was no way that it could ever come back to you. It escalated from there. . . . I did one, I thought that I'll give it a try and I ordered something very small, a DVD, £12, to see if it actually works. And when it did actually work I got a bit of a thrill out of it and then my friend started pushing me, this is the one that had the items going to his house. He later decided that he wanted to do it himself.

The fraudulent act was further self-rationalized by the offender's own mistaken belief that online card fraud was a victimless crime in which nobody was deceived and that the financial loss was borne by the banks. Unfortunately, this neutralization strategy or urban myth tends to be reinforced and perpetuated by the system for reporting fraud and billing disputes. Whereas the banks may appear to write off losses, they, in fact, tend to 'charge back' the loss to the merchants and retailers. These increased operational risks to the merchants are offset either by passing costs onto customers or by offsetting them against the savings made from the costs of terrestrial retail operations in terms of rental costs and also losses to merchandise through store-theft and in-store damage.

Card-not-present frauds originated outside the technology of the banking systems in changes made to the banking rules that allow retailers (initially in phone transactions) to take credit card details without the credit card being present. These changes in policy arguably took the credit card beyond its original purpose and opened the door to new types of fraud: 'The Internet has taken the credit card schemes further than they were ever intended for. It was never meant to be used for card-not-present transactions over the WWW. The acquirers had adapted the card system to be used as card not present,

but it was and still is a weak system and is therefore open to abuse'
(Respondent 1b – Wall, 2002b).[8]

Card-not-present transactions have become the mainstay of e-
commerce-based retail operations. Not surprisingly, there has been
a considerable increase in all losses incurred from card-not-present
frauds (CNPFs). Levi's (2000) statistics indicate that during the five
years between 1995 and 1999 there was a six-fold increase in CNPFs
from £4.5 million to £29.5 million. Much of this was due to a spate
of pre-payment mobile phone (airtime) frauds during the late 1990s
in which false credit card details were used to purchase mobile
phone credits. However, some of this loss was also due to internet-
based CNPFs (Levi, 2000). Early concerns about the rise in losses
due to internet activities have subsequently been substantiated. In
2001, the APACS card fraud loss statistics indicated that £7 million
(2%) of the £292 million losses in 2000 due to credit card frauds
were internet related (APACS, 2001a: 6; 2001b: 2). In 2005,
APACS calculated that all of the different forms of internet fraud in
2004 were responsible for 23 per cent (£117 million) of all losses
through credit card fraud (APACS, 2005c). These increases must
however be viewed against a background of a massive overall
expansion in global internet-based transactions during the early
twenty-first century, which also includes the administration of many
local, national and international services that were hitherto office-
based and range from insurance purchase to the purchase of travel
documents.

The virtual sting 2: arbitrage and other internet scams

Arbitrage/grey market exploitation

The global reach of the internet enables the exploitation of 'grey
markets' created by price differentials across jurisdictions (see
Granovsky, 2002). Moreover, the internet is a tool which allows
pricing differences to be identified from afar and the goods traded in
order to circumvent the manufacturer-, producer- or government-
authorized channels for the distribution of goods. Price differentials
can result from local differences in the costs of producing basic commodities, in currency exchange rates, or taxation (in VAT or import
tax) and lead to illicit cross-border trade in, for example, cigarettes,
alcohol, fuel and consumer durables, pharmaceuticals, and also
exotic rare animals and their skins and furs (BBC, 2005g; IFAW,

2005). Differentials can also be created by law (legal arbitrage) where goods that are illicit or restricted in one jurisdiction are purchased from jurisdictions where they are legal; such is the case with prescription medicines, sexual services, rare stones, antiquities and (allegedly) body parts.

A recent development in legal arbitrage has been the growth of the online gambling industry, which is rapidly gaining popularity across jurisdictions that have varying legal and moral attitudes towards gambling. The size of online gambling is illustrated by statistics released by GamCare, a UK-based charity addressing the social impact of gambling, which estimates that there are approximately 1,700 gambling websites on the internet (GamCare: www.gamcare.org.uk). Merrill Lynch estimated that the online gambling market had a turnover of $6.3 billion in 2003, which would increase to $86 billion in 2005 (Leyden, 2004g). The debate over online gambling has predictably focused upon its legality and morality, particularly in the US, 'which has both a puritanical streak running right through the national psyche and a thriving, and powerful, home-grown gaming sector' (Fay, 2005a). So the main thrust of this debate has been about increasing (US) jurisdictional control over the inter-jurisdictional aspects of running illegal gambling operations in and from other countries (Goss, 2001: 32).

In November 2004 a WTO (World Trade Organization) panel ruled that US federal and state laws were in breach of GATS (General Agreement on Trade in Services). In April 2005, the WTO reversed much of the ruling, making the (US) Wire Act, the Travel Act, and the Illegal Gambling Business Act all measures 'necessary to protect public morals or maintain public order' in accordance with paragraph (a) of Article XIV (WTO, 2005: para. 373 (D vi a)). The panel did, however, decide that offshore gambling operations were not being allowed the same access as US-based gambling operations and ordered the situation to be addressed (Fay, 2005a; Butterfield, 2005). What is certain about online gambling is its popularity – and an innate part of that popularity is the desire of punters to beat the system, either within its own rules (not dealt with here) or outside of them by defrauding the gambling operations. With regard to the latter, in 2002, Europay, MasterCard's partner in mainland Europe, claimed that one-fifth of losses due to online fraud were related to gambling (Leyden, 2002b). The revision of acceptable use policies by companies such as PayPal, who provide electronic payment transfers, so that customers are no longer allowed to subscribe to online gambling sites, combined with new security technology, will likely lessen incidents of online gambling fraud.[9]

Internet advertising frauds

New online commercial opportunities quickly become the focus of fraud. One such example is 'pay-per-click' advertising, where internet sites that display adverts receive a small fee from the advertiser each time the advertisement is viewed. Individually, these are minute payments, but they aggregate within a high volume environment. As a consequence, they have given rise to 'Click fraud', or 'bogus click syndrome' (Liedtke, 2005), which defrauds the internet advertising billing system. Unscrupulous website owners employ individuals to bulk click advertisements, sometimes outsourcing to third-world countries where labour is cheap and 'factories' of low-wage workers will click manually on web ads, often in circumstances where the boundary between wage-labour and coercion is vague. More common, however, is the use of bespoke software, such as 'Google Clique' which effects computer scripted clicking, to perform the same task. The Google Clique case took an interesting twist when its author, Michael Bradley, allegedly sought to extort $100,000 from Google in return for him not 'releasing a software program that he claimed would allow spammers to defraud Google of millions of dollars' (USDOJ, 2004).[10] Another related example is 'link spamming', which also exploits the burgeoning internet advertising industry. The aim of 'link spamming' is to link a keyword, such as 'pornography', with a particular website. Although it is not necessarily illegal (depending upon jurisdiction), it does often flout fair trade practice rules. Link spammers, or search engine optimizers as they often describe themselves, regularly spam websites and personal webblogs with blocks of text that contain key words to inflate the search engine rankings of websites that offer 'PPC – pills, porn and casinos' (Arthur, 2005).

Premium line switching frauds

Before broadband replaced the dial-in modem, a fairly common form of telephone billing fraud was premium line switching. Here visitors to unscrupulous websites, usually pornography related, would, during the course of their browsing, unknowingly become the victim of a 'drive-by download'. They would find themselves infected with a virus, a 'rogue dialler', that would automatically and discretely transfer their existing telephone service from the normal domestic rate to a premium line service and defraud them (Richardson, 2005c).

'Short-firm' frauds: exploiting online auction reputation management systems

Introduced to protect and guide users of auction houses, such as eBay, reputation management systems enable purchasers to rate vendors on their conduct during the sale. Vendors subsequently build up profiles based upon their customer feedback and past sales performance which enable potential purchasers to vet them before making bids. Good reputations are highly valued and maintaining them discourages dishonest behaviour by vendors and bidders. An interesting knock-on effect of these reputation management systems is the emergence of 'the short-firm fraud', which is the virtual equivalent of the long-firm fraud where trust is artificially built up, at a cost, by selling off some quality articles below their true value. Once a good vendor rating is acquired then a very expensive item is sold, often offline to a runner-up in the bidding war, and the vendor disappears once the money has been received.

The virtual sting 3: using e-commerce as a means to deceive individuals

Hand in hand with opportunities for e-commerce comes the potential to exploit them, with scams clinging tightly to the coat tails of technological innovation. Although the media by which offenders engage with victims have changed, and will continue to do so, history reminds us that the principles and practices of deception remain similar. These include the baiting of victims with attractive hooks such as cut-price goods or services far below the market value, 'better than normal' returns on investments, alternative cures to serious illnesses or rare drugs not available in the jurisdiction (Hall, 2005). From an analytical point of view, it is very hard to distinguish between enthusiastic, even aggressive marketing, bad business and wilfully criminal deceptions. What we can do, however, is outline the spectrum of deceptive behaviours related to e-commerce that are causing concern. Some of these categories will find resonance with the later analysis of spam content because that is where they originate. Particularly prevalent on the margins of e-commerce are the scams that sit on the border between aggressive entrapment marketing and deception, such as get-rich-quick schemes which tempt internet users to invest in financial products that they think will yield a substantial return. The potential for scamming is often fairly clear, if not obvious, but the US Federal Trade Commission (FTC), the UK's DTI and other sources of victimization statistics clearly show that even normally risk-averse internet users can fall victim to them.

Pyramid selling online

Pyramid selling schemes (also known as Ponzi) and their variants have been a successful scamming tactic for many hundreds of years and, like other lucrative scams, have found their way onto the internet in many ingenious disguises. Pyramid selling is an elaborate confidence trick which recruits punters, promises them a good return on investment and gets them to part with money. New recruits to the schemes are themselves encouraged by the fact that they can recoup their initial investment simply by introducing two or more new recruits to the scheme. Pyramid selling is a numbers game fuelled by the fact that the very early investors often do get a good return on their money and that their enthusiasm advertises its apparent authenticity, encouraging others to follow suit in anticipation of great gain. Because the returns are based upon new recruitment numbers rather than profit from product sales, as in the case of legitimate multi-level marketing practices, the pyramid selling schemes are doomed to fail. They merely redistribute income towards the initiators and the many losers pay for the few winners. The internet versions of pyramid schemes reflect the terrestrial versions, although the internet gives the scammer access to a larger number of potential recruits and the stakes are therefore higher.

There are many variations of the pyramid scheme. Some may use chain letters, others more imaginative devices such as the purchase of ostrich eggs, or a specific numbers of investments, works of art, in fact anything that generates numerators. All have the same distinctive recruitment features and exploit characteristics of the pyramid algorithm. The hook is usually greed and attracts those looking for a high return on investment but with limited means and a limited knowledge of business. However, there are also examples of exploitation of specific trust characteristics. The 'Women Empowering Women' scam operates through a chain letter distributed by email across women's friendship networks. It purports to be a 'gifting' scheme and appeals to women to donate gifts to other women and receive a return on investment for so doing (Levene, 2003). To be allowed to participate, new recruits first have to sign statements declaring their payments to be unconditional gifts to other women, which, frustratingly for law enforcement, makes the scheme legal despite considerable losses to participants.

Direct investment scams

Direct investment scams on the internet are legendary. Some focus on businesses while others target individuals. Some may be genuine – though misguided – attempts to stimulate business by providing recipients with a genuine investment service. Others are less genuine and seek to persuade interested recipients to part with money without receiving any service in return, or offer investors the opportunity to earn large incomes while working at home. In the latter case, victims are encouraged to send off a fee for a package of information that explains the scheme. If, indeed, they do receive anything at all, usually what they receive is worthless, impractical or may even involve them participating in a nefarious activity. Particularly vulnerable to these scams are the less mobile or the unemployed, or those who are house-bound such as single parents or carers.

Beyond the work-at-home schemes are the more harmful scams perpetrated by those purporting to be legitimate investment brokers who, upon sign up (sometimes also requiring a fee to join), produce free investment reports to customers which subsequently trick them into investing their funds in dubious stocks and shares. Another direct investment scam is the 'Pump and Dump' scam whereby investors playing the stock market are deceived by misinformation circulating on the internet about real stock. This information artificially drives up the price of the stock (the pump), which is then sold off at inflated prices (the dump). Research by Frieder and Zittrain in 2006 found that respondents to 'pump and dump' emails can lose up to 8 per cent of their investment within two days, whereas 'the spammers who buy low-priced stock before sending the e-mails, typically see a return of between 4.9% and 6% when they sell' (Frieder and Zittrain, 2006; BBC, 2006m).

Loans, credit options or the repair of credit ratings

A particularly insidious group of financial scams committed via the internet are those which prey upon the poor and financially excluded with promises to repair their credit ratings, provide credit options or credit facilities, credit cards with zero or very low interest, or instant and unlimited loans without credit checks or security. Such offers, if followed up, tend to come at a considerable cost to victims in terms of high interest rates or by trapping them into a nexus from which it is hard to escape. Even worse, the entrapment may lead to the victim becoming embroiled in a wider range of criminal activity to pay off the original debt.

Deceptive advertisements for products and services

Deceptive advertisements purport to sell goods at greatly reduced prices to hook the victims. Some simply fail to deliver, others sell substandard goods (e.g. reconditioned), others exploit grey markets (see earlier). The traditional (offline) deceptive advertising has tended to focus upon the sale of desirable consumer durables. However, a majority of deceptive online advertisements appear to be targeted at businesses and particularly business managers responsible for purchasing office, medical or other supplies and who might be attracted by the prospects of low costs. Typically, advertisements of office supplies offer specially priced print cartridges or greatly discounted computing and, in some cases, expensive equipment.

Other deceptive advertisements are aimed at the individual and offer a range of consumer durables or other branded goods or services at greatly discounted prices, bogus educational qualifications, appeals for money, usually to (fake) charities linked to obscure religious-based activities or organizations, or even soliciting donations to help victims of disasters. The events of September 11, the 2004 Boxing Day Tsunami, the 2005 London bombings (7/7 and 21/7), Hurricane Katrina, the Pakistan Earthquake and Asian bird-flu remedies each inspired attempts to exploit public sympathy to extort money by deception or to deceive recipients into opening infected attachments. In the case of the latter, within a few hours of the first London bombings on 7 July 2005, for example, the following spam message was circulated:

> From: breakingnews@cnnonline.com
> Subject: TERROR HITS LONDON
> Filename: 'London Terror Moovie.avi <124 spaces> Checked By Norton Antivirus.exe'
> 'See attachments for unique amateur video shots'

The trend continued into 2006 and websites purporting to show pictures of Slobodan Milošević having (allegedly) been murdered infected those accessing them with a malicious trojan called Dropper-FB (Leyden, 2006d). Upon clicking on the URL to see the news footage the host machine would become infected by a worm that rendered it receptive to remote administration as a zombie. In addition to the disaster spams are the fake foreign lotteries and prize promotions in which recipients, having been told in a spammed email that they have won a prize or entered into a prize pot, are directed to a website where they have to enter their personal information to release the prize. Often, a small administration fee is also required from the participant to enable them to proceed. In other instances, recipients may be drawn to the site (as with other spams) only to fall victim to a 'drive-by download'.

Entrapment marketing scams

Entrapment is the stage beyond deception. It locks the victim into a situation from which they cannot easily extricate themselves, with the consequence that may become repeat victims and their losses even greater. Entrapment can occur by being deceived into participating in some of the activities mentioned earlier, or by falling victim to one of the many entrapment marketing scams, of which there are many. The classic, often legal, entrapment marketing scam is one in which individuals are enticed to subscribe to a service by the offer of a free product, usually a mobile phone, pager, satellite TV decoder, etc. Alternatively, the subscriber may be seduced by the offer of a free trial, for example, to access sites containing sexually explicit materials, or by being given free lines of credit in new trial gambling websites. The key to the scam, and this is where many stay on the right side of the law, assuming that the content is legal, is that the onus of responsibility is on the applicant to withdraw. To withdraw from the service, free trial subscribers often have to give a prescribed period of advance notice and usually in writing; facts that may be obscured in rather lengthy terms and conditions. Because of this, subscribers can end up paying an additional monthly subscription.

Auction frauds

The popularity of online auction sites attracts fraudsters. Although auction sites advertise rigorous security procedures to build consumer trust, fraudsters still manage to exploit them. The US National Internet Fraud Information Center's internet fraud report for 2005 shows that auction fraud was the single largest category of reported fraud and constituted 42 per cent of the 12,315 complaints to its reporting website (NFIC, 2006). The fraudsters' key objective is to lure the bidder outside the well-protected online auction environment. In October 2005, three people were jailed for 'second chance' online frauds amounting to £300,000. They placed advertisements for items ranging from concert tickets to cars, some of which were genuine, others not. After the auction concluded, the fraudsters would get in touch with unsuccessful bidders to give them a second chance to buy the goods which they would be encouraged to pay for using money transfers; the bidders did not subsequently receive the goods (BBC, 2005n). Other examples of online auction-related frauds include the overpayment scam whereby the scammer (the bidder this time) intentionally pays more than the agreed sum. The payment cheque clears the banking system after a few days and the seller sends off the goods and refunds the overpayment. The fact that the cheque is counterfeit is usually not discovered until a few weeks later, leaving the victim liable for both losses.[11] In a variant of this scam, the buyer overpays the seller using a counterfeit cheque. The overpayment is then refunded by the seller before the cheque clears, but the goods are not collected – the seller retains the goods but loses the sum of the overpayment (Rupnow, 2003).

419 (Nigerian) advanced fee frauds

At the hard end of entrapment scams are the advanced fee frauds, called Nigerian because they originated in Nigeria and contravene Code 419 of the Nigerian Penal Code. Advanced fee fraudsters have cheated individuals and companies out of money for many years, but concerns have grown recently because of the increasing use of emails to contact potential victims. Furthermore, the risk to the individual increases dramatically in terms not only of potential financial loss, but also of personal risk.

> The e-mail scam . . . is a computer age version of a con game that goes back hundreds of years and is sometimes called 'The Spanish Prisoner.' Victims are contacted by a stranger who claims to have access to large sums of money. They are told that the money can only be accessed if they disclose the details of their bank account or put up an advance fee, but the promised funds never materialize. (Reuters, 2005)

Advanced fee frauds commence with the receipt of an official-looking letter, usually purporting to be from the relative of a former senior government official, who, prior to their death, accrued a large amount of money which is currently being held in a bank account within the country from which the letter was being sent. The sender of the following typical '419' letter invites the recipient to assist with the removal of the money by channelling it through his or her bank account. In return for collaborating, the recipient is offered $12 million, 20 per cent of the $60 million money to be transferred (see box 5.3).

Box 5.3   Example of a 419 (Nigerian) advanced fee fraud: excerpt from email

During the time my father was in the government with the late General Sani Abacha as the head of state, they were both involved in several deals that yielded Billions of Dollars . . .

During this period my father was able to make some good money for himself and kept in his private bank accounts . . . Right now, my father has been arrested and detained for interrogation. As the eldest son of my Father, I believe that I owe the entire family an obligation to ensure that the $60M is successfully transferred abroad for investment purposes. With the present situation, I cannot do it all by myself. . . .

I have done a thorough homework and fine-tuned the best way to create you as the beneficiary to the funds and effect the transfer accordingly. Is rest assured that the modalities I have resolved to finalize the entire project guarantees our safety and the successful transfer of the funds. So, you will be absolutely right when you say that this project is risk free and viable. If you are capable and willing to assist, contact me at once via email for more details.

Believe me, there is no one else we can trust again. All my fathers' friends have deserted us after exploiting us on the pretence of trying to help my father. As it is said, 'it is at the time of problems that you know your true friends'. So long as you keep everything to yourself, we would definitely have no problems. For your assistance, I am ready to give you as much as 20% of the total funds after transfer and invest a reasonable percentage into any viable business you may suggest.

Please, I need your assistance to make this happen and please; do not undermine it because it will also be a source of up liftment to you also. You have absolutely nothing to loose in assisting us instead, you have so much to gain.

Email (verbatim) received by author, 8 March 2001 (with similar ones on many subsequent occasions).

Once recipients respond to the sender, an advanced fee is sought to pay for banking fees and currency exchange. As the victim becomes more embroiled in the scam and pays out money it becomes harder to withdraw. Needless to say, the majority, if not all, of these invitations are bogus and are designed to defraud the respondents, sometimes for considerable amounts of money.

In a press release issued in July 2001, the National Crime Intelligence Service (NCIS) was concerned that the risk to the public from advanced fee frauds would rise through the increased use of emails. During a ten-month period in 2001, the West African Organised Crime Section of the NCIS conducted some research into victims of 419 advanced fee frauds. About 25,000 complaints (5,050 complaints by letter and 19,700 by email) were received during the research period from people who had been approached by fraudsters via letter or email. Interestingly, the volume of complaints contrasted sharply with the NCIS statistics for the number of victimizations reported during 2001. A total of 72 victims in the UK reported that they had fallen victim to 419 advanced fee frauds in 2001. This statistic does not provide much evidence of an increase in victimizations resulting from approaches by email. However, there are reporting disincentives at play here because many victims will usually destroy the letter or email that drew them into the fraud so that they are not subsequently accused of being involved in a conspiracy. But the incentives to report increase as the loss escalates, or worse, if victims feel that they are being personally threatened. It is therefore hard, if not impossible, to confirm whether or not there really is a grey figure of unreported advanced fee fraud. What is certain, however, is that the consequences of falling victim to an advanced fee fraud can be catastrophic on two counts. The first is financial. The NCIS calculated in 2001 that the victims of advanced fee frauds reported a total loss of £10.5 million, with the average loss per victim being £146,000. Even more worrying was that eight of the victims had lost £300,000 or more, with three of these each losing over £1 million. When these larger losses were removed from the statistics the average loss fell to £32,000. The experience in the US, compiled using a different methodology, also demonstrates large losses. The National Internet Fraud Information Center's internet fraud report of 2005 shows that 8 per cent, or 985 out of 12,315 fraud complaints were about Nigerian money offers. The average loss was just short of $7,000 or about £4,000. The second is the increase in personal risk. In a nasty twist, some individuals who travelled abroad in an attempt to recover their money have subsequently been kidnapped and a few have reportedly been murdered (BBC, 2001b). The jury is still out on the extent of 419 fraud victimization by email, but a number of interesting variations of the advanced fee theme have been found in emailed letters requesting loans rather than fees. In other examples, relationships are deliberately struck up on online dating services and then flight costs and other expenses are requested in advance by the correspondee to visit the person advertising on the dating services. These are all designed to elicit money in advance of any action.

Drug sales/health cures/snake oil remedies

The sale of prescription drugs through internet sites provokes widespread concern because of the potential dangers that can arise from the circulation of unregulated or even counterfeit drugs (Hall, 2005). Promises of quality goods, value for money, availability and also convenience of access would appear to be quickly shattered by broken promises and fraud. A poignant example is the booming international trade in Viagra, the anti-impotence drug (Cialis). In addition to the many Viagra emails that are thinly veiled attempts either to link-spam or to infect computers with trojans, the more plausible invitations, with trading address and other credible business credentials, often involve the illegal transport of drugs across borders to circumnavigate local prescription restrictions or exploit pricing differentials caused by taxes. Similar markets are also found trading steroids and other body enhancing drugs, such as slimming pills (Satchwell, 2004: 44). The growing use of the internet to sell counterfeit drugs is of great concern as it is exacerbating an already booming business and making it global (Satchwell, 2004). The World Health Organization (WHO) has estimated that about 8 to 10 per cent of all medicines available globally are counterfeit. Of particularly concern are stories that indicate, for example, that over 60 per cent of drugs sold in Nigeria were found to be counterfeit, some sold via the internet. An indication of the impact of counterfeit drugs upon a population is to be found in a report in the *Shenzhen Evening News* which stated that almost 200,000 people were alleged to have died in China during 2001 from taking bogus drugs (Satchwell, 2004: 44; Humble, 2005). These drugs are increasingly being procured over the internet, provoking demands for international regulation to verify the quality and legality of manufacture and also to authorize their purchase (WHO, 2004). The two primary concerns about internet drug sales relate to the regulation of mass sales, which is being addressed by the WHO, and of private sales to individuals – which is much harder to regulate.

Alongside the sales of pharmaceuticals is a robust market for alternative health cures and snake oil remedies which attempt to persuade buyer/victims that the product or service is to be trusted. Unlike the entrapment scams, however, which hook potential victims through their greed-driven gullibility, the snake oil scams play upon personal insecurities, or even the individual's ill-health. It is, of course, no surprise that individuals should seek longevity. The classical literature is full of tales of the quest to restore youth and to achieve immortality, going back 4,000 years to the Epic of Gilgamesh set in ancient Mesopotamia (Sandars, 1972: 97). Miracle cures became popular on the stalls of the Medieval English fairs and in the nineteenth century became the basis for the American medicine show (Anderson, 2000). It is therefore no surprise that the internet has become the site of the twenty-first-century virtual medicine show, feeding the same old personal insecurities and peddling miracle cures and snake oil, but on a global scale. Commonly found in email inboxes are offers to maintain and enhance vitality, youthfulness, health and longevity; miracle diets and potions; body enhancement lotions or operations to reduce body fat; lotions and creams to enlarge breasts, penises; to chisel body muscles (typically abs and peks). At the very bottom of the (moral) barrel are the bold claims of cures for cancer and other serious illnesses.

Virtual theft: cyber-piracy and 'stealing' informational intangibles

The ability of networked technologies to disseminate, share or trade informational (intellectual) property in the form of text, images, music, film and TV through information services has been one of the more significant developments of the internet. This property is informational, networked and also globalized, and its authors, or their licensees, have a right of ownership or control over it, including the right to receive payment for access to the content. Both the means of access to the services and also their informational property content have a market value which simultaneously creates opportunities and motivations for what has become known as cyber-piracy.

Informational services

Informational services deliver informational content to the user for a charge. The most popular way of stealing information services is to pay for them by using cloned, counterfeit or stolen credit card details. Alternatively, they can be accessed through account take-over when usernames and passwords have been obtained from legitimate users by shoulder surfing, dumpster diving or from electronic searches of computers, guessed/anticipated passwords, or even by using password cracking scripts. In circumstances where the technology permits, a legitimate subscription may be taken out and the access details then shared by a number of contributing individuals. Even where the source's information services lies offline, for example with satellite decoders, the internet can be used to obtain the information which will enable offenders to reprogram the security chips in access cards (see box 4.1). Finally, there are also a range of illegal information services in the form of P2P file-sharing networks which distribute and trade 'content' across networks of file sharers.

Intellectual property piracy and the internet

At the heart of the cyber-piracy debate is the ability of those who have legitimate control over the rights to digital intellectual property to maintain that control in their own interests. The problem is largely one of policing its usage, because digital property, whether in written, musical, or video form, has the unique characteristic of being stored as code and therefore being produced in its original form each time the file is run. Digital copies are identical, which creates new problems for controlling their dissemination in ways that preserve income streams. They are very different in nature to intellectual property that has been reproduced by analogue technology, such as vinyl records or film, which degrade in quality with each generation of copy. This characteristic emphasizes the value of the original artefact, but also installs an informal policing mechanism into the process. Without adequate controls in place the value of digital property can be lost very quickly. Consequently, running in parallel to the growth of the internet has been an increase in the number and complexity of intellectual property laws relating to trademarks, copyright and patents (see, for example, the debates over the changes in privacy and publicity laws in the US; Boyle, 1996; Madow, 1993; Wall, 2004). These laws have intensified the debates over piracy. The intersection of the medium of cyberspace and the more restrictive intellectual property laws have become quite a potent combination, especially at a time when, as Baudrillard observes, economic activity has become the outcome rather than the cause of cultural values and norms (Baudrillard, 1988, 1998). Importantly, the fact that productive ideas can now be put into place without the need for expensive mechanical manufacturing processes means that the monetary value of those ideas is further enhanced. These forms of intellectual property, trademarks, domain names and character merchandizing are becoming the real estate of cyberspace – especially where the IP is linked to the architecture of the internet (e.g. domain names, etc.). Thus the virtual terrain of cyberspace is marked by the struggle for control over this 'intellectual' real estate and its value increases in proportion to the strength of the legal and technological control that exists over its dissemination. The downside is that this control makes it all the more desirable as something to be acquired for use or to be sold on.

Intellectual property piracy follows the centuries' old practice of counterfeiting products by making copies of the original and then passing them off as originals. The trademark was introduced as a trusted sign to counter piracy by indicating to the purchaser that the product is genuine and produced by quality manufacturers (see Sherman and Bently, 1999). In the age of mass consumption the trademark, itself has acquired its own status and value as a brand, independent of the quality of work. For goods carrying trademarks, the internet has become a natural market place,[12] especially with the increasing popularity of e-commerce and internet auctions. These sites can be used to sell counterfeit branded *hard* goods, like Rolex watches, designer clothes and accessories, but also counterfeit branded *soft* goods that have been copied and packaged, or made available to download.

In many ways, these examples follow the *mens rea* (guilty mind – intent) and *actus reus* (guilty act) of traditional piracy and the primary concern of intellectual property right (IPR) holders is the loss of income when goods or services are purchased illegitimately. However, other new forms of counterfeiting are emerging solely within the confines of cyberspace, for example where pictures of a famous pop star are appropriated from (usually official) internet sites, or scanned from physical sources, or digitally created by 'morphing' different images together. The pictures are then packaged in a glossy, professional format with some additional explanatory text, then sold through some form of cyber-shopping mall or perhaps via a subject-specific internet relay chat group, typically to young customers who purchase them in good faith. To frustrate detection, the mall may be on a server in the US while the proceeds are paid into a bank account on the other side of the world. The whole operation might take as little as a few days so that, by the time the deception is detected, the proceeds of the scam have been removed from the bank account and the perpetrators gone.

Alternatively the images may be traded online for other similarly pirated informational products.

Informational piracy, as this form of cyber-piracy is more aptly described, differs from traditional piracy because it blurs the boundaries between criminal and civil actions. It is where owners' intellectual property rights (IPRs) in images, trademarks, copyrighted texts or general character merchandizing are threatened by theft or release into the public domain of the internet. The threat is not so much of loss of income, but of 'dilution', a term used in intellectual property law to describe the reduction in value through unrestricted use, but also to justify sustaining the intellectual property rights. The additional problem for IPR holders and for law is that the internet also facilitates new types of participatory consumption of informational properties. The appropriation of informational property may be motivated by libertarian (see Akdeniz, 1997),[13] artistic, moral, even educational reasons and not necessarily by the prospect of financial gain. See, for example, the three culturally different, yet significant, examples of the protection of intellectual property rights by the owners of Elvis Presley's imagery, the Tellytubby trademark and the pop group Oasis's copyright in Wall (1999: 120–3; and 2004) and more latterly the ferocity of the anti-MP3 and MP4 (copyright) anti-piracy compaigns. Although not explored in detail here, these and many more examples nevertheless demonstrate the gravity which owners of IPR attach to threats to their interests. They also illustrate the new dilemmas that IPR holders face with regard to the paradox of circulation and restriction in an environment of participatory consumption, which requires them to balance carefully their need to restrict the unauthorized circulation of their informational property to maintain income streams, while also allowing sufficient circulation of the property to allow the market to consume it as culture in the broadest sense and enabling it to reach new markets (Wall, 2004: 35).

Intellectual property piracy: music

Whereas P2P software has transformed information sharing, the invention of MP3 and MP4 file formats have respectively transformed the distribution of music and video. In the case of the former, as long as the appropriate P2P software is available, the music files can be downloaded to a computer's sound system, a portable MP3 player, or directly onto a CD-ROM or Mini-disc. The recording of music in a computer readable format was previously possible; however MP3 compression techniques reduced the files to manageable or transferable sizes. Consequently, devices from the early Rio Diamond MP3 player through to the more recent generation of iPods have been specifically designed to play MP3 files. Opinions on the morality and legality of MP3 are divided. On the one hand, the record companies and a few rock bands argue that the distribution of unauthorized MP3s is causing the death of popular music by giving away hard-earned and expensive properties and denying the authors the rewards they deserve. On the other hand, a strong counter argument is emerging that questions the claims of the music industry. A report by the Australian Institute of Criminology argued that the music industry cannot 'explain how it arrives at its statistics for staggering losses through piracy' (Greene, 2006). Evidence is also beginning to suggest that illicit MP3 downloads are in fact helping to promote music culture and also expand the capacity of the market. Not only can individual musicians now obtain immediate exposure to a much broader section of the public without having to become contracted to record companies, but MP3 has arguably stimulated the market for old as well as new popular music.

It is even alleged that CD sales are going up and not down. Oberholzer-Gee and Strumpf disproved the industry claims in their 2004 research into the impact of downloads on physical CD sales with the observation that 'downloads have an effect on sales which is statistically indistinguishable from zero' (Gibson, 2005; Schwartz, 2004; Potier, 2004). Furthermore, this claim is strengthened by the commercial success of recently introduced, and authorized, pay-to-use MP3 sites, such as iTunes, e-music and others, and, of course, the popularity of new MP3 playing hardware devices, such as the iPod. Further evidence of this trend is found in empirical research conducted in 2005 by Leading Question, which found that online file sharers actually buy more music, up to four-and-a-half times more, in legal downloads (Leading Question, 2005; Gibson, 2005).

Such counter claims illustrate the dynamics of a power play in which the recording industry's highly publicized private legal actions have been framed within a crime discourse to tame the MP3 download market. As soon as the MP3 technology began to gain popularity, legal actions were launched by the Recording Industry Association of America (RIAA) and British Phonographic Industry (BPI) on behalf of the music industry. They invoked copyright laws and brought law suits against MP3 bulk uploaders. Perhaps uniquely, the 16,000 or more cases were mostly brought against individuals, but few have actually gone to court, with the majority being settled privately (Vance, 2005). Accompanying these cases was a publicity campaign that simultaneously warned the public of the damage to the industry and also to society by suggesting that the proceeds of (mainly) CD piracy support organized crime. The impact of the actions and publicity has been to create the illusion of certainty of prosecution and to exercise a broad chilling effect upon illegal downloading behaviour.

Intellectual property piracy: video (film and television)

MP4, or MPEG-4, is a computer file compression format which, like MP3 for music, allows video, audio and other information to be stored on one file. Within a P2P network, MP4 files have transformed the dissemination of video, film and televisual materials. Newly released films can, for example, be illicitly videoed in cinemas and then converted into MP4 files, as can television programmes. Similarly, DVDs can be ripped into MP4 files. All can be sold or traded through illegal 'film portals' or across P2P networks. DVD manufacturers initially protected their products with a security device, however this was broken by a descrambling program, DeCSS, written by Jon Lech Johansen (also know as 'DVD Jon') so that he could watch his own DVDs on his Linux-powered PC. He also posted details of his descrambler on the internet which led to him being prosecuted 'largely on the behest of the Motion Picture Association of America (MPAA)' (Leyden, 2003b). The case for the prosecution argued that by sharing his DeCSS descrambler with others over the internet, Johansen made it easier to pirate DVDs and therefore had acted illegally. The case was thrown out by the Norwegian court on the grounds that the DVD scrambling codes had prevented Johansen from using his Linux PC to play back the DVDs that he had bought legitimately (Cullen, 2004: *Public prosecutor v Jon Lech Johansen*, 2003).

The failure to convict Johansen did not prevent the MPAA from continuing to protect its interests. Since 2004, legal actions have been brought against file sharers, particularly the film indexing sites and television download sites (BBC, 2005m). The latter action was significant because of the increased use of the internet as the broadcasting medium for television and the blurring of the boundaries between the two 'as TV-quality video online becomes a norm' (BBC, 2005b). Like the MP3 cases, the MPAA's actions were framed within an even stronger crime discourse that was driven by anti-piracy advertisements showing at the cinema and on DVDs and containing very vivid crime imagery which alleged that piracy supported organized crime and terrorism. As with the cases against individual music file sharers, most of the MP4 cases appear to have been settled privately. The actions and crime discourse have, as with MP3, created a chilling effect on downloading behaviour with evidence that the volume of downloads is decreasing, although it is an area that requires further research. These P2P related actions against individual infringers take place alongside legal actions against film websites that pose as legitimate film and music download services (BBC, 2005l).

Intellectual property piracy: software

The final aspect of IP piracy – and one that is currently a hot topic within cybercrime debates – is the illegal distribution of software over the internet. Illicit software was initially distributed though BBS bulletin boards and later across P2P file-sharing networks such as 'Drink or Die' (USDOJ, 2002; BBC, 2005d). The distribution operations were either for profit or for trading (not necessarily for profit) or to fulfil a broader ethic of helping the internet community. The latter function is often referred to as 'warez', which is a leet (l33t – see Glossary) speak derivative of (soft)wares, and is often used to signify copyrighted software that has been illegally offered for trade, but usually not-for-profit.[14]

The theft of virtual artefacts

The trade in 'game cheats' has been a longstanding practice. Cheats are virtual artefacts that enable players to map their way through computer games more quickly or gain access to hidden spaces within them. Some cheats exploit flaws in gaming programs, while others are strategically placed there by the game makers to sustain players' interest in the game. The problem with 'cheats' stems from the difficulty in identifying which are illicit and which are legitimate products of game designers. Perhaps the most infamous 'cheat' in recent years has been the software called 'Hot Coffee', which unlocked secret sex scenes in *Grand Theft Auto: San Andreas* (BBC, 2005f). Because of these additional scenes, the rating of the game was subsequently changed to 'Adult' which, along with the additional publicity attracted by litigation, helped to ensure that the game became one of the most popular of all time. Interestingly, there is also a growing online market in the sale or trade of other 'cheat' type activities outside the gaming world, such as assignments by students (plagiarism) on auction sites and P2P networks.

An interesting development in computer gaming is the increased criminal exploitation of gaming artefacts that have strategic import-ance in online role play gaming, for example in Project Entropia (project-entropia.com). Players need to obtain artefacts that sustain their place in their games and help them progress through it. The arte-facts are therefore highly desired because they represent not only high levels of ability and power, but also the hours of labour put into their construction. Because of this, players are willing to pay large amounts of real money for them. In 2004, a virtual island was sold on eBay for $26,500 (£13,700) and in 2005 a virtual space station went for $100,000 (£56,200) (BBC, 2005p). Consequently, the high values of these artefacts have generated a string of new criminal opportunities. Already there have been examples of buyers being defrauded through e-auction sales, artefacts being stolen from player's accounts by hackers, and even an 'online mugging' where a Japanese student was subsequently arrested for using automated bots in a 'first person shooter' game by making his avatar move faster than other players and shoot with pinpoint accuracy, thus attacking fellow players and steal-ing items (BBC, 2005j). The challenges that these forms of offending pose for criminal justice systems are considerable, not least because the victims can point to real economic harms done to them through the illegal use, or sale, of their 'virtual currency'. A key question is how best to legally represent the loss in the victims' interests. In their discussion of virtual property crimes, Lastowka and Hunter (2005: 300) argue that the analogy of theft is inappropriate because it implies the destruction of existing value. They favour instead, the language of offences such as 'counterfeiting' which takes into consideration the fact that the 'criminals' are actually creating illegitimate value (Lastowka and Hunter, 2005: 315).

Conclusions

This chapter has illustrated how inventive, reflexive and responsive computer-assisted or computer-mediated crime can be and also how close it sits to legitimate business opportunities. It shows how the virtual bank robbery, the virtual sting and virtual theft are areas of harmful/criminal activity that are rapidly evolving in step with tech-nological developments. As they evolve they create new challenges for law enforcement. For example, in the UK, the law is based on the understanding that machines cannot be deceived, only the people who use them; data cannot be stolen; fraud and deception are yet to be fully established as specific crimes; and trade secret theft is still not an offence (only the way that the information was obtained) in the UK. But is law the most effective local solution to what has become a global problem? The example of MP3 and MP4 file-sharing is a graphic illustration of where private corporate interests compete with the public interest and capture the crime agenda.

The bulk of this chapter has focused upon fraudulent behaviour driven by the desire for economic or informational gain. This profile will gradually broaden as new opportunities for offending are created by the convergence of networked technologies in the home, work and leisure, with those managing identity and location. Importantly, this new world of convergence will be characterized more and more by information brokering; 'information capital' will become increasingly more valuable. As a consequence, we shall probably see a further rise in the extent and breadth of information theft. Future debates on computer-assisted crime will therefore focus increasingly upon the rights relating to the protection of information and also the restoration of information and reputation once compromised.

6

Computer Content Crime: Pornography, Violence, Offensive Communications

How has criminal activity changed in the information age?
Part 3

Chapter at a glance

- **Obscene materials online (extreme pornography)**
  Sexually explicit materials
  Child pornography and the internet
- **Violent or harmful content**
  Hate speech, including racism and radical politics
  Violent imagery/murder video nasties
  Circulating information about making drugs and weapons
  Using websites to circulate information used in the
    organization of harmful action
  Circulating misinformation online
- **Offensive communications emails, chatrooms and blogging**
  Chatroom and discussion group communications (stalking
    and grooming)
  Blogging and blogsites
- **Can words actually harm?**
- **Conclusions**

Internet content today can be beneficial socially, culturally, educationally, politically. Rauterberg's meta-literature review of almost 400 relevant articles about the impact of the internet entertainment industry upon its participants concluded that when the content and context of use are properly designed the effects on users are very positive (Rauterberg, 2004: 51). Furthermore, it is content and context rather than the technology itself that influences behaviour. However, Rauterberg's findings also show that if the content and context of use are poorly or maliciously designed, then the outcomes can be very different – and even harmful. Such findings are not surprising and largely confirm what has long been assumed. But what is it about content that is harmful?

There are currently three substantive areas of concern about how informational computer content can harm people through words and imagery. The first part of this chapter will focus upon the impact of unhealthy and inappropriate materials on the individual, especially extreme sexual imagery such as child pornography. The second part considers the use of violent content to hurt people, particularly using hate speech, racism, or images of violence. Also included here is information that enables weapons to be made, the dissemination of dangerous skills and the deliberate use of misinformation. The third part examines the new generation of content deviance such as obscene or libellous emails and blogs, which is growing as online communities link to accessible and affordable broadband. The final part discusses the key concerns arising from the debate about harmful words and pictures and their effect upon conduct (social action), especially the borderline between harmful thoughts and harmful actions – between words and conduct (Balkin, 2004: 2090) – and also the tension between offensive content and freedom of expression.

Obscene materials online (extreme pornography)

Novelist Irving Welsh's character 'Sick Boy' succinctly outlines the relationship between the consumer society and pornography:

> we need tits and arse . . . because we're consumers. Because those are things we like, things we intrinsically feel or have been conned into believing will give us value, release, satisfaction. We value them so we need to at least have the illusion of their availability. For tits and arse read coke, crisps, speedboats, cars, houses, computers, designer labels, replica shorts. That's why advertising and pornography are similar; they sell the illusion of availability and the non-consequence of consumption. (Welsh, 2002: 450)

Sick Boy's last point – the illusion of availability without the consequences of consumption – is poignant here because it begins to explain the attraction of the internet as a medium for both distributing and consuming pornography. Pornography and technological

development have had a curious and contradictory long-term relationship, one which has involved the internet since the early 1990s
(Johnson, 1996: 217). A commonly held belief during the mid-1990s
was that pornographic materials could be accessed with impunity and
it was this that drew many people to the internet. Interest was fuelled
by the availability of new types of media delivery, such as the voyeuristic soft-core cam-girl sites like Jennifer Ringley's Jennicam.com.[1] The
cam-girl sites were made possible by the (then) unique ability of the
internet to converge textual and visual media in both real and chosen
time, and at relatively low cost. The cam-girl sites represented, if not
facilitated, a shift in the politics of self-representation to enable
women to express themselves on their own terms (Turner, 2004: 64)
and giving women a stake in the internet while further expanding the
market for it. While Jennicam may have retained its initial values,
much like a visual blog, many cam-girl sites were quickly absorbed
into the burgeoning online hardcore pornography industry brought
together by 'cyber-pimps', or financiers who resourced their web-
pages and linked them to cam-girl networks, sex portals and maintained their high positions in search engine rankings. Until 1999, the
word 'pornography' was the number one target for internet search
engines, a position which it held for almost a decade until it was
eclipsed by 'MP3' (Carey and Wall, 2001: 35). By 2005, both had
been superseded by 'Paris Hilton' (Wordtracker, 2005) as the most
popular search phrase.

Sexually explicit materials

The high level of demand for sexually explicit materials online subsequently encouraged the advancement of the technology that delivered
it. The virtual sex-trade quickly became an electronic sexual information service (imagery, stories, etc.) which, controversially, not only
pioneered the virtual transaction but also demonstrated the commercial potential of the internet to the business community. But it was the
fear of unrestrained access to sexually explicit or pornographic materials that fuelled public concern about the internet. Because sexually
explicit materials that arouse the viewer are not necessarily illegal, the
cyber-pornography/obscenity debate has been complicated by a lattice
of moral and legal issues. The most heated of these focuses upon the
extent to which children should be protected from the effects of
viewing obscene imagery. The test in the UK and other jurisdictions
as to whether pornographic materials are obscene is if they deprave
and corrupt the viewer: 'an article shall be deemed to be obscene if its

effect or (where the article comprises two or more distinct items) the effect of any one of its items is, if taken as a whole, such as to tend to deprave and corrupt persons who are likely, having regard to all relevant circumstances, to read, see or hear the matter contained or embodied in it' (s.1(1), Obscene Publications Act 1959 (UK)).

There are two fundamental problems in identifying obscene materials online. The first is to find the margin of appreciation between the individual's right of freedom of expression and the right of the state to protect its own cultures and values. To this effect, Article 10(1) of the European Convention on Human Rights reflects Article 19 of the United Nations Universal Declaration of Human Rights and empowers EU citizens with the freedom 'to hold opinions and to receive and impart information and ideas without interference by public authority and regardless of frontiers'. But Article 10(2) clearly explains that the burden of these freedoms, duties and responsibilities are prescribed by law and 'are necessary in a democratic society, in the interests of national security, territorial integrity or public safety, for the prevention of disorder or crime, for the protection of health or morals, for the protection of the reputation or rights of others' (see *R. v. Handyside v. United Kingdom, 1976; Paris Adult Theater I v. Slaton*, 1973 – the state should protect morals of society).

The second problem is to reconcile the considerable legal and moral differences in deciding which criteria should be applied to establish obscenity and depravation (see Chatterjee, 2001: 78) in a global medium such as the internet. In the UK, for example, individuals daily consume risqué images through the mass media which might be regarded as obscene in some societies; and sexual images that are permitted after the 9pm watershed on UK television, may be found on daytime TV in more permissive countries. In seeking to clarify the defining criteria, the European Commission's *Green Paper and Action Plan on the Protection of Minors and Human Dignity in Audio-Visual and Information Services* made the important distinction between situations in which children might gain access to legal websites with pornographic content and sites containing material depicting illegal, obscene, acts that are subject to penal sanctions (EC, 1997). The usefulness of the legal distinction is that it identifies the point at which self-regulation ceases and state intervention starts, particularly where moral and political agendas drive public opinions. However, it is complicated by the broadly held view that while the pornographic content of websites may not necessarily be illegal, it may nevertheless still be judged to be harmful to childrens' development (European Commission Select Committee, 1996: ch.1).

The emotionally charged nature of the debate over the regulation of obscene materials on the worldwide web has taken it in a number of different directions. Rimm's Carnegie Mellon Survey (1995), for example, alleged that the consumption of pornography constituted as much as half of all internet traffic, mostly through 'usenet' discussion groups. Rimm claimed to identify '917,410 images, descriptions, short stories, and animation downloaded 8.5 million times by consumers in over 2,000 cities in forty countries, provinces, and territories' (Rimm, 1995: 1849). The public reaction to this influential survey contributed to the moral panic of mid-1990s over the use of the internet, which persisted long after inconsistencies in the survey's methodology were exposed. Rimm's methodology was indeed deeply flawed – he had greatly overestimated the level of internet traffic in sexual materials by concentrating his data collection upon newsgroups and bulletin boards. In fact, when all forms of internet traffic were considered, it was later found that the overall percentage was less than 1 per cent, in contrast to the 83.5 per cent he had claimed (Wallace and Mangan, 1996). Yet, Rimm's survey findings made a lasting impact upon the debate over internet regulation and were instrumental in setting the emotional climate in the lead up to the passage of the Communications Decency Act 1996 (47 USC s.223) in the US, which was later partly overturned (*ACLU et al. v. Reno* (1997); Heins, 2001b). Rimm's findings appeared to give strong empirical support to the anti-pornography lobby who argued that pornography degraded women (MacKinnon, 1993) and was an assault on the moral fabric of society. For a while, the findings eclipsed the arguments of the pro-pornography lobby, who claimed that the availability of sexual materials on the internet would reduce sex crimes (Diamond and Uchiyama, 1999: 1, 18), of civil libertarians who defended the pornographers' right to freedom of expression, and of the advocates of *laissez faire* who believed that free market demand should determine the course of events. Although the moral panic has since subsided it still lurks in the background.

The different moral and political perspectives on pornography highlight the need to differentiate the types of pornographic content found on websites in terms of their risk to viewers. The majority of internet-based pornography is adult consensual pornography, whether it is softcore sexual imagery or even hard-core imagery depicting penetration and other sexual acts. Although subject to moral strictures, its consensual nature leaves it largely non-contentious within most western jurisdictions, and with some caveats, within the boundaries of law. Even 'extreme' pornographic materials depicting acts on the borders of consensuality are unlikely to be prosecuted so long as the acts are consensual (*R. v Brown*, 1993, 1994; *R. v Wilson*, 1996). It is only when there is clear evidence of violence against one or more of the parties by the other that an investigation may take place, and then usually only after a formal complaint has been made to the police. To illustrate this point, the UK's Crown Prosecution Service (CPS), which prosecutes on behalf of the Crown, argues that it is impossible to define all of the obscene activities that can be prosecuted, but it nevertheless lists the most common categories (reproduced in box 6.1).

Box 6.1   Commonly used categories in prosecutions for obscenity

- sexual acts with children
- sexual assaults upon children
- portrayal of incest
- buggery with an animal
- rape
- drug taking
- flagellation
- torture with instruments
- bondage (especially where gags are used)
- dismemberment or graphic mutilation
- cannibalism
- activities involving perversion or degradation (such as drinking urine or smearing excreta on a person's body)

Source: Crown Prosecution Service Charging Practice on Obscene Publications (as of January 2006), www.cps.gov.uk/legal/section12/chapter_e.html#10.

In deciding whether or not to prosecute, the CPS considers whether the allegedly obscene presentation is in written or visual form – the former is deemed to have a lesser impact than the latter. They also consider whether the presentation is personal or commercial; whether it was, or could have been viewed by a child or vulnerable adult; whether it could be readily seen by the general public in a public place or shop; whether or not the defendant has a similar previous conviction. The final consideration concerns the degree of participation by the suspect and the level of his or her knowledge of the contents of the material (s. 2(5) Obscene Publications Act 1959). Of crucial importance to the

prosecution process is that the publication is produced and dissemi-
nated within the country in question, which is a key problem in policing obscene materials on the internet. This current position in the UK
could change, however, following the 2005 Consultation on the
Possession of Extreme Pornographic Material, and subsequent plans
announced in August 2006 to make it an offence to possess images
depicting scenes of serious sexual violence and other obscene materials that arc currently illegal to publish in the UK under the Obscene
Publications Act 1959, but are accessible from abroad via the internet
(Home Office, 2005; 2006).

Child pornography and the internet

The most contentious type of online pornography is that which contains 'sexualised or sexual pictures involving children' (Taylor, 1999).
In the UK, the Protection of Children Act 1978 currently defines four
offences involving indecent photographs or pseudo-photographs of
children (Sentencing Advisory Panel, 2002: 2):[2]

> Under section 1(1) of the 1978 Act, it is an offence for a person:
> (a) to take, or permit to be taken, or to make any indecent photograph
> or pseudo-photograph of a child; or
> (b) to distribute or show such indecent photographs or pseudo-
> photographs; or
> (c) to have in his possession such indecent photographs or pseudo-
> photographs, with a view to their being distributed or shown by himself
> or others; or
> (d) to publish or cause to be published any advertisement likely to be
> understood as conveying that the advertiser distributes or shows such
> indecent photographs or pseudo-photographs, or intends to do so.

The possession of indecent digital photographs of children was
made an offence under section 160 of the Criminal Justice Act 1988,
while section 84(4) of the Criminal Justice and Public Order Act
1994 included possession of 'pseudo-photographs' (Akdeniz, 1997).
'Pseudo-photographs' had previously weakened the case for the
prosecution because of reliance on the fact that a child had been
abused in the construction of the picture (see further *R. v. Jonathan
Bowden*, 2000). Increased societal concern about child pornography
on the internet in the late 1990s led to section 41(3) of the Criminal
Justice and Court Services Act 2000 in which the possession of
an indecent photograph or pseudo-photograph of a child was made
an offence that would be tried in either the (lower) Magistrates'

Courts or (upper) Crown Courts, with a maximum penalty of five years' imprisonment on conviction (Sentencing Advisory Panel, 2002: 2).

Other common law jurisdictions have adopted legal considerations similar to those outlined above. However, the constitutional protection of freedom of expression in the US and elsewhere has meant that while the production and possession of child pornography is illegal, there are possible defences. Much of the debate therefore revolves around the definition of child pornography. In the US it is found under 18 USC 2256(8) (A–D) (following the case of *Ashcroft v. Free Speech Coalition* in 2002; Landau, 2002).

> (8) 'child pornography' means any visual depiction, including any photograph, film, video, picture, or computer or computer-generated image or picture, whether made or produced by electronic, mechanical, or other means, of sexually explicit conduct, where—
> (A) the production of such visual depiction involves the use of a minor engaging in sexually explicit conduct;
> (B) such visual depiction is, or appears to be, of a minor engaging in sexually explicit conduct;
> (C) such visual depiction has been created, adapted, or modified to appear that an identifiable minor is engaging in sexually explicit conduct; or
> (D) such visual depiction is advertised, promoted, presented, described, or distributed in such a manner that conveys the impression that the material is or contains a visual depiction of a minor engaging in sexually explicit conduct.

At the core of public and legal concerns about child pornography is the ability of investigators and prosecutors to determine when imagery contravenes the law. In order to standardize classifications that enable the assessment of images in both the investigation and the court process, the UK Sentencing Advisory Panel (2002) collapsed the University of Cork's COPINE 10 point classification for describing the range of pornographic images of children down to five levels to make it more applicable – see box 6.2.

While these UK classifications have found support in the international law enforcement and legal communities and overlap with the tests applied in the US, they also display some fundamental differences. In the US, a key factor in determining whether or not child pornographic imagery is obscene is whether or not it displays 'lascivious exhibition'. Many US courts apply the six-part 'Dost test' (box 6.3) from *United States v Dost* (1986) to determine whether a picture constitutes a 'lascivious exhibition' (Adler, 2001: 262).

Box 6.2   Classifying images depicting child pornography

Level 1: images depicting erotic posing with no sexual activity;
Level 2: non-penetrative sexual activity between children or solo masturbation by a child;
Level 3: non-penetrative sexual activity between adults and children;
Level 4: penetrative sexual activity involving a child or children, or both children and adults;
Level 5: sadism or penetration of or by an animal.

Source: Sentencing Guidelines Council, 2006: 102; also see Sentencing Advisory Panel, 2002: 6, para. 21.

Box 6.3   The Dost test for lascivious exhibition

[I]n determining whether a visual depiction of a minor constitutes a 'lascivious exhibition of the genitals or pubic area' under [18 USC] S 2255(2)(E), the trier of fact should look to the following factors, among any others that may be relevant in the particular case:
(1)   whether the focal point of the visual depiction is on the child's genitalia or pubic area;
(2)   whether the setting of the visual depiction is sexually suggestive, i.e. in a place or pose generally associated with sexual activity;
(3)   whether the child is depicted in an unnatural pose, or in inappropriate attire, considering the age of the child;
(4)   whether the child is fully or partially clothed, or nude;
(5)   whether the visual depiction suggests sexual coyness or a willingness to engage in sexual activity;
(6)   whether the visual depiction is intended or designed to elicit a sexual response in the viewer.

Source: *United States v. Dost* (1986: 832).

Whereas the Sentencing Advisory Panel's classifications tend to deal primarily with matters of fact, the 'Dost test' requires some degree of interpretation, which is not particularly useful when the meanings of what constitutes child pornography are 'not always quite so clear' (Taylor, 1999). What makes the pictures attractive to those with a sexual interest in children is only partly their content; the most important factor is the sexual fantasy and personal meaning that the content invokes. While the law can define the boundaries of behaviour – for example, possession of sexualised child images, including morphed imagery, is illegal in the UK – it leaves much room for interpretation, especially with regard to where the public interest lies in terms of risk. In other words, where does the danger lie? It is therefore important to understand more about why child pornography is produced, collected and consumed and all indications are that this task will require us to think beyond the legal definition of child pornography (Taylor and Quayle, 2003; Krone, 2004: 1).

Child pornography is by no means a product of the internet – it has been a problem for many years and there is much historical evidence to indicate that adult sexual interest in children dates back to ancient times. Within the context of this discussion, however, it is important to ascertain whether or not the internet has had a transformative impact on child pornography, and if so, how. Taylor and Quayle (2003) draw on the COPINE research to demonstrate that the internet creates the social, individual and technological circumstances that enable an individual with an interest in child pornography to feel safe in expressing their sexual fantasies and, in some cases, realities. First, networking technologies create a socially self-justifying online community for consumers of child pornography in which otherwise deviant values are shared or even encouraged. Secondly, the internet also allows individuals to gain access to pornographic material and to communicate with others from the privacy of their own home, giving them a feeling of security and also a sense of control over the medium, plus the choice over whether or not their involvement is going to be passive or active (M. Taylor, 1999). This illusory distance between participants and their perceived non-consequences of consumption, particularly through the possibility of anonymity through using false or fantasy identities or encryption, are further stimulated by the fantasies invoked by the imagery: 'the 50-year-old can present himself as a teenager . . . the weak as strong' (M. Taylor, 1999). The concern here is that these fantasies may eventually be acted out in online interactions with children or even in person, following meetings arranged online (Krone, 2004: 3). This game can, of course, be played both ways because the same media also enables police officers to pose as children in 'sting' operations.

Thirdly, perhaps the main impact of networked technology on child pornography has been to provide new and increasingly effective methods of distributing child sexual imagery. Particularly significant has been the transition from dial-up BBS (bulletin board services) to

P2P (peer-to-peer) networks. P2P distributed qualities facilitate the rapid dissemination of imagery, while simultaneously enabling those with an interest in such images, or a more general sexual interest in children, to organize themselves more effectively. Crucial to the effectiveness of this organization is the P2P networks' dependency upon its participants to allow uploads from their public folders, combined with the membership requirement of many closed child pornography networks to submit a pre-specified number of images and demonstrate a willingness to exchange them. Fulfilling this condition not only makes all those involved in the network complicit in the act, but it also makes them feel complicit, further tying them in to the network while also encouraging the collecting of images as an end in its own right.

Some idea of the scale of demand for child pornography and also of the organization of its distribution can be gleaned from the yield of policing operations against the consumers of online child pornography. 'Operation Ore' was the UK police response following supply by the FBI of the details of 7,200 British suspects who had subscribed to a Texan subscription portal. *Landslide*, the portal's name, gave subscribers access to 300 child pornography sites for about £21 per month (Sherriff, 2004). The UK side of the operation resulted in 3,744 arrests, with 1,848 people being charged of whom 1,451 were convicted. A further 493 were cautioned and a total of 879 investigations were undertaken. In all, 109 children were rescued from abusive homes[3] (Cowan, 2005). Rather controversially, approximately 35 of those investigated have since committed suicide (Howie, 2006), and Leppard (2005) and Campbell (2005a, 2005b) have subsequently highlighted flaws in the evidence process. However, the sheer size of the whole *Landslide* subscription database, which contained the names and credit card subscription details of 390,000 subscribers across 60 countries, illustrates the globalized scale of the problem (Jewkes and Andrews, 2005: 49), and 'Operation Ore' was by no means the first such police operation. In 1998, 'Operation Cathedral' was launched against a paedophile ring called the Wonderland Club (after Alice in Wonderland) and 750,000 child pornography images were seized (Creighton, 2003: 3). In the subsequent analysis of these images, it was found that more than 1,200 different children were involved; however, only 18 were identified and discovered – three in the UK (Downey, 2002). This illustrates the complexity and resource intensity of the policing operation.

It is therefore interesting, and of some concern, that despite the potentially serious nature of the offences, Edwards (2000) found that only a small number of cases of possession of illegal images were eventually proceeded with in the courts, especially the Crown Court. It is only the more serious offences of possession with intent to distribute and taking an indecent photograph that can be tried either in the Magistrates Court or Crown Court (Edwards, 2000: 19). Another possible reason for the apparent shortfall in the prosecution of the more serious forms of offending is that the technology allows relatively few individuals, the more serious offenders, to control large databases across a number of illicit operations, simultaneously giving the impression that the offender population is more numerous. This latter point further emphasizes the need to differentiate between the different levels of risk posed by individuals so that resources into the investigation of offending can be efficiently allocated.

Drawing upon COPINE's research into collections of child pornography traded online, M. Taylor (1999) found three types of sexual material. The first are erotica, pictures of children in the form of personal snapshots, or advertisements for children's clothes. They are not necessarily sexual and not necessarily illegal, but the format of the collection may reveal the compiler's sexual interest in children. The second type depicts images of child nudity. Some will be collections of pictures taken covertly, pictures posed in sexual positions (soft pornography); others will be drawn from nudist and artistic publications. As is the case with erotica, these may not individually be illegal, but nevertheless indicative of a sexual interest in children. The third category is explicit sexual materials and those classed as obscene. While this is a very useful classification for imagery, it says little about the risk from offenders. Krone's (2004: 3) typology of online child pornography offending, outlined in box 6.4, specifically seeks to achieve this further goal. Particularly useful is his delineation between individuals whose sexual interest in children is confined to fantasies and those who actually abuse children. Krone takes into consideration the type and nature of the individual's involvement, the level of networking, the immediate security risk to children and the nature of the abuse.

What Krone usefully shows is that there are quite distinct groups among consumers of child pornography, each of which displays different levels of risk to the community. The first three groups – browsers, fantasists and trawlers – display very low levels of networking and it is likely that much of their activity will remain internet-based, distanced and private in thoughts, rather than actions. Furthermore, they are likely to be of less immediate risk to children. The others, however – the collectors, groomers, abusers, producers and distributors – are

---

Box 6.4   Krone's typology of online child pornography offending

1 *Browsers* respond to spam or accidentally fall upon suspected sites. They knowingly save material. Browsers tend to be lone operators and do not network.
2 *Private fantasists* consciously create online text or digital images for their own use. They tend to be lone operators and do not network.
3 *Trawlers* actively seek child pornography through openly available browsers. Trawlers tend to be fairly lone operators, but may engage in low-level networking.
4 *Non-secure collectors* actively seek material through peer-to-peer networks. They are high-level networkers, but do not tend to engage any security measures in so doing.
5 *Secure collectors* actively seek material, but only through secure networks and engage high levels of security to avoid being detected. They are high-level networkers and are willing to exchange collections to gain access to new sources.
6 *Groomers* cultivate online relationships with one or more children, but they may or may not seek material as in 1–5 above. They are more likely to use pornography to facilitate abuse.
7 *Physical abusers* abuse children who they may have been introduced to online. As with the groomers, they may or may not seek material in any of the above ways. They are more likely to use pornography to facilitate abuse.
8 *Producers* record their own abuse of a child, or that of others. Or they may induce children to submit images of themselves.
9 *Distributors* may distribute imagery at any one of the above levels.

Source: Based on Krone, 2004: 4 (table 3).

---

clearly prepared to put their thoughts into action and therefore pose a greater risk to children because of their willingness to become involved in networks of like-minded individuals.

Making such distinctions is important for efficient resource allocation, but this is understandably an issue that also scares people. Public emotions run very high when it is felt that children have been abused. As a consequence there is a high level of media sensitization that subsequently politicizes the policing of child pornography and paedophiles. Hewson believes that viewing child pornography has become equated in the public eye with criminal responsibility for rape and has worrying implications for liberty and also law. Of principal concern is that the current tendency towards wholesale condemnation of offenders is chilling critical debate about its actual impacts, while the strict measures being imposed are actually fuelling interest in the very thing that they are seeking to suppress (Hewson, 2003). It also raises the much broader and extremely contentious philosophical issue identified by Adler, though not discussed in this book, that: '[c]hildren and sex become inextricably linked, all while we proclaim the child's innocence'. The main problem for Adler is that 'sexuality prohibited becomes the sexuality produced' (Adler, 2001: 273).

Much further work is required to understand whether or not an individual's continued involvement as a browser or fantasizer will simply satisfy his or her curiosity (see Diamond and Uchiyama, 1999), or whether it erodes the browser's moral bind, gradually releasing them from the moral constraints of conventional order (Matza, 1964). Proponents of this widely prevailing 'drift theory' predict that the paedophilic *weltanschauung* would progress the individual's lusts and sexual appetite up the scale of deviance. Yet, this 'ideology of paedophilia', which has emerged as a public moral response that automatically labels and demonizes all offenders, can cloud the understanding, investigation and resolution of the problem. This is particularly so in regard to understanding where the line is to be drawn between thoughts and actions. Clearly, the answer to whether or not those whose sexual interest in children does not go beyond fantasizing are a different group of individuals from those who actually abuse children has profound implications for the effective targeting of finite resources at the people who pose the greater risk to children. Such understanding is crucial in an area so emotionally charged because it is arguable that the former may need help, whereas the latter may deserve prison.

Violent or harmful content

Informational content can violate individuals or social groupings by singling them out as a target for hate and then reinforcing that hate through threats and implied violence. While such activities do not necessarily have an immediate and direct physical manifestation, the victim can, nevertheless, feel the violence of the act and can bear long-term psychological scars as a consequence. Violence can be expressed directly through hate websites: peddling violent imagery; providing information about the manufacture of drugs, bombs and weapons; offensive email communications through blogsites; and cyber-stalking/grooming in 'public' chat rooms. The ways that words and images impact upon individuals are discussed later.

Hate speech, including racism and radical politics

There is some academic controversy about the precise meaning of 'hate speech' because of the different actions that it involves, such as hate, bigotry, prejudice, exclusion (see O'Connor, 2003: 62). However, a definition derived from various commonly cited sources is that it is a form of speech that is uttered intentionally to degrade, exclude, intimidate or incite violence or prejudicial action against another person based on their race, ethnicity, national origin, religion, sexual orientation or disability. Online hate speech expresses much the same characteristics, but is exercised online and is therefore informational, networked and global. Of key importance to the criminological debate over online hate speech is the point at which the informational content crosses the line between thoughts and action and when the words become actual threats (Rothman, 2002: 1). This is discussed later.

The internet is host to some very disturbing hate speech, and responses to it vary across jurisdictions. Perhaps one of the most dramatic examples is holocaust denial, as illustrated in the case of *R. v. Zundel* (1992). Zundel, a Canadian, attempted to rewrite Jewish history by denying that the persecution of the Jewish people by the Nazis had ever taken place. Zundel was originally prosecuted in 1988 for 'publishing false news' but his conviction was later overturned on appeal because the false news law was subsequently judged to have contravened the Canadian Charter of Rights. He subsequently moved the offending website to a server in the US, where it came under the protection of stronger freedom of expression laws. Zundel is not alone and other websites are also devoted to the issue of holocaust denial (see Greenberg, 1997: 673) along with many more directed towards hate-speech. In January 2003, a protocol against racism and xenophobic material on the internet was added to the Council of Europe's Convention on Cybercrime (COE, 2003). Although the US ratified the Convention on Cybercrime in 2006, it is unlikely that this additional protocol will be signed in the near future because it is inconsistent with the US constitutional right to free speech.

Violent imagery/murder video nasties

The UK Obscene Publications Acts are not solely restricted to sexually explicit materials and can include materials that represent extreme violence, though cases of non-sexual obscene materials are few in number and may also be dealt with under legislation such as the Video Recordings Act 1984. Networked technology easily lends itself to the distribution of extremely violent imagery, especially in video format. Concerns were voiced during the 1990s about the online distribution of 'snuff movies' – films that purport to depict sensationally and for the gratification of others actual deaths, usually of women while performing a sexual act (Harding, 2001).[4] Initially sold illegally as complete movies in video format and later reduced to web video clips, snuff movies are designed to convince viewers that 'they are privy to something rare and exclusive'. FBI investigations in the mid-1990s concluded that snuff movies were likely to be bogus and that the murders depicted in them were staged, a conclusion that is now the conventional wisdom on the subject. 'I've not found one single documented case of a snuff film anywhere in the world. I've been searching for 20 years, talked to hundreds of people. There's plenty of once-removed sightings, but I've never found a credible personality who personally saw one' (Ken Lanning, FBI Training Academy, cited by McDowell, 1994; also in cited in Harding, 2001).

Concerns about violent pornography persisted following the death of a British teacher, Jane Longhurst, in 2003 at the hands of a man who was allegedly obsessed with violent pornography. The case brought the issue to the fore, and in 2006 the UK Government announced that it would seek to make the viewing of violent pornography illegal (Home Office, 2006). Following this announcement, a study of violent pornography available online conducted by the BBC came to the conclusion that although the material viewed was extremely convincing, it mainly appeared to be faked (Oliver, 2006), thus opening up the controversy about the impact upon individuals who view violent sexual imagery.

Some insight into the impact of non-sexual violent imagery online can be obtained by examining the emergence since the 2003 'Gulf War' of a chilling genre of 'execution' videos that depict the murder of foreign nationals, such as British citizen Ken Bigley in April 2005, who had been kidnapped by Islamic groups based in the Middle East. The recordings were made available through various websites and show the victims being forced to make a humiliating public plea for their lives before being executed in cold blood. Unlike the snuff movies, which were designed to be sold, these execution videos are primarily instruments of cyber-terror because they are intended to further the maker's political agenda, spreading fear and outrage across the victims' communities, while also galvanizing their own supporters. In addition, the recordings subsequently became widely circulated by net users on the internet as a spectacle and a curio.

In his short article, Walker (2004) briefly summarizes the popularity of murder videos as being primarily due to viewers' curiosity: '[a] lot of it's to do with the taboo of seeing stuff we're not supposed to'. This curiosity is excited by the cold and calculating quality of the act and has stirred the rantings of the conspiracy theorists who claim that the videos are faked to serve anti-Muslim interests. So people watch just to see if it is real! (*Illuminati News*, 2004). The motivations of the host sites to show these recordings vary. Some use the viewers' curiosity to increase the volume of visitors to their site, while others may further a moral or political agenda either in support of the action or against it. Korean pro-liberation groups, for example, have released video footage of public executions in North Korea to demonstrate the barbarity of the incumbent regime and promote their own cause (CNN, 2005). Alternatively, other sites containing gruesome imagery may actively seek to uphold their right to freedom of expression, especially those located within the US.

Circulating information about making drugs and weapons

Discussion about crime, its commission and the technology required to achieve it occurs in news groups, internet relay chat forums and blogsites. The topics vary considerably and their potential for influencing individual action is even more contentious than that relating to obscene or violent content. At one end of the spectrum is the circulation of information outlining sophisticated technologies designed to circumnavigate existing infrastructural frameworks.[5] For example, Pryce, the hacker mentioned earlier, stated that he used bulletin boards to get software and gain access to hardware.

'I used to get software off the bulletin boards and from one of them I got a "bluebox", which could recreate the various frequencies to get free phone calls,' he said. 'I would phone South America and this software would make noises which would make the operator think I had hung up. I could then make calls anywhere in the world for free'. (Ungoed-Thomas, 1998: 1)

At the other end of the spectrum is bomb-talk, which ranges from the circulation of instructions on how to make a bomb or other weaponry to the deliberate targeting of groups with a view to committing a violent act (see Wallace and Mangan, 1996: 153). Perhaps the most vivid example of the latter was the supposed use of the internet by members of various militias in the planning of the Oklahoma bombing (Deflem, 1997: 5) and, more recently, by Richard Reid, the 'shoe bomber' (BBC, 2002a). Similarly, the manufacturers of the devices used in the London Bombings of 7 July and 21 July 2005 are alleged to have got the recipe for the acetone peroxide-based explosive from the internet. There is, however, some controversy about this claim because while the formula may be available, the extremely volatile nature of the substance requires specialist expertise in the manufacturing process to stabilize it and prevent a premature explosion. As one of the correspondents to Bruce Schneier's security weblog soberly commented: '[t]rying to make explosives from instructions downloaded from the internet is pretty stupid. Explosives are something you don't generally want to try to make (or even handle) without proper training' (posted 5 August 2005, 9.36 am).[6] This reveals once again the need to be able to differentiate between thoughts and actions and truths and untruths in assessing risks – a dialectic that characterizes just about all things internet and crime. Also relevant here is the fact that because talk about crime is regarded as speech, it is often given freedom of expression protections, for example under the US Constitution and Canadian Charter of Rights,[7] even though the intent behind the harmful speech might conflict with criminal codes.

Using websites to circulate information used in the organization of harmful action

Websites can be used to organize harmful actions by, for example, announcing details of meetings and gatherings or even identifying specific targets towards which hate should be directed. In the organization of such activities, a range of bodies of law are contravened: notably public order or conspiracy. Where physical harm occurs, laws protecting the person are invoked. Sometimes referred to as cyber-thuggery,[8] specific examples include the following.

Nuremberg files The American Coalition of Life Activists (ACLA), a pro-life group, collected personal information both about doctors who performed abortions and their supporters. It passed this information to an anti-abortionist who loaded it onto a website. Some of these 'named' individuals were subsequently attacked in a brutal manner and after each attack the authors of the website struck through the names of the dead and highlighted the names of the wounded (Maynard, 2001: 41; Gey, 2000: 541). In the subsequent court case, *Planned Parenthood v. ACLA* (2001), the issue of thought versus action featured prominently. The court concluded that the website's speech made it easier for the abortion providers to be identified, to the point that it could be seen to encourage the attacks. However, this was not judged to be sufficient enough to warrant conviction because the actual statements on the website did not mention violence nor did they specifically threaten the doctors with harm. The statements were judged to be part of a public discourse and therefore not considered to have constituted a threat (Maynard, 2001: 42).

Racist websites (organizational)   Websites may host racist content and also be used to organize groups by recruiting and disseminating information about events. They mostly comprise political and religious extremist groups.

Flash-mobbing and protest groups   Flash-mobbing uses networked communications technologies to organize people spontaneously. It began as series of fairly surreal, even pointless, stunts to gather people together, such as congregating in a toy store. However, flash-mobbing has since been utilized by those with political agendas to organize spontaneous protest, for example, in some (but not all) of the anti-G8 protests. Although flash-mobbing and protest may have some protection under freedom of expression laws, it is frequently treated with hostility by those with authority for maintaining order.

Criminal gang organization   Criminal gangs are known to use the internet to circulate information about themselves and also to publicize their symbols and achievements. The websites can also be used to organize physical or online gatherings, with the details often deeply hidden to all but members within the servers. In some cases, the information might be hidden by encryption, although such action is more likely to arouse outside interest. The groups involved may include paedophile gangs (Hayward, 1997), software piracy gangs (see 'Drink or Die' cases: Shenon, 2001; BBC, 2005d; USDOJ, 2002), football supporter gangs (BBC, 1999b), street gangs (Chicago Crime Commission, 2000)[9] and organised crime gangs (Computing, 2005).

Circulating misinformation online

In a world that relies heavily upon information, misinformation can have a very powerful impact upon opinion and action, especially when deliberately used to mislead populations in order to change agendas. At one end of the spectrum are perhaps employees spreading damaging rumours about their employers; then, towards the middle, hoax virus announcements or 'gullibility viruses' which 'socially engineer' and trick individuals into deleting part of their computer's operating system, for example; the spread of malicious gossip stories perpetuating various urban legends or reinforcing stereotypical viewpoints; and at the other end there is the calculated and distributed circulation of misinformation circulated on a grand scale to shape the political agenda (see the section about information warfare in chapter 4).

Offensive communications emails, chatrooms and blogging

The growth of interactive forms of mass communication online increases the potential for their being abused. Offensive online communications can take many forms. They can be email communications 'spammed' to 'profiled' address lists, or they can take place through internet forums, chat rooms or blogsites. The intensity of offensiveness varies from bullying and blackmail to threats of physical violence.[10] Some idea of the extent of the problem was exposed by a 2006 MSN/YouGov survey, which found that 10 per cent of UK teenagers were victims of online bullying (BBC, 2006d). Serious offensive online communications are taken very seriously by law, especially where there is a clear intent to harm or offend the recipient. The following case study of offensive communications under UK law demonstrates the breadth of law which covers such acts. Threats to kill tend to demonstrate clear intent and therefore fall under the Offences Against the Person Act 1861 (s. 16). However, emails that are threatening, offensive, indecent or obscene in nature, or deliberately cause annoyance or anxiety, may still constitute an offence under the Telecommunications Act 1984 (s. 43, 1a and 1b) if serious enough in intent. In addition, further offences may be committed under the Malicious Communications Act 1988 (s. 1) or the Obscene Publications Act 1959 (s. 1(2)) if the emails also carry offensive and threatening attachments or embedded obscene pictures. The offending becomes even more serious if a clear intent is displayed through repeat communication by different technologies – for example, if the harassing messages are first sent by email then followed by phone calls over a relatively short period of time. In such cases, the sender may breach the Protection from Harassment Act 1997 (ss. 1, 2 and 7).

Where the emails are sent to a publicly accessible email list and cause 'harassment, alarm or distress' to the recipients by using words or other visible representation that are threatening, abusive or insulting 'within the hearing or sight of a person', the senders could be breaching the Public Order Act 1986 under either section 4 or 5. Furthermore, if the content and manner of the communication demonstrates the sender's hostility towards the victim's membership, or presumed membership, of a racial group then they may constitute racially aggravated offences under section 28 of the Crime and Disorder Act 1998. The final type of offensive email is the defamation arising from a libel that seeks to ' "vilify a person" and bring that person into "hatred, contempt and ridicule" '.[11] Most libel cases in the UK are brought under civil proceedings; criminal prosecutions brought under the common law are rare because the harms tend to be better covered by other criminal laws.

Chatroom and discussion group communications (stalking and grooming)

Chatrooms are online forums which allow individuals to chat to fellow members in real time. They evolved from the usenet newsgroups (prefixed by 'alt.') into internet relay chat (IRC). The main difference between the two is that chatrooms operate in real time while newsgroups work in chosen time through the posting of messages and responses to those messages. Chatrooms provide, for all involved, a readily accessible peer group with similar interests. They are forums for living out a 'second life' away from everyday routines, giving participants an opportunity to express themselves more freely, communicate with like-minded others and indulge in their fantasies, but are often subjected to policing, or moderation if acceptable behaviour policies are breached. For younger people, the lure of the chatroom is partly based upon the pragmatics of being able to 'play out without going out'. Chatrooms allow internet users to resolve the tensions of adolescence, namely by enabling them to conform with parental rules while communicating with and making new friends with similar interests. But chatrooms are also clearly demarcated spaces to which young people lay emotional claim through their participation with peers on their own terms and not those of their parents. This 'boundary formation' has led to public concerns about the dangers that younger people face in chatrooms, particularly because of the higher levels of trust they appear to place in their peers with whom they communicate. Not only are there societal concerns about young people's potential exposure to pornographic or other morally dangerous materials, but there are also specific parental concerns about their children being groomed online by individuals (usually adults) who wish to do them harm. Yet, Walker and Bakopoulos (2005) found in their research into patterns of internet usage that young people also expressed surprisingly similar priorities and concerns about online safety to adults: 'In the main they were concerned about security rather than pornography, which they saw as amusing rather than harmful'. This finding may allay some concerns, but it was also found that younger people tended to spend more time in chatrooms than their parents were aware of, thus increasing the potential for stalkers or groomers to establish trust relationships with them.

Chatroom and discussion list communications can be a contributory factor in 'cyber-stalking', which is where individuals become singled out as a target for subsequent harassment because of some characteristic or vulnerability that they have revealed in their online discussions. The key to dealing successfully with cyber-stalking lies in being able to decide where to draw the line between the genuine threat and the nuisance. This challenge, and the need to be able to resolve it, became apparent in two early internet cases which, in retrospect, could only loosely be described as examples of stalking. In the renowned Jake Baker case (*United States v. Alkhabaz*, 1997) during the mid-1990s, Baker was prosecuted after publishing fantasy rape-torture and snuff stories on the 'alt.sex.stories' newsgroup. In one story called 'Doe', Baker named the victim as one of his fellow students (Wallace and Mangan, 1996: 63). Baker had not stalked the girl in the real sense of surreptitiously tracking his victim; in fact, he had not even contacted her. Moreover, it was later suggested that the girl's real name was only used because one of the syllables in it rhymed with the popular name for the male phallus. Yet, he had caused her and the others who had read the story considerable worry. In the other case, 'Mr. Bungle' hijacked fellow characters in a virtual environment called LamdaMoo, 'spoofing' their words and actions and perpetrating 'acts of fictive sexual assault against the virtual reality denizens of LamdaMoo' (MacKinnon, 1997). Although none of the participants in the virtual community believed that actual bodily rape had occurred, some of the participants felt that the 'attack' was beyond fiction and they experienced a violation of their 'cyborg bodies' (see further Dibbell, 1999: 11). While 'Jake Baker' and 'Mr Bungle' brought cyber-stalking to the fore, the growing popularity of real-time internet relay chat quickly gave it a harder edge.

In a 1999 BBC interview, Parry Aftab, founder of CyberAngels, which is based upon the Guardian Angels model, identified three main cyber-stalking scenarios. The first was spouse abuse or revenge following the breakdown of a relationship, where offensive material is sent by email to the former partner's friends and employers. The second was the souring of internet relationships forged in a chatroom. The information shared by two people in better times was subsequently used against one of them by the other, or possibly they each used it against each other: '[p]ictures can be morphed onto pornographic pictures and emailed to employers, postings can be made which make the victim look like she is offering sexual services, giving her telephone number' (BBC, 1999a). In Aftab's third category were those who take pleasure at targeting anyone they can scare, very often children and vulnerable groups in society. At their least harmful, this third group are simply bullies; at their worst, they could be grooming for offline contacts.

Often mistakenly referred to as cyber-stalking (see Finch, 2001), internet grooming is the befriending and manipulation of children or vulnerable people online, usually in chatrooms. Groomers have the deliberate intention of gaining the confidence of their victims so that they can subsequently transfer the relationship into the offline world where the abuse can take place. Internet grooming has been of great concern for many years and with some cause. A search of the BBC news website, for example, using the key words 'internet grooming' throws up about 100 separate cases of relevant investigations or prosecutions. It was the dramatic real-time unfolding of the Studabaker case in 2003–4 which placed the issue of online grooming in the international headlines. Former US Marine Toby Studabaker had carefully groomed a 12-year-old girl in an internet chatroom, and then met up with her in Manchester before flying to Paris with her. The abduction generated considerable media attention and Studabaker was eventually tracked down and arrested in Frankfurt before being extradited to the UK for trial. He was subsequently convicted and sentenced to four-and-a-half years in prison (BBC, 2004d). The Studabaker case not only raised public awareness of the issue of grooming, but it also eased the passage of the UK Sexual Offences Act 2003, which strengthened the existing law against grooming.

Blogging and blogsites

'Blogs', or weblogs, are internet diaries or personal journals shared with an online audience. They emerged in the mid-1990s following advances in web publishing shareware. Diverse in format, blogs are multimedia formats with a combination of text, video and image and sometimes music. Some express the blogger's personal thoughts; others are interactions between blogging friends, interest or occupational groups. Bloggers discuss topical or political news items or issues, or journeys through illness, religion, or even sexual exploration. As with most internet activities, blogging can also be used to express grievances or to enrol public support for their cause; see, for example, 'The Queen of Sky', a former air hostess who was sacked for displaying photographs of herself taken aboard her employer's airplane (Oates, 2004b). Or it can be used as a tool of political resistance, as in the case of the 'Baghdad Blogger' (BBC, 2004f), or as a sort of hybrid newsgroup to share experience of conducting a illicit or criminal activity (hacker blogs) – see, for example, 'Belle de Jour', a self-confessed prostitute who regaled her readers with 'stories of the night' (BBC, 2004g).

The important thing about blogs is that they are more than just the blogger's personal reflections on a range of issues; they bring together individuals who share similar views who, in most cases, can also contribute to the blog. Blogs therefore demonstrate considerable potential for transmitting good and bad information very quickly. Most contain weblinks to related information and also to other blogs. Together, this network of blogs, or 'blogroll', forms an interconnected blog environment, a 'blogosphere', in which information and debate can escalate rapidly and virally, creating a frenzy of sometimes heated discussion. According to Wikipedia and other similar sources, these 'blogstorms or swarms' occur when 'a large amount of activity, information and opinion erupts around a particular subject or controversy in the blogosphere'. Although the terminology sounds futuristic, the blogosphere constitutes a distributed network of information sharing which can provide alternative information flows to the regular media and create a conduit for constructive and informative discussion and debate. However, in rapidly galvanizing opinion, blogging can quickly distort information, often with adverse effects, thus providing potential 'content' manipulators with access to large numbers of internet users, despite the high level of mediation and self-policing by users.

Can words actually harm?

Of crucial importance to ascertaining the level of risk posed by offensive communications is the ability to differentiate thoughts and actions – words and conduct – in societies which value freedom of expression. It is essential, therefore, to be able to understand the ways in which the words and images that constitute content on the internet impact upon the individual. Do they simply satisfy the viewer's informational or sexual needs or curiosity? Or do they contribute to the erosion of the individual's moral bind by reaffirming and justifying deviant thoughts and then gradually exposing them to more extreme fantasies or imaginary experiences that subsequently become embedded in the individual's psyche as 'normal', thus bridging the mental divide between thoughts and actions? The main theoretical push towards understanding the power of words has been 'speech act theory' (Austin, 1962; Searle, 1969), though not within the context of crime. Only a few, most significantly Matsuda et al. (1993), have specifically sought to theorize and understand 'words that wound', and speech act theory has now been applied to understanding pornography (Thurley, 2005) and to the study of cybercrimes (Williams, 2001, 2003).

With some variations over time, speech act theory distinguishes between illocutionary and perlocutionary acts of speech. *Illocutionary* speech acts perform an act: for example when a police officer says 'I arrest you . . .', a legal process is invoked. *Perlocutionary* speech acts, on the other hand, result in actions that can be very different to the words spoken, such as when a person is being persuaded to do something that subsequently leads to an action. In practice, however, the distinction is not so easy to make because speech types are not so easily disaggregated. In fact, both actions are 'performatives' which may operate simultaneously. But we can use this theory to deconstruct acts of cybercrime such as phishing. Phishers firstly perform a locutionary act by sending an email in which they present themselves to their victim as legitimate by displaying the official symbols and signs, such as a credible letter using official bank formatting and logos. Once the letter has gained the recipient's attention, then the wording – the illocutionary act – which uses the language of authority (e.g. bank speak), employs perlocutionary tactics to persuade and instruct them to comply with the request to reconfirm their personal information and financial details on the phisher's website.

Similarly, in the debate over the impact of pornography, speech act theory has usefully illuminated the discussion about the impact of pornographic text. A number of authors, including MacKinnon (1993), Langdon (1993) and Stark (1997), have argued that pornography is a performative utterance. This is because the locutionary, perlocutionary and illocutionary acts, though separate and simultaneous, are necessary for an utterance to be properly considered to be performative. 'The medium of presentation is the locutionary act, the reiteration of the subordination of women and sexual arousal is the perlocutionary act, and most importantly, assent to, legitimization of, and depiction of the subordination of women is the illocutionary act' (Thurley, 2005).

However, Thurley observes that MacKinnon and Langdon employ a very narrow definition of pornography which focuses only upon erotic material that subordinates women. Were they to broaden their definition, then the illocutionary act would disappear, refuting the argument that pornography is performative. This form of critique challenges the line of argument that led to the passing of the short-lived Communications Decency Act 1996 in the US (see Heins, 2001a, 2001b) by highlighting the broader range of expression found in pornography. Speech act theory can then provide a tool for analysing online communications in chatrooms and discussion lists, as well as blogging, to identify the words that wound.

Conclusion

This chapter has explored patterns of offending relating to the three distinct areas of obscene, violent, and offensive online content. It has demonstrated the breadth of these patterns and also the seriousness of their intent. Just because offending behaviours take place online does not mean that they are trivial or less serious. But the impacts of words and imagery are much more subtle than many of the grander theories that draw upon relationships between variables. Words and images involve a delicate interplay between thoughts and actions, and some have the capability to wound while others do not. This point was only too clear in the cases of Jake Baker and 'Mr Bungle' described earlier. Online personal contact was absent in these cases so the words and mental images became all the more important. Applying Austin's speech act theory to the 'Mr Bungle' case, Powers (2003) argues that it 'is possible to have real moral wrongs in virtual communities . . . [and that] people can act in virtual communities in ways that both establish practices and moral expectations, and warrant strong identifications between themselves and their online identities'. Williams (2001) makes this point more forcefully by stating that most types of abuse online are manifested textually and the reliance by internet users on that same text to create and maintain their identities online makes them all the more psychologically vulnerable to textual attacks. 'The notion that "real" and "virtual" phenomena are inexorably connected indicates that these online abusive acts affect "actual" lives. The ability for online injurious illocutions to convey physical violence in text affords them "extra-performative muscle", where "traditional" forms of violence are re-engineered to function online' (Williams, 2001: 164).

So, not only do online words have the capability to victimize and wound, but their effects are intensified when the online medium communicates via text and through image, thus highlighting the need to be able to assess the risk that the informational content poses to the individual (see further Balkin, 2004). This issue will become more relevant and pressing as new and diverse forums for communication emerge that lay participants open to new online risks. This conveniently brings us to the next chapter on the automation of offender – victim engagement.

7

Cybercrime Futures: The Automation of Offender–Victim Engagement

How is criminal activity continuing to change in the information age?

Chapter at a glance

- **Online offender–victim engagement within virtual environments**
- **Automated offender–victim engagement online through unsolicited bulk emails (spams)**
  Bulk email list compilation
  The contents of unsolicited bulk emails
  Victims
  Direct entrapment through spamming
  Mechanized entrapment
  Automated entrapment
  The victim response
  Spammers
- **Automated offender–victim engagement online through malicious software**
  Worms and viruses
  Blended threats
  Botnets and cybercrime waves
- **Conclusions: towards a new (third) generation of cybercrime**

As the previous chapters have illustrated, online victimization mainly results from opportunities arising from the exploitation of vulnerabilities in technological, organizational or legal systems of regulation. It was very apparent in those prior explorations of system integrity, computer-assisted and informational content crime that each was increasingly becoming automated in different ways by malicious software and code (typically trojans and viruses). Also apparent was the gradual convergence of the individual threats to form composite automated delivery mechanisms that rely upon a combination of social engineering (via spams) and software, such as the 'blended threat' to facilitate victimization by offenders. The motivations to use these devices are by no means novel. As in the real world, offenders such as burglars and thieves actively minimize their risks of being caught by seeking out the vulnerable premises that lack security and/or have open or broken windows that allow entry. On the internet, much the same principle applies – would-be intruders look for a different type of open or broken windows, namely the vulnerable flaws in the Microsoft Windows operating system that can allow intruders in. Indeed Wilson and Kelling's 'broken windows' metaphor (1982: 29) is particularly appropriate here because if not mended quickly the broken windows signal the vulnerability of the computer's contents. They invite not only unauthorized entry but also re-entry and the eventual take-over of the system. Sophos estimated in July 2005 that insecure PCs with Windows operating systems have a 50 per cent chance of being infected by an internet worm within just 12 minutes of coming online (Sophos, 2005d; Ward, 2005b).

This chapter focuses on how criminal activity is continuing to change in the information age. It will illustrate how the automation of offender–victim engagement via malicious software represents a step-change in the transition towards the third generation of true cybercrime. In this new era of cybercrime, neither offender nor victim knows each other, nor ever intends to become entangled with each another. Only the system vulnerabilities and flaws, combined with happenstance, bring them together, rather like fish to bait. This is post-traditional hacking because hackers as we knew them have become a very small part of a much bigger picture. It is a process that creates a new generation of informational problematics in understanding the relationship between offenders and their victims, but also a new generation of cybercrime. The first part of the chapter briefly overviews the victimizations arising from participation within virtual environments as touched upon earlier in chapters 4, 5 and 6. The second part explores the spam industry to identify what spams seek to achieve and how they are achieving it. The third part explores the automation and convergence process through blended threats and botnets that are introduced through spams and other mechanisms.

Online offender–victim engagement within virtual environments

To recap on issues raised previously, as soon as virtual environments emerged then new forms of online offending in those environments quickly began to evolve. *Virtual worlds and communities* created and inhabited by participants have fallen victim to the sabotage or vandalism of their virtual constructions (Williams, 2003). *E-auction sites* have initiated a range of internet scams and internet frauds which include payment card scams, account take-overs, advance fee frauds, counterfeit goods and vendor crime (non-delivery). *Chatroom and online discussion groups* have provided opportunities for offensive communications, grooming and the stalking of participants. *Bogus websites* ensnare browsers; *wi-fi*, it is alleged, makes users vulnerable to 'evil twins' – bogus websites. *Blogs* (weblogs) can be 'toxic', in that their links can be used to infect browsers when they download materials from blogs (Leyden, 2005d). The list lengthens as new environments emerge and evolve. However, while it is significant that these offender–victim engagements each take place in environments mediated by networked technologies, it is also important to note that the offending patterns – the *actus reus* and *mens rea* and basic *modus operandi* – appear not to be so far removed from offline behaviour. The environments tend to generate many new opportunities for symmetrical one-to-one victimizations, even though they may be separated by jurisdictional, geographical, social, sexual or ethnic boundaries. However, the harmful behaviours and offending patterns tend to have their roots in offline behaviour. The large numbers of e-auction frauds, for example, reflect more the number of online participants than the ability of the technology to reach large numbers. Consequently, the remainder of this chapter focuses upon automated offender–victim engagement arising initially from unsolicited bulk emails, the crimes they solicit and the step-change in victimization caused by the botnets they create.

Automated offender–victim engagement online through unsolicited bulk emails (spams)

Nowhere is the automation and asymmetry of the offender–victim relationship more evident than with spamming. It is currently the primary and most prevalent means by which offenders actively seek to engage with potential victims online. As the direct progeny of the internet, spamming embodies its transformative characteristics; it is informational, networked and global. It also places considerable productive power, some would say destructive power, in the hands of a few spammers – the 'empowered small agents' mentioned earlier (see Rathmell 1998: 2; Pease 2001: 22). By enabling one individual simultaneously to reach a massive audience across an infinite, global span, spamming is a significant 'force multiplier' (Perry, 1998) and represents a marked shift in the division of criminal labour. Yet, few would ordinarily regard spamming as a cybercrime. The reasons for this are twofold. First, there is an overall lack of knowledge and understanding about spam, which is not assisted by its rather demeaning and simplistic name and a general tendency by experts to regard it simply as a technical problem. Secondly, there is a long-standing lay person's expectation that cybercrimes are serious and dramatic, when in fact their main threat lies in their aggregation. Individually, they tend to be *de minimis* and therefore particularly difficult to police conventionally for reasons outlined in the following chapter (Wall, 2007). To complicate matters further, spamming itself not only constitutes an illegal criminal act in many jurisdictions, but it is also commonly the precursor to further offending because it provides offenders with the means to ensnare victims either by social engineering or though infections via viral payloads. The latter is problematic because although spamming itself tends not to be regarded initially as serious, it can subsequently lead to more significant forms of victimization that are serious. So, within the context of this study, spams are illustrative of true cybercrime and therefore an 'indispensable prism through which social structure and process may be seen' (Lyon, 2001, quoting Abrams, 1982: 192).

For the handful of souls who still need reminding, spamming is the distribution of unsolicited bulk emails that deliver invitations to participate in schemes to earn money, obtain free products and services, win prizes, spy upon others, obtain improvements to health or wellbeing, replace lost hair, increase one's sexual prowess or cure cancer. The term 'spam' derives from the Monty Python 'Spam Song' sketch in which Spam, Hormel Foods' canned pork product made popular in World War II, dominated a café menu and was sung repeatedly to the point of absurdity by a group of Vikings. It is therefore 'something that keeps repeating . . . to great annoyance' (*CompuServe Inc. v. Cyber Promotions* (1997); Edwards 2000: 309; Khong 2001).

In support of spamming are arguments based upon upholding rights to free expression and the need to promote legitimate commercial activity. There is also a claim that by continually challenging security systems, spams help to contribute towards overall improvements in internet security. In so doing, they support an entirely new anti-spamming wing of the cyber-security industry and therefore create new occupations. But, the pros outweigh the cons. The industry that spamming has created is also the main source of virtual 'insecurity'. More significantly, spams rarely, if ever, live up to their promises and they degrade the overall quality of virtual life. Unlike terrestrial junk mailings, which support postal services, spamming actively impedes the efficiency of email communications. It chokes up internet bandwidth and reduces access rates and overall efficiency, costing internet service providers and individual users lost time through their having to manage spams and remedy the problems they give rise to, such as infections by viruses (Wood, P., 2004: 29–31). More importantly, spams introduce new risks to recipients in the form of unpleasant payloads, potent deceptions or harmful computer viruses and worms, and their relentless attack dispirits internet users. Research by Pew (2004) found that spam was causing increases in levels of personal distress and also that growing numbers of internet users were becoming disillusioned with email. Before looking at the impacts of spams and their payloads it is important first to take an overview of the spam industry. It can, in fact, be broken down into three quite different enterprises: the compilation and production of bulk email lists which are then sold on to spammers, the subsequent use of email address lists to spam recipients, and the use of networks of remote-controlled PCs to distribute them (botnets) (Wall, 2005b).

Bulk email list compilation

The current legal method of compiling email lists in EU countries (under Directive 2002/58/EC) is to require individuals to opt-in to email lists through voluntary subscription. More commonplace, however, is the illegal compilation of email address lists. One such method is to obtain email addresses by bribing employees of ISPs and organizations hosting mail lists. In 2005 a former AOL employee pleaded guilty to stealing 92 million names and email addresses from the ISP's customer database. He sold the names for $28,000 to an individual who bought them to promote his offshore gambling site before selling them on to other spammers (Oates, 2005; BBC, 2005i). Another method is to use 'spider-bots' and other malicious software (including pop-up adware) to gather email addresses automatically (Wall, 2005b). Of course, the automation of the compilation and production of bulk email lists does not stop here. In this current climate of rapid change, the whole process is rapidly being 'deskilled' and automated by remote administration tools and 'botnets' which are bypassing the collection of addresses and directly exploiting the address books of infected machines, as we shall see in the next section.

The economics of list compilation are relatively simple. Individual email addresses have no perceivable worth, but when aggregated with 10, 20, 40 or 80 million others they accumulate value. Spammers tend to use email addresses from lists sold to them in CD-ROM format by bulk email compilers. Two familiar examples of this practice are shown in box 7.1.

Relatively few spams from these CD-ROMs are likely ever to reach the recipient because most of the addresses will either be out of date or inactive. However, the economy of spamming is such that only a few responses are needed to recoup costs and make a profit. Ironically, some of the major victims of the spam list compilation industry are themselves intending spammers who have been duped into buying expensive CD-ROMs of unvalidated and useless email addresses.

Active email addresses have a much higher value, which increases further when profiled by owner characteristics. In common with advertisements, spams containing information relevant to the recipient are most likely to obtain a positive response and result in a successful transaction. 'We specialize in successful, targeted opt-in email marketing. MORE THAN 164 CATEGORIES UNDUPLICATED Email Addresses!! ** business Opportunity seekers, MLM, Gambling, Adult, Auctions, Golf, Auto, Fitness, Health, Investments, Sports, Psychics, Opt-in Etc.'

A routine, yet effective, strategy to confirm that an email address is active while also yielding important information about the recipient is to send out 'spoof spams'. These can be transmitted by one of three methods. A blank email may be sent which requests an automatic response from the recipient's computer upon opening, or it may include offensive subject content or make preposterous claims that incite the recipient to 'flame' the sender. Alternatively, the spoof may include the option to 'deregister' from the mail list, providing the spammer with important information about the recipient whilst possibly embroiling them in a 'remove.com' scam whereby they end up paying recurrent 'administration charges', apparently for an email preference service, without any proof that the service they are buying works (see below). In each case, the spammer obtains confirmation that the email address is valid and may also receive some important information about the recipient such as personal, occupational or commercial details. Email replies frequently reveal much information about the

---

Box 7.1   Two examples of bulk email lists for sale on the internet

Example 1

200 MILLION EMAIL ADDRESSES FOR ONLY $149
You want to make some money? I can put you in touch with over 200 million people at virtually no cost. Can you make one cent from each of theses names? If you can, you have a profit of over $2,000,000.00. That's right, I have over 200 Million Fresh email addresses that I will sell for only $149. These are all fresh addresses that include almost every person on the Internet today, with no duplications. They are all sorted and ready to be mailed. That is the best deal anywhere today! Imagine selling a product for only $5 and getting only a 1% response. That's OVER $10,000,000 IN YOUR POCKET !!! Don't believe it? People are making that kind of money right now by doing the same thing, that is why you get so much email from people selling you their product. . . . it works! I will even tell you how to mail them with easy to follow step-by-step instructions I include with every order.
I will send you a copy of every law concerning email. It is easy to obey the law and make a fortune . . . To make money you must stop dreaming and TAKE ACTION.

Example 2

'MULTILEVEL MARKETING OPPORTUNITIES: Email Addresses 407 MILLION in a 4-disk set
** Complete package only $99.95!! **'
'WE WILL SEND Successfully Emails 1.Million ADDRESSES =Only $99.95!!
Nowhere else on the Internet is it possible to deliver your email ad to so many People at such a low cost.100% DELIVERABLE Want to give it a try? Fill out the Form below and fax it back:'

Source: Spams received by author, Tuesday, 6 November 2001.

---

sender, such as where they work, for example, 'ac.uk' denotes that they work in a UK university and gov.uk in a UK government office, or 'nameofbusiness'.com in business. Email signatures that are automatically included in replies reveal even more specific personal information.

A survey of spams received in the five years between 2000 and 2004 (Wall, 2003, 2005b) found that only a relatively small

---

Box 7.2   Unsolicited bulk email contents

Clearswift 2004–5 categories (in italics) alongside those from Wall (2002):

Health: Health cures / snake oil remedies
Finance: Income generating claims / loans, credit options or repair credit ratings
Products (direct): Offers of free or discounted products, goods and services / product adverts / information
Pornography: Pornography and materials with sexual content
Other (gambling, spam related, scams (phishing)): Surveillance / scares / urban legend / opportunities to win something, online gambling options / jokes and news items

---

proportion, possibly just over 10 per cent of all spams, were plausible attempts to inform recipients about products or services. The remainder lacked plausibility, suggesting that spammers were either short on business acumen, victims of unscrupulous spam list builders, or they deliberately intended to deceive the recipient into parting with money or information, or to download a trojan. Approximately one-third of all spams received appeared to be 'spoof spams', many generated by link spammers, which were never intended to convey a message. Their purpose was simply to invoke a response from the recipient and thus validate the address and provide additional information.

The contents of unsolicited bulk emails

The following analysis of spam content not only outlines the types of risks that recipients face, but also strengthens the argument that many spams are implausible and are actually vehicles for victimization. The analysis is a qualitative breakdown of the contents of spams received in one account during the first two years of a longitudinal study into spams. It illustrates the complex and multiple flows of information that spamming generates. The categories also find a resonance in Brightmail's *Slamming Spam* (2002)[1] and other spam surveys such as Clearswift's monthly spam index. The categories are set out in box 7.2 alongside the categories from Clearswift's 2004–5 monthly spam index. In figure 7.1 the data provided by the Clearswift monthly spam index between June 2003 and July 2005 have subsequently been aggregated and plotted to illustrate the trends in spamming activity during the period.

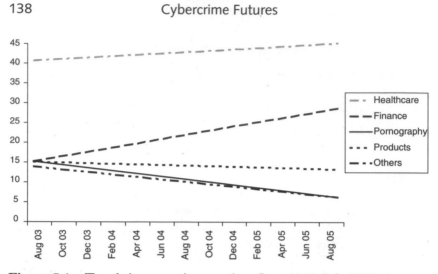

Figure 7.1   Trends in spamming practices, June 2003–July 2005 (percentage of all spam received)

Source: Secondary analysis of monthly Clearswift statistics, www.clearswift.com.

The secondary analysis of the monthly Clearswift spam data over the period 2003–5 (figure 7.1) illustrates two distinct trends in the distribution of different types of spam. Against the backdrop of a rise in the volume of spam, there has been an increase in the percentage of spams related to health care and personal finance, and a decrease in the percentage of those related to pornography, products and services and those falling under the category 'other'. The contents of these categories are described below and many will be familiar from discussions in earlier chapters, especially chapter 5.

Health cures / snake oil remedies   Spammers who advertise health cures or snake oil remedies prey upon vulnerable groups like the sick, elderly, poor and inadequate. Examples include the following offers: (a) miracle diets; (b) anti-ageing lotions and potions; (c) the illegal provision of prescription medicines; (d) expensive non-prescription medicines at greatly discount prices (such as Viagra); (e) hair loss remedies; (f) various body enhancement lotions or potions to effect breast, penis, muscle enlargements or fat reduction, etc.; (g) operations to effect the above; (h) cures for cancer and other serious illnesses.

Income-generating claims   These contain invitations to the recipient, supported by unsubstantiated claims, to take up or participate in lucrative business opportunities. Examples include the following: (a) investment reports and schemes; (b) lucrative business opportunities such as pyramid selling schemes, including ostrich farming schemes; (c) earning money by working at home; (d) 'Pump and Dump' investment scams; (e) emailed Nigerian Advanced Fee scams; (f) invitations to develop websites and traffic for financial gains; (g) phishing using emails that purport to be from a legitimate bank requesting confirmation of personal details; (h) pharming, the next generation of phishing.

Loans, credit options or repair credit ratings Examples include the following propositions: (a) instant and unlimited loans or credit facilities, instant mortgages, often without the need for credit checks or security; (b) the repair of bad credit ratings; (c) credit cards with zero or very low interest; (d) offers which purport to target and engage with people whose financial life, for various reasons, exists outside the centrally run credit-rated driven banking system.

Advertisements/information about products and services Some of these advertisements are genuine, others are blatantly deceptive. Examples include advertisements for the following: (a) office equipment and supplies, especially print cartridges; (b) greatly discounted computing and other equipment; (c) medical supplies and equipment; (d) branded goods at greatly discounted prices; (e) educational qualifications; (f) internet auction scams, whereby an advertisement containing information about the auction is spammed; (g) bulk email lists.

Offers of free or discounted products, goods and services, including free vacations For recipients to be eligible for these free or discounted offers, they usually have to provide something in return, such as money, a pledge (via a credit card) or personal information about themselves, their family, their work or their lifestyle. Enticements include the following: (a) free trial periods for products or services as long as the recipient first signs up to the service, and leaving it to the recipient to withdraw from the service; (b) free products, such as mobile phones, pagers, satellite TV, if the recipient signs up to the service for a specified period of time; (c) cheap grey market goods which exploit import tax or VAT differences between jurisdictions by selling items such as cheap cigarettes, alcohol, fuel; (d) spams which sell goods across borders from jurisdictions in which the goods are legal to those where the goods are either illicit or restricted, such as the case with prescription medicines, body parts, sexual services, rare stones, antiquities.

Pornography This and other materials with sexual content include the following: (a) invitations to gain access to a website containing sexually explicit materials; (b) invitations to join a group which is involved in sharing images and pictures about specific sexual activities; (c) invitations to webmasters to increase their business traffic by including invitations to obtain access to sexually oriented materials on their sites. Many of these spams contain entrapment scams.

Opportunities to win something, online gambling options Examples include: (a) notification that the recipient has won a competition and must contact the sender so that the prize can be claimed, or they might have to provide some information before the prize can be received; (b) offers to enter a competition if information or money is provided; (c) free lines of credit in new trial gambling websites. These are generally also disguised forms of entrapment marketing (see above).

Surveillance software, devices and information This category is hard to disaggregate from the mischief section below. The two are included together in box 7.2 because it is hard to tell whether the information and products are genuine or not. Examples include: (a) scare stories about the ability of others to keep their internet use under surveillance to coerce recipients into buying materials (books, software, etc.) on how to combat internet surveillance and find out what other people know about them; (b) encouraging recipients to submit their online access details purportedly to find out what others know about them; (c) recommending a web-based service for testing the recipient's own computer security; (d) encouraging recipients to purchase spyware that allegedly equips them to undertake internet surveillance upon others.

Hoaxes, urban legends, mischief collections Examples include the following: (a) spams that appear to be informative and tell stories that perpetuate various urban legends; (b) hoax virus announcements or 'gullibility viruses' that seek to convince recipients into believing that they have accidentally received a virus and then provides instructions on to how to remedy the problem, deceiving them into removing a system file from their computer; (c) messages which appear to be from friends, colleagues or other plausible sources that deceive the recipients into opening an attachment which contains a virus or a worm; (d) chain letters which sometimes suggest severe consequences to the recipient if they do not comply, or the letters may engage the recipient's sympathy with a particular minority group or cause, for example, single mothers, or women in general (the Sisterhood Chain Letter scam); (e) email-based victim-donation scams that emerge on the internet soon after a tragic event; (f) invitations to donate funds to obscure religious-based activities or organizations; (g) links to hoax websites, such as Convict.Net which originally started as a spoof site, but was so heavily subscribed by former convicts that it eventually became a reality.

Jokes and news items   A final category of spam, though very small in number, but increasingly of strategic importance to the spammer's art, are spams that deliberately contain legitimate text such as jokes and news stories. These serve the dual function of reducing the recipients' irritation and making them feel more tolerant of spam if they believe there may be something of value within them, while also 'unbalancing' anti-spam products designed to filter out irrelevant or illegal messages (Sophos, 2005b).

These categories resonate with the three substantive groups of cybercrime outlined in chapters 4, 5 and 6: computer integrity crime, computer-assisted crime and computer content crime.

Victims

The burning question about spams is what impact they have upon the recipient. Of course, the first thing that springs to mind from the above typology is that there is little new because they appear to follow tried and tested fraudulent routines which attempt, with varying degrees of success, to entrap and defraud. Not only do most criminal and civil justice systems already have legal remedies for most of these deceptions, but the deceptions are also no strangers to criminal justice professionals or the general public. What is new, however, is the way that offenders try to ensnare their victims. The content categorizations and detailed descriptions of the activities illustrate quite vividly the extent to which information is being manipulated to assist offending. The content analysis also indicates some significant differences in the global scope, span and penetration of populations of potential victims. Three main techniques of deception and entrapment are currently being employed: direct entrapment through spamming, mechanized entrapment and automated entrapment.

Direct entrapment through spamming This is direct engagement with victims through spams on a one-to-one basis. Individuals, duped by the invitation or proposal delivered in a spam email, become embroiled in an exploitative relationship with a fraudster who could be geographically located anywhere on the network. The inevitable outcomes are the 'scams', frauds and deceptions described earlier in the content analysis. Inducements include get-rich-quick schemes, access to pornography sites, free goods, snake oil remedies/health cures, credit repairs, surveillance software and online gambling. Particularly interesting examples of direct engagement through spamming are some of the variations of advanced fee fraud, described above in chapter 5. These illustrate the evolution of deceptive criminal behaviour from the terrestrial to the online world, and also the 'social engineering' that is employed to 'hook' the victim and get them to respond to the invitation.

Mechanized entrapment This is a variant of entrapment marketing in which potential victims subscribe online to 30-day or three-month free trial offers of informational services ranging from access to pornography sites to news, chat-line, dating or other internet services. Applicants are usually required to supply their credit card details. The applicant then receives free access to the service for the prescribed period of time, but must then actively withdraw from the service, otherwise it will be automatically assumed that he or she wishes to continue and billing to the credit card will commence. At their least invidious, users may be requested to enter into land mail correspondence with the service provider to confirm their intention to withdraw. At their worst, once enticed into receiving a service, recipients seeking to disengage from it might be given mild indications or even warnings that if they cease accepting the service then information about their subscription could be made public – for example, a confirmation letter will be sent to their home address. A popular urban myth currently circulating, though hard to corroborate, is that owners of online pornography sites have reimbursed overcharged fees to complainants by using personal cheques that bear the provider's name and very graphic sexual imagery in the background print, which acts as a strong disincentive to submit the cheque for payment at the complainant's bank.

A good example of complicit mechanized entrapment is the 'remove.com' scam. Fed up with receiving nonsensical spams, recipients are encouraged to click on to a service advertised in the offending email that promises to remove them from bulk email lists.

To join the removal service, which allegedly ensures their continued privacy, recipients are asked to provide details of their identity. Usually a small 'administration' charge is also requested, paid via credit card. This payment is often a recurring one, though this fact tends to be buried in lengthy terms and conditions. In practice, recipients are rarely supplied with the service they seek, but it is impossible for them to confirm conclusively that the service to which they have subscribed actually delivers what it promises, so they continue to pay the very small recurring charge, typically about $2.95 or more every month or so, as the following complaint reveals:

> I made the hideous mistake yesterday of registering my email addresses with http://www.[REMOVED].org after receiving several spams claiming to honor remove requests sent there. Within 24 hours, I am now receiving a marked increase in spams containing the [REMOVED] tagline, plus I am actually getting spams that were relayed BY the [REMOVED].ORG server. (After all, by following the [REMOVED] 'remove' procedure, which uses an email verification, I allowed them to validate that my server accepted email from the [REMOVED].ORG server.)[2]

Automated entrapment   Typically, this is where the individual is deceived, by a spam message or adware, into downloading malicious software. Before adware (pop-up) blocking protection became commonplace, users were often infected when they tried to close down or delete rogue advertisements or other dialogue boxes that appeared on their screen. In other instances, the 'drive-by download' might be entirely automated, triggered either by adware or web uploads. In July 2006 an infected adware attack on social networking sites such as MySpace.com and others exploited an old Windows security flaw on unpatched computers. Some 1.07 million users were infected with spyware that secretly tracks internet usage at the same time as showering infected users with pop-up advertisements (Krebs, 2006b; Leyden, 2006g). In these cases the machine was deceived into downloading malicious programs without the user's knowledge or consent.

The risks to online users from malicious spams are potentially serious. Furthermore, the fact that spammers are sustaining such a high volume of mail shots despite more restrictive legal regulation demonstrates the extent to which the spam industry circumnavigates or even exploits the trans-jurisdictional capabilities of internet technology. This suggests strongly that spamming will continue to thrive despite existing laws and therefore calls into question the effectiveness of legal interventions against spam, such as the EU directive (Article 13) which is now enshrined in the legislation of EU member states to prohibit unsolicited email. Arguably, if we need stronger law it should be formulated and enforced in the countries in which the majority of spams originate, namely in the US, which has introduced some legislation, and countries in the Far East.[3]

The victim response

The victims of malicious spam content are very hard to identify because they are such a heterogeneous group of internet users, which is possibly their only common characteristic. There is also the more general problem of under-reporting. Many victims often do not know to whom they should report their victimization, or they may be too embarrassed, or individual losses may be small and the victims are prepared to tolerate the loss. In other cases the victimization may not be criminal, with just inconvenience or upset to endure. Indeed, an analysis of ISP complaints statistics over an 18-month period in the early 2000s, when the volume of spams grew exponentially, found recipients' self-assessment of risk to be very reflexive. The complaints statistics in table 7.1 were provided by a telecoms provider who at the time hosted about 70 ISPs. During the 18 months of the survey, there was a quarterly decline in complaints about unsolicited emails, from just below half (48% of all complaints) to less than a sixth (16%). Yet, the overall number of complaints did not increase markedly compared with the massive rise in internet usage during this period (ofcom, 2005a; 2005b; 94). During this period there was a shift away from concerns about the 'nuisance' of the spams towards more serious

Table 7.1   Complaints to internet service providers, 2001–2002 (percentage of all complaints received)

2001–2002	Quarter 1	Quarter 2	Quarter 3	Quarter 4	Quarter 5	Quarter 6
Spam and abusive email	48	35	23	19	24	16
Other	49	59	60	65	71	59
Virus	3	6	17	16	5	25
Total (%)	100	100	100	100	100	100
Numbers of complaints	8,101	6,174	6,764	8,606	8,642	10,255

Source: Anonymous ISP.

concerns over receipt of viruses. These data strongly suggest that internet users ceased to regard all spams as a threat and began to view them more as a nuisance to be coped with – usually by deleting the offending spam mail (see Wall, 2003). In so doing, recipients were replicating patterns of personal risk assessment and avoidance behaviour grounded in experience, in ways not dissimilar to those found offline (Wall, 2002b). These findings are supported by research conducted in the US by the Federal Trade Commission, which found that users are becoming generally more tolerant of spam (BBC, 2005q), but this may be because, as WebWatch found, nine out of ten users surveyed (mostly in the US) had taken at least one security measure because of their concerns about cybercrime (PRAI, 2005: 18; BBC, 2005o).

While spams may be perceived as a declining threat to those who are internet savvy, they nevertheless pose a greater danger to the more vulnerable communities in society: the poor; newly redundant; those in remote locations; those with learning difficulties; 'newbies' who lack experience of the internet to be able to judge between the plausible and less plausible invitations; the terminally sick ever hopeful of some relief from their pain; the poor single parent who sends off his or her last £200 for a 'work at home' scheme; youths who seek out 'cheats' for their computer games. Another particularly vulnerable group are the newly retired who possess all of the internet fraudsters' most desired characteristics – impatience to invest their retirement lump sums and lack of computer knowledge and savvy. Novel forms of spamming, particularly those employing tactics based upon deception, such as phishing, pharming, 'gullibility viruses' and more recently vishing (using VoIP), frequently catch large numbers of internet users who are unaware of new risks until they are informed by word of mouth, local IT support, web or media reporting. The offenders therefore have a particular interest in keeping one step ahead.

Spammers

It is worth turning at this point to the offenders (spammers) and pondering who they are. In contrast to the sheer volume of spam in circulation, the overall number of spammers is surprisingly small, which is a graphic reflection of the power that networked technologies place in the hands of the few. A single spammer can reach many millions of recipients. Wood estimated that 'more than 80 per cent of global spam originates from fewer than 200 known spammers in the USA' (2003:

Box 7.3   Typology of spammers originating unsolicited bulk emails

Honest vendors advertise their various products and services through spams.

Misguided vendors are in search of a 'quick buck' and are often victims of spam list builders.

Internet entrepreneurs are the backbone of the legitimate internet industry and comprise website developers and e-commerce marketing managers.

List builders range from those who compile and sell profiled and validated email distribution lists to those who generate bulk email lists regardless of the wishes of the recipient.

Protesters are individuals or groups who use spamming as a means of making what they argue is legitimate protest; see for example, the Electronic Civil Disobedience Theatre mentioned earlier (p. 61).

Artists are individuals who see spams as a vehicle for the free expression of their creative artistry.

Pranksters are individuals and groups who view spamming as a 'fun' way of achieving an effect. There are many examples of 'spoof emails' which are linked to spoof sites, such as Convict.net. Care has to be taken to differentiate them from spammers who use jokes to impress on recipients that spams may have some value.

Smugglers seek to exploit cross-border price differences and advertise their wares via spams.

Link spammers (search engine optimisers) are paid to spam websites with emails containing key words and blogs to inflate search engine rankings (see chapter 5).

Dishonest vendors seek to entrap and defraud internet users.

4; also see Spamhaus.org). A further analysis of received spams suggests that the spammers are also fairly heterogeneous, although it is very important to discern here between the originators of the spam messages and those who distribute the spams. The former may pay the latter to distribute them. The originators of spam emails have been broken down according to the following typology (see box 7.3) to enable a more accurate assessment of the overall risks that they present.

At one end of the spammer spectrum are the honest vendors who seek to advertise genuine products and services. They are estimated to send out as few as 10 per cent of spams. At the other end, however, are the dishonest vendors whose aim is to entrap and defraud. Somewhere in the middle are the misguided vendors, protesters, pranksters, smugglers, artists, list builders (Wall, 2002b) and link spammers. It is also important to remember that many spammers, for example, the misguided vendors, are often themselves victims of spam list-building frauds. These findings show that not all spammers are rational actors who seek to maximize benefits while reducing their costs (Savona and Mignone, 2004: 4). Only some are, which has implications for the simple blanket application of spam solutions based on rational choice theory. The characteristic that spammers and their victims each appear to have in common is the internet; therefore it is in the governance of behaviour on the internet where the solution to spam must lie (see chapter 9).

Automated offender–victim engagement online through malicious software

If spamming marked the beginning of a step-change in offender–victim engagement online, then the attachment of malicious software in viral payloads to spams consolidated it. Today there is a very close relationship between spamming and viral payloads in the form of trojans containing worms and viruses which exist to perpetuate victimization. The final section of this chapter outlines this relationship.

Worms and viruses

A computer worm is a piece of software that propagates itself across a network by exploiting security flaws. This characteristic distinguishes it from viruses which tend to infect static files and therefore require the actions of users to assist with their propagation. As a consequence, viruses are slower to reproduce and there currently exists an arsenal of anti-virus software to counter them. However, Weaver et al. (2003) found that the practical distinction between worms and viruses is becoming less clear as their sophistication increases. Contagion worms, for example, fall under the definition of viruses because although they do not require user activity to activate them, they are transmitted by 'otherwise unconnected user action'.

Weaver et al. (2003) provide useful insights into the world of the worm. First, worms need to find a machine to infect and to this end a number of mechanisms of *target discovery* are employed: scanning worms, such as 'Code Red I', which exploit security holes;

pre-generated hit-lists of probable victims installed in the code; externally generated target lists maintained and communicated to the worm by an external (meta) server; internal target lists using local topological information to identify new targets; and passive worms that wait for victims to contact them, or rely upon user behaviour. Secondly, to transport them to the target, worms need a *carrier*, which is usually embedded in, or appended to, existing messages. Thirdly, worms require an *activation* mechanism to trigger executable files. These may be recipient activated, for example after he or she is lured by a seemingly credible news story or pornographic picture, internet joke, or gossip to click on links which subsequently download and activate trojans (BBC, 2004h). In other cases, where infection has already occurred, activation may be automatically linked to necessary computer activity such as the login script, scheduled processes such as auto-updating, or self-activation by attachment to running services. Fourthly, worms deliver *payloads* in the form of software code carried by the worm to the propagation routines, which is tailored to the attackers' particular motivation (e.g. information theft, revenge, etc.; see above). Consequently, the list of potential payload types is long. Some may not actually be functional but simply impede the function of operating systems, while others may identify vulnerable machines to a potential remote administrator or even install privileged back doors on victim machines (Code Red II) for later use. The payload may also create spam-relays across infected machines to transmit spams. One of these, SOBIG, also redirected web requests through domain name servers to randomly selected (HTML) proxy machines. Code Red and others also contained a denial of service attack tool which targeted specific sites. The list of payloads continues: collecting particular types of information; installing remote controls (Schechter and Smith, 2003) for sale or rent; damaging data. Finally, there are the various impacts that payloads can have on the physical world by controlling physical objects, activating phone systems to effect physical denial of service, or damaging systems, such as by including reflashing routines that damage Flash Roms.

What Weaver et al. (2003) demonstrate in their work is the diversity of worm and virus attacks. Furthermore, and very importantly, the most successful, trojans such as Code Red, were multi-modal (or 'blended') and employed a number of distinctly different ways of delivering the above payloads to penetrate defences. Named after the original Trojan horse, trojans are programs hidden inside apparently innocuous links and attachments which, once introduced into a host system, can be triggered to deliver worms and viruses that distort information, cause damage or even system failure. 'Logic bombs', a type of trojan, activate once predetermined criteria are met, such as a specific date or after a system has been accessed a specified number of times. The best known of these is 'Michelangelo' which only activates on Michelangelo's birthday. Ransomware, such as Archiveus (see p. 64 above), automatically encrypts files until a ransom has been paid and a password is released to stop the operation.

The period of time, or 'lag', between the identification of a flaw, its exploitation and a solution or 'patch' was once measured in months, but this has reduced to weeks and is now often hours: '[w]arnings are getting shorter; the time between knowledge of vulnerability and its exploitation and propagation of virus has decreased' (Geer, 2004). In October 2005, for example, 'Mocbot', a botnet client that exploited a vulnerability in Microsoft's 'Plug and Play' system, was released only two weeks after the issue of the Microsoft update, 'repeating a recent pattern of shorter and shorter release cycles by the bad guys' (Leyden, 2005l). Trojans and the malicious codes they deliver can be shut down quickly, either by upgrades to 'patch' vulnerabilities in operating systems or by anti-virus software updates; however, the authors of malicious code play on the fact that there will always remain a large number of unprotected computers. Also working against the security patches is the fact that the freely accessible open source nature of many new worms and viruses means that as one is gradually eradicated by technological means, new variants tend to emerge, and new methods of delivering them are invented. New variants of worms have been found in jpeg and other files (BBC, 2004h). Alternatively, 'pop-up' ads, otherwise known as the 'pop-up parade', 'pop-up hell', 'the Java trap', or the 'spam cascade', themselves the product of infections by adware, have been known to deliver malicious code that hijacks the user's session, usually with pornographic websites (Leyden, 2004d). Alternatively they 'mouse trap' the screen by showing a full-page advertisement whilst removing the menus bars, or they might 'browser hijack' the computer so that it keeps being directed towards a predetermined URL.

Blended threats

A major development in malicious software in recent years has been the emergence of the 'blended threat', which employs simultaneously – through multiple infection – a combination of attack techniques that make the viruses and worms even more potent and also much harder to detect. 'Blended threats' (Naraine, 2005) are meta-trojans that contain multilayered viral infections which 'combine the characteristics of viruses, worms, Trojan Horses, and malicious code with server and Internet vulnerabilities to initiate, transmit, and spread an attack. By using multiple methods and techniques, blended threats can rapidly spread and cause widespread damage' (quoted from www.symantec.com; also see Ingle, 2004). Once installed, mass-mailing worms, such as VBS.Gaggle.D and its variants, will automatically overwrite and infect a number of files in order to protect themselves, often using rootkit technology to hide their presence on infected systems (Leyden, 2006f). They will also institute multilayered attacks by sending out messages through the host's email system, installing back doors to enable remote administration as part of a botnet and capturing keywords or passwords (Naraine, 2005). To confuse recipients, and avoid detection, these activities may be 'timed' so that particular functions are carried out over predetermined periods of time, such as specific hours on certain days of the month. Box 7.4 illustrates the characteristics of blended threats.

Once a PC has succumbed to remote administration and has become a zombie, it can be used to send out mass mailings through the recipient's email browser's address book; some trojans will also harvest personal details and return them to the infector. The trojan evades virus checkers by hiding itself in various system files and regularly generates new clones so that the computer, if cleaned, can re-infect itself. Of great concern is the possibility and eventual probability that new generations of cybercrimes, described above, will be able to cross-infect the different operating systems of converged technologies. There are already signs of this taking place. The Cabir worm, for example, was specifically aimed at PDAs (Personal Digital Assistants) and other mobile devices. Digital picture formats, such as jpeg and bmp photos, have recently been configured to deliver viruses (Sieber, 2004: 113). Text spams are already a nuisance on mobile phones and it is only a matter of time before the attachments carry malicious software (Leyden, 2005g).

Botnets and cybercrime waves

The purpose of infecting numerous PCs with remote administration software is to create a (bot)network of zombie computers that can be controlled at a distance. These botnets comprise lists of IP addresses of infected computers and are valuable commodities because of the power they can place in the hands of the remote administrators to deliver a range of harmful malcode and software. For this purpose they

Box 7.4   The characteristics of a blended threat

- Causes harm: launches a Denial of Service (DoS) attack at a target IP address, defaces web servers, or plants trojan horse programs for later execution.
- Propagates by multiple methods: scans for vulnerabilities to compromise a system, such as embedding code in HTML files on a server, infecting visitors to a compromised website, or sending unauthorized email from compromised servers with a worm attachment.
- Attacks from multiple points: injects malicious code into the .exe files on a system, raises the privilege level of the guest account, creates world read and writeable network shares, makes numerous registry changes, and adds script code into HTML files.
- Spreads without human intervention: continuously scans the internet for vulnerable servers to attack.
- Exploits vulnerabilities: takes advantage of known vulnerabilities, such as buffer overflows, HTTP input validation vulnerabilities, and known default passwords to gain unauthorized administrative access.

Source: http://securityresponse.symantec.com/avcenter/refa. html# blended threat.

can be hired out, sold or traded. As the graph lines in Figure 9.1 demonstrate, this form of 'parasitic computing'[4] creates problems for regulation and law enforcement because of its high level of automation. Successive generations of malicious software rely less and less upon human action to be activated. Currently, spams are thought to constitute about two-thirds of all email traffic (Leyden, 2003a; MessageLabs threat stats) and along with pop-ups and web ads, pose a major obstacle to effective internet usage and its further development. To circumvent technological countermeasures, spammers have increased dramatically the volume of spam attacks by using botnets to distribute ratware (sometimes known as a botnet client). Remote administration mailing trojans (ratware) randomize the content of each spamming campaign to create unique messages and evade checks by content-based anti-spam software (Sophos, 2005c). An idea of the scale of these enterprises was revealed in October 2005 when it was found that a foiled botnet operation had put approximately 1.5 million computers and servers under its control for use in DDOS attacks (Sanders, 2005). Sophos calculated that as much as 60 per cent of all spam originates from compromised, zombie computers (Sophos, 2005e). The cycle of automation, which starts with the distribution of ratware, is represented graphically in figure 7.2.

The botnets are the major contributor to what are currently being understood as 'cybercrime waves' (*High Tech Magazine*, 2003). The nature of this automated cybercrime wave is such that it, and others like it, leave behind traditional concepts of crime mapping. Indeed, the exponential growth in infections caused by ratware and their subsequent mutations, suggest that a cybercrime wave actually shares more characteristics with a storm than a wave or a disease model algorithm. Consequently, better analogies might be found in the meteorological terminology of internet storms (Seife, 1997: 477) or

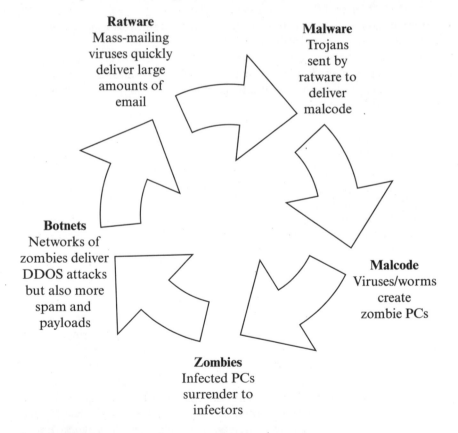

Ratware
Mass-mailing
viruses quickly
deliver large
amounts of
email

Malware
Trojans
sent by
ratware to
deliver
malcode

Botnets
Networks of
zombies deliver
DDOS attacks
but also more
spam and
payloads

Malcode
Viruses/worms
create
zombie PCs

Zombies
Infected PCs
surrender to
infectors

Figure 7.2   The cycle of automating online offender–victims engagement

blizzards (Leyden, 2005k; see further McQuade, 2006a: 99–108). For the purposes of this analysis the concept of 'wave' suffices.

Evidence of the existence of cybercrime waves caused by the rise in the number of botnets can be found in the explosion in the volume of spams between mid-2002 and early-2004 (see figure 9.1 in chapter 9). This 'explosion' is reflected in the numbers of distinct spam streams circulating between 2003 and 2006. Figure 9.1 shows an exponential rise in the stream of spam between July 2002 and May 2004. This rise is also recorded by others; see, for example, the graphs provided by the Distributed Checksum Clearinghouse (DCC) website (see Race, 2005: 3). After May 2004 the monthly levels of spam remained much the same until December 2005 when, in one month, the number of spams in circulation doubled. They have since reduced, but rest at a much higher monthly average. This stream of spam reflects a sustained increase in the number of botnets. While there exist methodological differences in the generation of data about spams, there are broad patterns of consensus in the various reports by Sophos, Clearswift and DCC. Nevertheless, calculating the number of spams is not an exact science because of the distributed nature of the internet. But what these trends do demonstrate is that the problem is not going away and, if anything, the increase in botnet-driven spam is continuing (Lemos, 2006).

The botnet-creating trojans originally belonged to a family of spybot worms called 'agobots' (or gaobots) and their more recent variants the 'phatbots'. Both are typically distributed through internet relay chat (IRC) to infect, though not exclusively, the Microsoft Windows operating systems. Because the authors of agobot made the malicious code 'open source' and freely accessible, there now exist many thousands of variants of the worms. Although the compromising of computers by viruses such as the NetSky variants and predecessors is by no means new, the creation of worms such as Bagle and MyDoom along with agobot trojans have proliferated the overall number of botnets (Leyden, 2004c). MessageLabs plotted the ratio of viruses to emails as part of their series of threat statistics and found correlations between infection peaks by the Sobig.F worm in September 2003, MyDoomA in January 2004 and Bagle vs Netsky between February and September 2005 (MessageLabs.com). They estimate that almost one in every fifty emails carries a virus – a figure that appears to have remained fairly constant since February 2004. Figure 9.1 illustrates the level of the step-change in the volume of botnet-assisted attacks that took place between mid-2003 and early 2004 and were received by one account. The same curve is also found over the same time period replicated in other independent data on viruses detected by MessageLabs (see Race, 2005: 1; Wood, 2003) and the Distributed Checksum Clearinghouse (Race, 2005: 3). These independent statistical analyses draw upon independent sources of data and also measure different, but contributing, points of data to reveal and verify the trend.

The return on investment for 'bot herders', as remote administrators are often called (Krebs, 2006a), is high, which probably explains the aggressive growth in botnets. Stiennon estimates that personal computers illegally infected with 'adware' – software that displays unrequested marketing material, usually as pop-up banners – generates an average of about $3 per infected computer (Stiennon, 2005). While the overall level of financial gain has been contested by Leyden (2005b), Stiennon's findings of individual loss nevertheless indicate a considerable financial yield to 'bot herders'. 'One company, Claria, revealed that their software resided on 40 million PCs and they generated $90 million in revenue a year. Another company, Avenue Media, claimed they had 2 million infected machines that generated $7 million annually. An average of $2.95 per-infection-per-year' (Stiennon, 2005).

This is a very fast game in which the object of the exercise is to remain one step ahead of the 'security patch' to prolong the crime harvest, although as stated earlier, many PCs remain unprotected. The time-line for mass infections of computers is now very short and has reduced to a matter of hours. MessageLabs' analysis of the W32/Sobig.F virus, which was first seeded in August 2003, found that it took 17 hours from first identification to reach a peak of almost 130,000 infections at which point the virus was contained (Wood, 2003: 6). The virus not only mass emailed addresses collected from files with the wab, .dbx, .htm, .html, .eml, .txt extensions, but it also stole confidential system information, including passwords (Wood, 2003). Wood succinctly sums up the change in the use of viruses and spam through botnets. Whereas viruses and trojans 'used to be parallel threats to email security, we are now experiencing their convergence. Virus writers are starting to use ratware to seed initial copies of viruses. Spammers are including trojans and automatic connection to porn sites in spam messages' (Wood, 2003: 2).

Conclusions: towards a new (third) generation of cybercrime

The combination of spamming and malicious attachments that result in the formation of botnets has further changed the division of labour in the organization of cybercrime. By automating the offenders' engagement with their victims, asymmetric relationships become possible whereby one offender can simultaneously victimize many. While the overall incidence of offending has increased, the number of offenders (spammers) has allegedly remained more or less the same, providing evidence of the increased power of networked technology. However, this observation may hide new types of alliances that are currently being forged across different offending skill sets (BBC, 2003d). Furthermore, there is also renewed concern that organized crime gangs are becoming involved in cybercrime by employing spammers, hackers and virus writers to orchestrate a phishing or pharming attack: 'the script kiddies are making way for Mr Big' (Leyden, 2006c). In this sense, the new generation of cybercrime is becoming much more organized at a higher level than its predecessors and motivations for offending have changed from white to black hat.

> Viruses written to make headlines by infecting millions are getting rarer. Instead programs are now crafted for directly criminal ends and firms are tightening up networks with defences to combat the new wave of malicious code. The growing criminal use of malware has meant the end of the neat categorisation of different sorts of viruses and malicious programs. Before now it has been broadly possible to name and categorise viruses by the method they use to spread and how they infect machines. But many of the viruses written by criminals roll lots of technical tricks together into one nasty package. (BBC, 2005a)

The reorganization of offending behaviour will continue as technologies continue to converge. This new generation of offending is still developing and knowledge of offending patterns is only just becoming understood. One certainty is that while the medium for offender–victim engagement is likely to change, many of the practices will nevertheless remain familiar. However, another certainty is that many more surprises will emerge in the future, particularly as P2P-type technology creates new platforms for criminal activity as it links up networks of users across different types of networked technologies. As for spamming, only time will tell whether it will survive in its present form, but the indications are that as long as there remains value to be gained from the activity the spammers will continue to ply their trade. They will find new and innovative ways of evading technological and legal attempts to stop them and carry on exploiting new automated forms of communication to seek their ends, thus enabling offenders to engage with potential victims and to perpetuate the infection cycle. Such news does not bring much cheer to those whose job it is to regulate harmful internet behaviour and enforce the law. The automation of victimization changes the nature of the relationship between law and social action and also the dynamics of order maintenance and law enforcement, which is the subject of the next chapter.

8

Policing Online Behaviour: Maintaining Order and Law on the Cyberbeat

How is cyberspace policed and by whom?

Chapter at a glance

- **The challenge of cybercrime for the public police**
  'De minimism'
  Nullum crimen disparities
  Jurisdictional disparities
  Non-routine activity and police culture
  Under-reporting
- **Locating the public police in the networks and nodes of security within cyberspace**
  Internet users and user groups
  Online virtual environment managers and security
  Network infrastructure providers
  Corporate organizations and corporate security
  Non-governmental, non-police organizations
  Governmental non-police organizations
  Public police organizations
- **The role of the public police in policing cyberspace**
- **The neo-Peelian agenda: renegotiating the public police role in policing cyberspace**
  Multi-agency cross-sector partnerships
- **Conclusions: the challenge of cybercrime for the police–public mandate**

The contents of the preceding chapters clearly constitute a thematic and descriptive justification for policing the internet to maintain order and enforce the law. Given that networked computing power has increased the offender's reach and overall capacity to exploit criminal opportunities with a high aggregate return on investment, it is hardly surprising that concerns about law and order have long dominated debates about the internet. These concerns are perpetuated by the future shock (public feelings of helplessness or anxiety) generated by the poisonous combination of society's increasing reliance on networked technologies, the necessary steep learning curve demanded of users, and the popular public misperception that internet misuse cannot be controlled. Indeed, the fact that there appear to be hundreds of thousands of reported cybercrime incidents each year compared with very few prosecutions would seem to substantiate fears that attempts to control internet behaviour are failing. In earlier chapters we saw, for example, that during the first decade following the introduction of the Computer Misuse Act 1990 in the UK there were only about 100 or so prosecutions against hackers and even fewer convictions. This disparity is not only to be found in the UK, but elsewhere in the world (see Smith et al., 2004). Despite the low prosecution rates, the UK Police and Justice Bill 2006 sought to further increase the penalties for computer misuse to a maximum of ten years in prison (Bill 119–EN, 2005–6).

Does this mean that the law has failed? Is there perhaps something about cybercrimes that makes them so different that they subvert traditional justice processes? Yet, if the internet is apparently so criminogenic, then why are more cybercrimes against individuals not reported to the police or other responding organizations? Why is there so little 'chatter' in the form of personal stories about victimization across traditional pathways of communication (friendship, kinship and professional networks) verbally, by email, or by letter? And if the prevalence is really so great, then how does life online continue to thrive? Or could it simply be the case that many of these apparent 'victimizations' are low impact infringements that are either ignored, or resolved technologically? Remember that the more criminal behaviour becomes mediated by technology and distanced from social interaction, the more effectively it can be governed by the same technologies (and *de facto* less by law). This hypothesis begins to question seriously the role of law in the information age and ask whether or not the code itself has effectively become the law – a theme introduced in the early writings on cyberlaw (see Lessig, 1999). Or could it be that the majority of internet harms are actually being 'policed' by other means of behavioural governance. Central to this discussion is the need to understand the role of the public police in the policing of cyber-space.

This chapter focuses upon the maintenance of order and law enforcement on the internet in past and present events. It argues that policing online behaviour and cybercrime prevention cannot be reduced to a discussion about legal rules and regulations or techno-logical solutions, because policing, as in the terrestrial world, has to be understood in terms of broader frameworks of behavioural govern-ance. The policing of cyberspace can therefore be best analysed within a compliance framework composed of a multi-tiered order-maintenance assemblage of networks and nodes of security that shape behaviour online. The first part identifies the challenges that the public police face if they are to maintain their role in policing the internet. The second part maps out the networked and nodal archi-tecture of internet policing in terms of networks of security that con-tribute to policing harmful behaviour in cyberspace, and then explores how the public police are situated within them. The third part argues that some of the contradictions faced by 'the police' have been reconciled by the reconstitution of a neo-Peelian policing agenda across a global span. While this may (re)situate the police in the polic-ing of cybercrime, it nevertheless creates a range of fresh instrumen-tal and normative challenges.

The challenge of cybercrime for the public police

The relationship between the public police and technology is long-standing and complex and explains much about the positioning of the public police in late modern society. On the one hand, the police in Western industrial societies were created in the early nineteenth century as a response to the social disorder caused by the technolo-gies that brought about the industrial revolution. On the other hand, their responsive and localized nature always meant that the police fell behind in their access to, and use of, technology. Indeed, a long-standing complaint made by police officers and law enforcement agencies is that they do not have the technologies to keep up with criminals, especially with regard to offences that require what Brodeur has termed a 'high policing response' (Brodeur, 1983; Sheptycki, 2000: 11). For over a century, readers of the *Police Review* (*and Parade Gossip: Organ of the British Constabulary*, as it was origin-ally entitled) and other contemporary police journals were regularly told by police officers that they lacked the resources to obtain the latest technologies that would help them catch offenders. In those days, the police wanted new forms of transport (bicycles, automobiles, then helicopters) and new types of communications (telephones, radios). More recently, complaints have focused upon obtaining modern IT equipment, the latest software and high specification broadband links. Of course, such complaints inevitably backfire as they make good news copy and result in, often unfounded, allegations of police ineffectiveness, which ultimately reinforce the police-originated myth that criminals are ahead of the game. But, while historical themes can be drawn out, what distinguishes the modern debates from those of old is not just access to the latest technology and skill sets, but access to technology that facilitates networked policing, including access to relevant networks of security. The main problem for the police is, therefore, to reconcile the historical fact that operationally and organizationally they are local, whereas cybercrimes are globalized.

It is one thing, however, to have the technological capabilities and another to be able to utilize them. There are a number of institutional obstacles to achieving this task. The public police, like the other criminal justice agencies, are reactive and also deeply conservative institutions that have been moulded by time-honoured traditions, and therefore they do not respond readily to rapid change. Furthermore, part of this innate conservatism stems from the police also being symbolic expressions of state sovereignty. So, one way that police forces generally respond to new forms of criminal behaviour, while preserving their symbolic and organizational conservatism, is through the formation of specialist units into which officers with appropriate specialisms are placed. While this tactic constitutes an actual and visible response, it nevertheless tends to marginalize the problem it sets out to solve and runs the risk of preventing the broader accumulation of organizational and professional experience across the force in dealing with the issue at hand. Ultimately, it is the presence of a relevant body of specialist knowledge and expertise within a police force (and whether the other officers know about it) that can determine the success of the organizational and occupational response to new public concerns.

Cybercrimes introduce a new global dimension to the relationship between police, technology and the public because they clearly fall outside the traditional localized and even national operational purview of police. Their global and interjurisdictional reach and the new forms of technological crime organization they represent are markedly different to the daily police crime diet. As a direct

consequence, cybercrimes challenge, if not contradict, the traditional
Peelian policing paradigm which has long defined the local police–
public mandate and shaped the organizational and professional priorities of the police, while framing their 'constitutional' position
within the broader framework of policing society. This reminds us
that the public police were originally introduced by Peel to 'keep the
dangerous classes off the streets' by managing the present to maintain local order and investigating past events to enforce laws and
ensure that the criminal justice processes were invoked where necessary. These are still their primary functions today, though performed
in much more complex late modern societies (Critchley, 1978;
Manning, 1978; Reiner, 2000: ch 2; Wall, 1998: 23). Modern police
agencies remain largely responsive to complaints from the public;
they tend to deal with routine matters and are subject to tight budgetary constraints that restrict the immediate allocation of major
resources to emerging matters, and therefore their responsive capability.

The limitations of the Peelian paradigm and transnational crime
have long been understood and a number of strategies have been
employed to resolve the contradictions between the two. At a procedural level, there has been the use of 'soft law' (see Trubek and
Trubek, 2005) in the form of international harmonization and police
coordination treaties, such as the Council of Europe's Convention on
Cybercrime which does not create law, but harmonizes the relevant
criminal laws, police investigative procedures and mutual assistance
arrangements of the signatory states (COE, 2001). At an organizational level, a range of national/federal and international police organizations (e.g. Europol, Interpol) exist to complement locally organized
police forces – the hallmark of public police in most Western liberal
societies. They coordinate the investigation of crimes occurring across
jurisdictions and police force boundaries, collect intelligence and
investigate organized crime. Despite these procedural and organizational responses, cybercrimes continue to challenge the police in a
number of ways.

'De minimism'

The first challenge is the *de minimis* trap – the 'law does not deal with
trifles' (*de minimis non curat lex*). A common characteristic of many
cybercrimes is that they lead to low-impact, bulk victimizations
that cause large aggregated losses which are spread globally, potentially
across all known jurisdictions. Consequently, they fall outside the

traditional Peelian paradigm of policing dangerousness (risk popula-tions), which frames the police–public mandate. Since local policing strategies often depend upon decisions made at a local level about the most efficient expenditure of finite resources (Goodman, 1997: 486), it is often hard to justify the 'public interest' criteria that would release police resources for the investigation of individual cybercrime victimizations.

Nullum crimen *disparities*

The second challenge is the problem of *nullum crimen* legal dis-parities in interjurisdictional cases (*nullum crimen sine lege* – no crime without law). Protocols, including the COE Cybercrime Convention and the establishment of multi-agency partnerships and forums (see later), assist in facilitating interforce cooperation, but they rely upon the offence in question being given similar priority in each jurisdiction. If, for example, a case is clearly a criminal offence for which the investigation carries a strong mandate from the public, such as the investigation of online child pornography, then resourc-ing its investigation is usually fairly unproblematic from a police point of view. However, where there is not such an implied mandate, for example with offences *other* than child pornography, then resourcing becomes more problematic, especially if the deviant behaviour in question is an offence in one jurisdiction but not another. Of course, the other interjurisdictional problem is that there may be cultural differences in defining the seriousness of spe-cific forms of offending, or some offences may fall under civil law in one jurisdiction and criminal law in another, as is the case in the theft of trade secrets, which is a criminal offence in the US but a civil offence in the UK. In the UK, only the manner by which trade secret theft takes place falls within the criminal law (see Law Commission, 1997).

Jurisdictional *disparities*

Faced with a jurisdictional or evidential disparity, police or prose-cutors engage in a sort of policing arbitrage and use their resource-fulness to 'forum shop' (Braithwaite and Drahos, 2000) to increase the prospect of maximizing the potential for obtaining a conviction (Wall, 2002b). This process was very evident in *United States of America v. Robert A. Thomas and Carleen Thomas* (1996) where the prosecutors 'forum shopped' to seek a judicial site where they felt a conviction would best be secured. They chose Tennessee rather than California because of the greater likelihood of conviction. In R. v. Fellows; R. v. Arnold (1997) the investigation was passed from the US to the UK police because the former believed that the latter was more likely to gain a conviction because the defendants were resident in the UK. These cases illustrate some successful examples of interjurisdictional cooperation and both cases were relatively unproblematic because they concerned extreme pornography. Where cooperation tends to fall down is with the more contentious types of non-routine offending. Either the gravity of the offence may be recognized in only one jurisdiction and not the other, or the police will simply not pass on the case because they claim ownership over it.

Non-routine activity and police culture

The fourth challenge is routinization, which affects the capacity of the police to respond to 'non-routine' criminal activity. Since public policing tends to be based upon local and 'routinized' practices that define occupational cultures, working patterns, skill-sets and experiences – and ultimately the scope of professional policing – difficulties can arise when non-routine events occur (Reiner, 2000; Wall, 1997: 223). Internet-related non-routine events include cross-border investigations, or types of deviant behaviour not normally regarded as criminal by police officers.

Routine events are important in the construction of a police occupational culture because they generate stories that are told to others and this 'figurative action' can eventually structure the way that police officers interpret events (Shearing and Ericson, 1991: 481). Police occupational culture is the accumulation of the collective 'routine' experience of police officers and it is an important component of police work. With appropriate safeguards in place to prevent corruption and unfairness in the application of law, it enables officers to make sense of the world they have to police and enables them to apply the law appropriately (McBarnet, 1979).

Without this cognitive map police officers have little occupational understanding of the environment they have to police. But since cybercrimes are unique events for most officers, police culture does not assist them; in fact it can confuse rather than illuminate. Police officers tend to draw upon the 'cynical' application of conventional wisdoms (Reiner, 2000) – recall the earlier vignette about the recurring century-old call for more technological resources to fight crime.

It is therefore understandable that street police officers, who have close contact with the public, are unlikely to see the internet in terms of its potential for the democratization of knowledge and growth in active citizenship (Walker and Akdeniz, 1998) or the levelling of ethnic, social or cultural boundaries. Rather, they are more likely to see it as an area characterized by risk (Shearing and Ericson, 1991: 500) and the criminal 'other' (Garland, 2001). The internet therefore becomes understood as a place where criminals, notably paedophiles, Russian gangsters, fraudsters and other contemporary folk-devils, ply their trade. Although police forces have made great advances in their awareness of technology during the past decade, a cultural dissonance between traditional occupational culture and the demands created by the internet prevails, which allows the view to persist among many officers that 'cyberspace is like a neighbourhood without a police department' (Sussman, 1995: 59).

Under-reporting

A fifth, and most revealing challenge, is the under-reporting of cyber-crimes to the police – an issue that was briefly discussed in Chapter 2. Victim reporting practices create demands upon and contribute to defining the nature of policing services and their provision. Comparisons between reporting practices, police recording procedures and prosecutions reveal some startling information shortfalls (Wall, 2002b). The various cybercrime surveys mentioned earlier (Experian, CSI/FBI, the (UK) DTI and many others), all of which use reputable methodologies, indicate a large volume of victimizations, estimated at tens of thousands each year. This contrasts sharply with the findings of empirical research conducted for the UK Home Office in 2002 (Wall, 2002b) which found that relatively few internet-related offences were reported to the police (Wall, 2005a), a finding echoed in the analysis of answers to the British Crime Survey's internet-related crime questions (Allen et al., 2005). A detailed study of crime databases in one police force, followed up by interviews with reporting centre staff, revealed that approximately 120–150 internet-related offences per 1 million recorded crimes had been reported to the police during one year and most of these were reasonably minor frauds, mainly credit card related, over which no further action was taken.[1] When extrapolated to the national figures (taking into account the relative sizes of police forces), a figure was obtained of about 2,000–3,000 internet-related offences per year throughout England and Wales that were reported by the public to the police (Wall, 2003:

132). Even if these figures increased five- or tenfold, the reporting rate would still be relatively small.

This apparent under-reporting could be interpreted simply as evidence of low public expectations of the ability of the police to resolve internet-related crimes. Yet, despite a gradual erosion of public confidence in the police during the past few decades, policing in the UK, US and Canada is still primarily consensual and the public still regards them as a primary emergency service. Furthermore, in recent years, catalyzed by – though not wholly attributable to – the tightened security following the events of September 11, 2001 (Levi and Wall, 2004: 196), there are now in existence a range of international and national police organizations that address cybercrimes. There also exist national intelligence models, for example, in the UK the National Intelligence Model (NIM) (NCIS, 2000: 8), which structures the collection of intelligence about all crimes, including low-level losses, to construct a national or international picture of criminal activity. Whether the NIM would pick up the very minor *de minimis* cybercrimes is debatable, but the key issue is that a criminal intelligence model now exists in the UK to link the local with the national and international, whereas five years ago none existed. In addition, many of the larger local police forces/services have for some time possessed the capability to respond to internet-related complaints from the public. Some also possess local facilities to investigate computer crimes and conduct the forensic examination of computers to search for digital evidence to establish offenders' motives or whereabouts in traditional criminal code offences. Much of this evidence is located in computers, internet traffic data and mobile phone records. Finally, there are a growing number of online web portals in both the UK and the US through which the public can report victimizations.[2] In the UK, the Police Information Technology Organization (PITO) provides a range of online services through which non-emergency minor crimes can be notified to UK police forces (police.uk). The same site also has links to the US Internet Crime Complaint Center operated by the FBI and National White Collar Crime Center, and also RECOL.ca, a Canadian facility for reporting economic crime online.

While many of the above reporting facilities are fairly recent interventions and are yet to be embraced fully by the public, there also currently exist many systematic disincentives to reporting cybercrime arising from the challenges mentioned earlier. One inventive method adopted by law enforcement agencies to address the issue of under-reporting by businesses was the introduction of confidentiality charters. The UK's National Hi-Tech Crime Unit (NHTCU), for example, introduced a reporting hotline and confidentiality charter in 2002 to assure businesses that their reporting of crime would remain confidential (NHTCU, 2002; Thomson, 2002). The charter was discontinued in April 2006 when the NHTCU was absorbed into the Serious Organized Crime Agency (SOCA) (Bennett, 2006). Businesses, like individuals, now have to report to local police stations, which raises the long-standing concerns about reporting behaviour articulated elsewhere in this book.

What we have here is a combination of different factors that can explain the under-reporting of cybercrime victimization to the police. Most are clear evidence of the influence of the Peelian paradigm driving public expectations of the police and suggest that cybercrimes simply do not fit into the broader public perception of what the police actually do. This contrast in perceptions is exacerbated by the reassurance gap between what the police and the media perceive as the problem and the 'signal events' (Innes, 2004: 151). Signal events exert 'a disproportionate impact upon public beliefs and attitudes when compared with their "objective" consequences' (Innes, 2005: 5) and can distort public perceptions and increase levels of fear about cybercrime. These 'signal events' may not necessarily constitute a major infraction of criminal law, or necessarily a minor one, but 'nonetheless disrupt the sense of social order' (Innes, 2004: 151). In the case of cybercrimes they are often spam-driven low-impact bulk victimizations which users commonly experience repeatedly and which disrupt their internet use. When personal experience of these 'events' mixes with media-derived knowledge of more serious, though much less prevalent, forms of victimization, public perceptions of levels of cybercrime and the dangerousness of the internet increase. The police gaze, therefore, tends to focus upon crimes committed online where offenders are 'dangerous', such as paedophiles and also the more notorious hackers. The dangerousness of the former is undisputed; however, it is more contestable with regard to the latter as the earlier discussion in chapter 4 illustrated. It is increasingly apparent that the under-reporting of cybercrimes to the police is a reflection of the diverse nature of the provenance of the individual acts of cybercrime described earlier. Put simply, relatively few internet-related crimes are reported to the police because most are resolved elsewhere by the victims themselves, or by the panoply of other types of organization or groups involved in the regulation of behaviour in cyberspace.

Locating the public police in the networks and nodes of security within cyberspace

The public police role has to be understood within a broader and largely informal architecture of internet policing, which not only enforces norms, rules and laws, but also maintains order in very different ways. Understanding this position facilitates more realistic expectations and understanding of the police role, and also helps to identify the wide range of cross-jurisdictional and cross-sector net-worked issues that the police have to embrace in order to participate in the policing of the internet. They are 'networked' because new technologies have accelerated the growing tendency towards net-working sources of security (Johnston and Shearing, 2003; Dupont, 2004). Table 8.1 outlines the principal interest groups that constitute the nodes of networked internet governance. Without making any specific empirical claims, a distinction is made between the 'auspices' (entities that authorize governance) and the providers of governance (Shearing, 2004: 6) which shape internet behaviour (see further Wall, 2002a, 2007). They are referred to here as an 'assemblage' after Deleuze and Guattari (1987) and also after (Haggerty and Ericson, 2000: 605), because of the way that those who constitute the nodes 'work' together as a functional entity across the network, but do not necessarily have any other unity.

Internet users and user groups

Internet users and user groups combine to exert a very potent influence upon online behaviour, through censure, usually after the occurrence of 'signal' events or crimes. More extreme behaviours may also be reported (in the UK) to relevant authorities, such as the Internet Watch Foundation, Trading Standards or directly to the police, either in person or through one of the many crime reporting websites. In addition, individual internet users may take individual action, for example, for online defamation (as in *Keith-Smith v. Williams* (2006), see Sturcke, 2006; Gibson, 2006), or employ a range of software solutions to prevent themselves from becoming victims of cybercrime, solutions that range from the use of firewalls and encryption that protect personal space, through to the application of spam filters and virus checkers. Working on a self-appointed mandate, the internet users are simultaneously auspices and providers of governance.

Among the internet users are a number of interest groups formed around specific issues who 'police' websites that threaten or offend

Table 8.1   The internet's order-maintenance assemblage

Type (governance providers)	Population served	Sanctions (auspices)
Internet users/user groups – includes CyberAngels, Adult Sites Against Child Pornography (ASACP), Spambusters, eBay	All internet users within interest group	Moral censure, cold-shouldering, lobbying, reporting, hacktivism
Online virtual environment managers and security – for online role playing/game playing, chatrooms, discussion lists, e-auction rooms, cyberworlds	Members of online environments	Removal of access rights, exclusion from the environment when community norms or laws are transgressed
Network infrastructure (ISPs) – internet service providers, ISP orgs, domain name registries	Subscribing users/ clients	Withdrawal of internet service, introduction of control software such as spam filters or content management
Private (corporate) security – banks, telecommunications, corporate entities	Own private interests/private clients	Withdrawal of services, civil recovery
Non-government, non-police hybrids – Internet Watch Foundation, CERT, CAUCE	All internet users	Withdrawal of participation, financial sanctions, reporting to police
Governmental non-police – customs & excise, security services, intelligence, trading standards	All internet users, business	Financial sanctions, prosecution (civil or criminal)
Government-funded public police – police forces, national specialist units	All internet users	Criminal prosecution

them. Largely transnational in membership and operation, these tend to be self-appointed and possess neither a broad public mandate nor a statutory basis. Consequently, they lack formal mechanisms of accountability for their actions which themselves may be intrusive, illicit or even illegal. Nevertheless, they appear to be fairly potent. A number of examples of virtual community policing already exist. In addition to the various complaint 'hotlines' and the development of software to 'screen out' undesirable communications (Uhlig 1996), some netizen groups have sought to organize internet users around particular issues. The names of the following anti-child pornography sites reveal their particular mission. CyberAngels seek generally to protect children online; others are dedicated to combating child pornography: 'Ethical Hackers Against Pedophilia', 'Pedowatch', 'Se7en', 'Internet Combat Group' and 'Morkhoven'.[3] The final group, The Association of Sites Advocating Child Protection (ASACP) (originally known as Adult Sites Against Child Pornography) is dedicated to the elimination of child pornography from the internet through its reporting hotline (AIN, 2005). Other active user-groups exist to combat a range of issues, such as spamming and phishing.

The principle of peer-policing by internet users is now enshrined in e-commerce through vendor rating systems, of which the most well known is eBay's online auction trading partner profile rating system. Each eBay member has his or her own profile determined by customer feedback on past sales performance. The rating system enables prospective purchasers to identify the less trustworthy sellers, thus policing undesirable behaviour within the forum: '[l]earning to trust a member of the community has a lot to do with what their past customers or sellers have to say!'[4]

Online virtual environment managers and security

As virtual environments become more popular, the need to maintain order within them becomes more pressing. To this end, most virtual environments now employ moderators or online security managers to 'police' the behaviour of their online community. The moderators ensure that community members adhere to acceptable behaviour policies and prevent discussions from becoming disruptive, libellous or being hijacked. These online security managers are collectively emerging as a new stratum of behaviour governors. A useful example of online moderation is found in the virtual world 'Habbo Hotel' which describes itself as: 'a virtual Hotel, where teenagers can hang out and chat'. It is constantly monitored by trained, police-vetted,

moderators[5] and 'hotel guides' drawn from within the online community. The values and norms (auspices) that moderators maintain,
as in other environments, combine the interests and norms of the particular online community with the legal and corporate responsibilities
of the virtual environment 'owner'. The sanctions that moderators
can invoke when community norms or rules are broken include 'time-
outs', the temporary removal of access rights if the offending is minor,
or permanent exclusion from the environment if it is serious. While
these 'policing' practices are generally effective in upholding community norms, they are limited in scope, especially when the offending
behaviour 'crosses the line' into more serious offending. Then the
concern becomes whether or not the correct action has been taken.

Network infrastructure providers

The network infrastructure providers, typically the internet service
providers (ISPs), influence online behaviour through 'contractual
governance' (Crawford, 2003; Vincent-Jones, 2000). This function
is effected through the terms and conditions (auspices) of their
contracts with individual clients – the internet users. The terms and
conditions are largely the product of the market, the law and the
ISP's commercial interests. The ISPs are also subject to contractual
governance through the terms and conditions laid down in their own
contracts with the telecommunications providers who host their
internet services. In addition, ISPs can, because of their strategic
position in the communications networks, also employ a range of
software solutions to reduce offending online. Most typical of these
are robust security systems accompanied by sophisticated professional spam filters.

The ISPs have a rather fluid status because although they are physi-
cally located in a particular jurisdiction, they tend to function transna-
tionally (Walker et al., 2000: 6). The liabilities of ISPs vary under
different bodies of law and have yet to be fully established (see
Edwards and Wealde, 2000; Lloyd, 2000, Rowland and Macdonald,
1997), although cases such as *Godfrey v. Demon Internet Ltd* (1999)
and the *League Against Racism and anti-Semitism and The Union of
French Jewish Students v. Yahoo Inc. and Yahoo France* (2000), *In Re:
Verizon Internet Services, Inc.* (2003) (Wired, 2003) have exerted a
'chilling' effect upon ISPs' actions and have made them very risk
averse. The fear of civil sanctions encourages ISP compliance with
many of the regulatory demands made of them by the police and other
state bodies. Consequently, ISPs tend to tread carefully and are fairly

responsive to police requests for cooperation. In addition to being wary of their potential legal liabilities, ISPs are also fearful of any negative publicity that might arise from their failing to be seen to act responsibly. The general rule of thumb that appears to be adopted across many jurisdictions is that liability tends to arise when the ISP fails to respond to requests to remove offensive material, whether obscene or defamatory, once it has been brought to their attention following a complaint (*People v. Somm*, 1998; *Godfrey v. Demon Internet Ltd.*, 1999; Leong, 1998: 25; Center for Democracy and Technology, 1998: 3). ISPs tend to organize themselves both within specific jurisdictions and across them with a further level of transnational organization, for example the Commercial Internet eXchange, the Pan-European Internet Service Providers' Association (EuroISPA) and Internet Service Providers' Consortium (mainly US). These transnational organizations focus primarily upon technical/practical and commercial issues germane to ISPs. In addition to the ISPs are the (regional/national) domain name registries which allocate domain names under the oversight of ICANN (the Internet Corporation for Assigned Names and Numbers), an international non-profit corporation formed to assume responsibility for the IP (Internet Protocol) address space allocation, protocol parameter assignment, domain name system management, and root server system management functions. ICANN also resolves disputes over domain name registration.

Corporate organizations and corporate security

Corporate organizations protect their corporate interests by exercising contractual governance over their members (both employees and clients) and also any other outsiders. In addition, corporate security organizations may also employ a range of software solutions, not just to protect themselves, but also to identify and investigate abnormal patterns of client behaviour. Contractual terms and conditions threaten the removal of privileges, or private or criminal prosecution in the case of more serious transgressions. A graphic example of the corporate exercise of contractual governance is found in the demise of Jennicam.com, one of the original and most popular of the cam-girl sites. Jennicam's collapse was blamed upon a change in the acceptable use policies of the online payment service PayPal, which also affected online gambling.[6] Similarly, charities and card issuers have lobbied the UK government to change the data protection laws to allow them to cancel the credit cards of those using them to purchase child pornography online on the grounds that it breaches the issuers' terms and conditions of use (BBC, 2006h). Along similar lines, online stores, such as those operated by Yahoo or Hotmail, are ceasing to enter into buyer–vendor arrangements where the seller has an easy-to-set-up webmail account (Leyden, 2006e). In March 2006 the Financial Coalition Against Child Pornography was formed to make it impossible to profit from child pornography operations on the internet. The coalition brought together a range of organizations involved in website service delivery and online payment systems to 'share information about websites that sell child porn and stop payments passing to them' (BBC, 2006a). Views vary, however, upon the effectiveness of shaping behaviour through acceptable use strategies and it is therefore likely that they will be more effective for some rather than others. For example, in the case of sites distributing sexual content there is clear evidence of their immediate tactical effectiveness, as with the collapse of Jennicam. However, the sheer market demand for sexual materials on the internet suggests some resilience against regulation.

Following the widespread mass integration of IT within most organizational structures from the 1980s onwards, and notably since the growth of e-commerce during the late 1990s, the security departments of commercial, telecommunications and other related organizations have been strengthened to protect their interests. As e-commerce grows, it is anticipated that corporate security organizations will become major players in policing the internet. However, because their primary function is to police their own 'private' interests, it is hard to assess their overall impact on policing because of their low 'public' visibility. Importantly, they tend to pursue a 'private model' of justice because the public criminal justice system does not offer them the model of criminal justice that they want (Wall, 2001b: 174). Consequently, their relationship with the public police is often minimal. Yet, the latter are organizationally ambivalent about this relationship because they resent the loss of important criminal intelligence, but simultaneously appear happy – from a managerial point of view – not to expend scarce and finite police resources on costly investigations.

Non-governmental, non-police organizations

Non-governmental, non-police organizations are a growing legion of hybrid public/private arrangements that contribute directly to the order-maintenance assemblage by acting as gatekeepers to the other levels of governance, but also contributing towards (cyber) crime prevention. The Internet Watch Foundation, for example, provides governance under the auspices of a mandate from the UK ISPs and UK government. One of its principle functions is to bring to the attention of ISPs any illegal materials reported to its hotline, particularly child pornography, the eradication of which is one of the objectives of the Foundation. If deemed actionable following a judgement made against set criteria by a trained operative (see chapter 6), the IWF takes appropriate action either by informing the offender's ISP, alerting comparable hotlines in the offender's jurisdictions, or, if serious enough and within the UK, it may pass on details of a website directly to the police. The IWF also contributes more generally towards cybercrime prevention and public awareness. It was formed in December 1996 with the endorsement of the Metropolitan Police, Department of Trade and Industry (DTI), Home Office and the associations of the ISPs, such as the Internet Service Providers Association and the London Internet Exchange (Uhlig, 1996). The standing of the Internet Watch Foundation has increased and it has become the quasi-public face of internet regulation in the UK, more notably since its relaunch in 2000.

Another example of a non-governmental, non-police organization is the Computer Emergency Response Team (CERT) based at Carnegie Mellon University in Pittsburgh. It was created in 1988 in the aftermath of a devastating attack by the Morris Worm which highlighted the internet's vulnerability by bringing much of it down. Located at the Software Engineering Institute, a federally funded research and development centre of Carnegie Mellon University, the purpose of CERT was to combat unauthorized access to the internet. Its programmers would log reported hacks and carry out the initial investigations. If security breaches were found to be too complicated to deal with in-house, they were farmed out to an unofficial 'brains trust' (Adams, 1996) and to the relevant public police organizations if an offence was serious and could lead to prosecution. In 2003 CERT joined the Arlington-based US-CERT team created by the Department of Homeland Security as part of the national infrastructure protection programme. Prior to the partnership, CERT (Carnegie Mellon) had become the model for many similar computer security organizations throughout the world. CERT was based within a non-governmental public institution but initially funded by a combination of private and governmental resources.

Although the non-governmental, non-police organizations are mainly private bodies, they often perform public functions. However, they tend to lack the formal structures of accountability normally associated with public organizations and sometimes find themselves the subject of public concern.

Governmental non-police organizations

Governmental non-police organizations provide governance under the auspices of regulations, rules and law through charges (levies), fines and the threat of prosecution. Not normally perceived as 'police', they include agencies such as customs, the postal service, and trading standards organizations. In addition, these agencies may employ a range of software solutions to protect themselves and also assist in investigations. They also include a higher tier of agencies that oversee the implementation and enforcement of national internet infrastructure protection policies. Some national governments, such as Singapore, China, Korea and Vietnam, have at one time or another, and with varying degrees of success, actively sought to control their citizens' use of the internet. They have either required users to register with governmental monitoring organizations or sought to directly control internet traffic in their jurisdictions through government-controlled ISPs (Center for Democracy and Technology, 1996; Caden and Lucas, 1996; Standage, 1998).

At the national level there are multi-agency cross-sector organizations, or forums with a remit to protect the electronic infrastructure either through active interventions or through the co-ordination of the activities of bodies at an international level. In the UK, for example, the National Infrastructure Security Co-ordination Centre (NISCC) oversees the protection of the critical national infrastructure and covers the following sectors: telecommunications, energy, central government, financial, transport, emergency services, water and sewerage, and health services. Announced in December 1999, NISCC is an interdepartmental organization which coordinates and develops 'existing work within Government departments and agencies and organizations in the private sector to defend the Critical National Infrastructure (CNI) against electronic attack'. NISCC is also responsible for UNIRAS (The Unified Incident Reporting and Alert Scheme) – the UK CERT equivalent which gathers information about IT security incidents in government departments and agencies. Most EU members have infrastructure protection agencies with similar functions to NISCC and there are emerging a number of EU-wide agencies, such as ENISA (European Network and Information Security Agency) whose role is to support the internal market by 'facilitating and promoting increased co-operation and information exchange on issues of network and information security'.

The US Department of Homeland Security (DHS) was created in the aftermath of September 11, 2001. The DHS brought together twenty-two previously disparate domestic agencies into one department to protect the nation against threats to the US homeland. Among these agencies was the National Infrastructure Protection Center (NIPC) which, since 1998, had articulated the National Infrastructure Protection Plan of which the internet was part. The NIPC brought together representatives from US government agencies, state and local governments, and the private sector in a partnership to protect the nation's critical infrastructures (PDD, 1998). Within the NIPC many state-funded non-police organizations were also involved in policing the internet to resolve specific problems. For example, the US Postal Service has a responsibility for the cross-border trading of pornography and the US Securities and Exchange Commission is responsible for dealing with fraud.

There is a final level of very important and influential governmental non-police organizations which set regulatory policy (often secondary legislation). They are the departments of government that are responsible for trade, and therefore tend to carry the e-commerce portfolios: in the UK, the Department of Trade and Industry; in the US, the Federal Trade Commission.

Public police organizations

Public police organizations draw upon the democratic mandate of government to impose governance by maintaining order and enforcing law. They play a comparatively small, though nevertheless significant, role in enforcing criminal sanctions upon wrongdoers online. While they are located within nation states which impose criminal definitions through the law of the jurisdiction, the public police are nevertheless networked by transnational policing organizations, such as Europol and Interpol, whose membership requires formal status as a police force (see Sheptycki, 2002). In most Western countries, the public police are organized locally, but there also exist national police organizations that deal with the collection of intelligence and the investigation of organized crime. Within the local police services, several specialist individuals or groups of police officers are trained to respond to internet-related complaints from the public (Davies, 1998). Some police forces set up their own units, while others enter into strategic alliances with other police forces to provide such services.

In the US, policing is delivered by about 17,000 independent local police forces (the actual number varies according to the definition of police used). At a national and cross-state level, jurisdiction lies with the Federal Bureau of Investigation, although the US Secret Service – once a bureau of the Treasury, but since March 2003 part of the Department of Homeland Security – also carries a responsibility for investigating crimes 'involving U.S. securities, coinage, other government issues, credit and debit card fraud, and electronic funds transfer fraud' (US Secret Service, Duties and Functions). In the UK, policing is delivered by about 55 main local police forces (the number again varies slightly depending upon how they are defined). Each police force now carries a capability to respond to local internet-related crimes, although the capability varies as some are more developed than others, or a strategic alliance has been forged with a neighbouring force. At a national level, the National Criminal Intelligence Service (NCIS) was, until 2006, responsible for providing intelligence on serious offences, such as child pornography, which cross police force or international boundaries. From April 1998, the investigation of such offences came under the National Crime Squad (NCS), a role previously held by the various regional crime squads. Both NCIS and the NCS were respectively defined by the Police Act 1997, parts I and II. In April 2001, the National High Tech Crime Unit (NHTCU), part of the NCS, became operational to protect the UK's critical infrastructure from offences such as paedophilia, internet fraud and any other national-level offences. In April 2006, the Serious Organized Crime and Police Act 2005 brought together the NCS, NCIS, the drug trafficking investigations and intelligence branches of Customs and Excise, and the organized immigration crime component of the Immigration Service to form the Serious Organized Crime Agency (SOCA). The NHTCU became SOCA's e-Crime Unit.

The significance of presenting internet governance in terms of the order-maintenance assemblage/compliance framework is that its starting point is one of order and compliance, rather than disorder and unlawful resistance. Indeed, the terms 'order' and 'law' have been deliberately reversed here to break the conceptual link that has increasingly bound the two concepts since the late 1970s (Fowles, 1983: 116; Wall, 2000). Resistance, in the form of harmful behaviours, must be understood within the compliance framework that defines it rather than outside it (see Hermer and Hunt, 1996: 477). Furthermore, the assemblage model also has major implications for the framing of policy: the distributed nature of the internet does not allow governments the privilege of monopoly control over either the internet or user behaviour. Although, the order-maintenance assemblage itself, or parts thereof, can be the subject of international policy, such as the European Commission's 1997 action plan for promoting the safe use of the internet (EC, 1997), better utilization and development of the existing assemblage could lay the foundations for a more effective and more broadly democratic, structure of governance. To effect this strategy, however, a plural approach is required that combines a complex web of interrelated legal, regulatory, normative and technological measures.

The role of the public police in policing cyberspace

The answer to the earlier questions about the effectiveness of the role of the public police in cyberspace is quite simple: they only play a very small part in overall policing of the internet. This is not, however, to say that cyberspace goes unpoliced. As Robert Reiner has observed more generally: 'not all policing lies in the police' (Reiner, 2000). Similarly, Stenning and Shearing have argued that the public police are neither in control of, nor are they necessarily at the centre of, the governance of crime because there are so many other actors involved (Stenning and Shearing, 2005: 167). It is also important to bear in mind that the poor visibility of traditional police performance indicators that measure online order, for example, contrasts sharply against high levels of police science which can catch infringers by using surveillant technology. This debate is taken forward in the next chapter.

The governance of online behaviour is characterized by a sense of order that results from the complex order-maintenance 'assemblage' of networked nodes of security described earlier. These networks not only effect compliance, but they also continually shape virtual behaviour (Wall, 1997, 2001b: 171; 2002a: 192; Walker and Akdeniz, 1998: 8; Newman and Clarke, 2003: 160). In so doing they transcend the 'state/non-state binary' (Dupont, 2004: 76) and also state sovereignty (Shearing, 2004: 6). The term 'assemblage' is particularly useful in this context to explore the relationships between nodes and also within them. In some of these networked relationships there may be consensus about the policing process, while in others the consensus may be in the outcomes or goals achieved. Consequently, there is a replication of the bifurcation found in terrestrial policing between the maintenance of order and the enforcement of law. By separating the two, some sense can be made of the rather conflicting messages emerging in debates over policing the internet. Networked security, for example, exploits the 'natural surveillance' implicit in networked technologies to enable both primary and secondary social control functions to operate. It also tends to mediate, to some extent, global disparities arising from national or jurisdictional legal differences in definition.

Furthermore, looking at the policing of the internet in this way exposes countervailing tensions and helps to unravel the apparently rather tangled role of the public police. On the one hand, the overall public police role is comparatively small, with the other networks playing the larger role in policing and regulating online behaviour. As indicated above, since many cybercrimes fall outside traditional police crime diets they become unproblematic from a police resourcing point of view – they simply do not get resourced. On the other hand, the public police not only tend to lay claim culturally (in an organizational and occupational sense) to a greater ownership of policing the internet than 'they actually own', but more importantly, they are also expected to do so by the public because of their traditional consensual relationship with the state and the citizen. In most common law countries, the public still regard the public police as an emergency service. So, even though the public police do not actually police some parts of cyberspace, an echo of their Peelian heritage reminds them of their symbolic duty to protect the public from danger.

We see in the debates over the policing of the internet a replication of the terrestrial reassurance policing debate (Crawford and Lister, 2004), though with a slight twist. Whereas the reassurance policing debate is borne out of the 'increasing recognition that the police alone cannot win the fight against crime and disorder nor meet the public's seemingly insatiable demand for a visible policing presence' (Crawford and Lister, 2004: 413). When shifted into cyberspace, the debate takes for granted that the police alone cannot win the fight against crime, but nevertheless demands a more visible policing presence. This raises important questions as to how they deal with those challenges.

The neo-Peelian agenda: renegotiating the public police role in policing cyberspace

The earlier discussion situated the police as a relatively minor, but important, player in the broader network of security that constitutes the policing of cyberspace. By outlining the various challenges faced by local police with regard to globalized offending online, the preceding analysis suggests that the police are in fact fairly ill-equipped organizationally, occupationally and culturally to deal with it. However, that is only part of the story. As Crawford and Lister (2004: 414) have observed, during the past decade or so we have witnessed the increasing pluralization of terrestrial policing. The 'public police are becoming part of a more varied and complex assortment of organizations and agencies with different policing functions together with a more diffuse array of processes of control and regulation' (Crawford and Lister, 2004: 414). They show that while 'much policing is now taking place beyond the auspices' of the public police (p. 426), it would be premature to view the partnerships that form plural policing as facilitating a form of 'networked governance'. In the British terrestrial policing context, '[t]he reality, at the moment at least, is that crime and disorder partnerships remain state-dominated institutions' (p. 426). But these observations can still inform our understanding of the police role in cyberspace because of its networked and nodal architecture. The earlier discussion about situating the police demonstrated considerable pluralism in the policing of cyberspace beyond the auspices of the public police. However, the emerging role of the police as (digital) information brokers (Ericson and Haggerty, 1997) has led, during the past decade, to a new neo-Peelian role for the public police in which the original Peelian principles and values are promoted, but within the networks and nodes of multi-agency cross-sector partnerships, forums and coalitions. Just as ideas about crime have become globalised, then so have ideas about policing.

Multi-agency cross-sector partnerships

Three main tensions arise in the order-maintenance 'assemblage' outlined above which public police forces have to reconcile in their working relationships or partnerships with others. These are the *public to public* police tensions, which have to be resolved in order to facilitate working relationships between public police forces and agencies, both formal and informal, at local, national and international levels. More problematic are the *public to private* tensions in relationships between public police and private organizations, and, thirdly, the tensions arising from *private to private* relations between private organizations which effectively exclude the public police (see McKenzie, 2006).

To varying degrees, multi-agency cross-sector partnerships and forums help resolve some of the potentially destructive conflicts between private/commercial and public policing interests. They also mediate potential 'turf wars' between different police agencies that can impede cooperative efforts between organizations and levels of cooperation between individuals. Traditionally, the tensions between the commercial and public sectors arise because the primary function of the former is to police their own 'private' interests. In so doing they pursue a 'private model' of justice that does not expose publicly their organization's weaknesses and thereby maintains the confidence of the market. The public criminal justice model, on the other hand, is public and the prosecution of offenders is carried out in the public interest and in the public gaze – not a model of criminal justice that many corporate entities want (Wall, 2001b: 174). Within the public sector are found equally destructive tensions between different policing agencies. Not only do 'turf wars' take place between national and local police forces for ownership of cases, but there are also distinct contrasts between the organizational and occupational ethos of law enforcement and police agencies that can damage the collective effort. Such contrasts are highlighted in Gorman's (2003) analysis of governmental responses to the September 11 terrorist attacks. Gorman argues that the 'FBI [are] from Mars, and the CIA from Venus . . . it's not that [FBI agents and CIA officers] don't like each other . . . they're really different people . . . they have a hard time communicating' (2003: paras 1, 4).

Through what is effectively a form of 'peacebuilding' (J. Wood, 2004: 41), the purpose of multi-agency cross-sector partnerships is to build up networked trust relationships that engender a willingness to share information. Although these partnerships tend to be driven by internet security and law enforcement initiatives, it would be wrong simply to assume they are the product of formal policy and also that they are necessarily dominated by state law enforcement imperatives. The following three examples from North America, involving many similar enterprises, illustrate how the partnerships, forums and coalitions of interest can vary in terms of their being multi-agency or cross-sector, or both, and also how the boundaries between them can overlap. POLCYB (the Society for the Policing of Cyberspace), for example, is both multi-agency and cross-sectoral, existing to share information across micro-networks of trusted individuals and agencies to promote cooperation between sectors while actively inviting international involvement from law enforcement, corporate entities and interest groups. The High-Tech Crime Consortium (HTCC), on the other hand, is more multi-agency than cross-sectoral. Largely internet based, it provides a closed forum for law enforcement and security officers – mostly, but not exclusively, from North America – to discuss matters within a secure environment. Whereas POLCYB tends to discuss policy-end issues face to face, HTCC is more about sharing information, day-to-day problem solving, providing solutions and identifying emerging problems. Other forums are much looser coalitions or friendship associations of law enforcement and security experts. The AGORA security group, for example, encourages informal cross-sector relationships and provides a face-to-face environment for information exchange between members/associates about internet-related security matters. In a similar manner to POLCYB, the discussion about information sharing in AGORA tends to take place at a policy or procedural level rather than specifically sharing substantive intelligence data; for example, developing ideas about security issues and good practice, but also identifying, even agreeing (pre-policy) possible acceptable limits for data storage about economic transactions and internet traffic flows and also the standards to be employed in responding to requests to store and/or provide data. However, the networked trust relationships established within the forums also facilitate the subsequent sharing of intelligence, including information about commercial victimizations and related criminal intelligence. Importantly, the personal and occupational interests of the members indicate a substantial cross-over of membership between the three partnerships.

The tightening of security after September 11 brought together multi-agency partnerships driven by specific national policies or legislation and drew together relevant aspects of (governmental and non-governmental) agencies under the auspices of a coordinating body. Appel (2003) provides a very detailed and useful list of the many private–public cybercrime-related multi-sector partnerships operating in the USA which are associated with the Department of Justice and the Department of Homeland Security. The nearest EU-wide equivalent is the European Network and Information Security Agency (ENISA). In the UK, the key coordinating organization is the National Infrastructure Security Co-ordination Centre (NISCC), which coordinates the principal agencies. In the US context, Appel argues that public–private collaborations are currently working in many states, counties, regions and cities, and cites many examples of effective solutions with many different approaches that involve law enforcement, business, private security, government and academia (Appel, 2003).

Specific emerging concerns have also stimulated demand for specialist coalitions to be set up by a broad range of interested organizations, often with some governmental input. One such example is the CNSA (the Contact Network of Spam Authorities) which coordinates efforts under the EU anti-spam directive. Existing on the margins of policing, though within the broader subject of EU-wide responses to spamming, which includes spam generation as well as spam content, the anti-spam enforcement authorities of thirteen European countries (Austria, Belgium, Cyprus, the Czech Republic, Denmark, France, Greece, Ireland, Italy, Lithuania, Malta, the Netherlands and Spain, with others invited to join) have agreed to work together to investigate complaints about cross-border spams from within the EU. However, since the majority of spam originates outside the EU, it is planned that the CNSA will work in cooperation with other countries 'both bilaterally and in international forums like the OECD and the International Telecommunication Union' (European Commission, 2005). In 2004, a similar agreement was reached between the US, UK and Australia to coordinate anti-spam efforts (electricnews, 2005). Another example of such a coalition is the Anti-Phishing Working Group (APWG), mentioned in chapter 5, which now has about 2,000 members.

It is very difficult to assess the effectiveness of these partnerships and forums in achieving their respective tasks because there are few visible performance indicators and the multiple flows of information generated between the many nodes in security networks can paint different pictures at different points. However, by creating environments of openness through the establishment of trust, then the networks created by the partnerships, forums and coalitions facilitate the flow of essential information to the nodes. At the centre of the establishment of trust appears the 'police' link.[7] A brief examination of the composition of the many partnership management boards indicates a mix of law enforcement and other organizations. Their activities, mainly conferences, workshops and meetings, also display a similar balance. What comes across very strongly, from a cursory examination of their activities, is that former and current police officers clearly play an important, though not always leading role in these multi-agency and cross-sector partnership forums. But there remain, as yet, a number of unanswered questions about the nature of their role because the actual working of the partnership operation often lacks oversight and transparency – although discretion, of course, is one of the main reasons why the partnerships work. Also relatively unknown is the extent to which the non-police contacts in these networks of trust are themselves former police officers. Again, a brief look at the composition of the boards of these agencies and their working parties suggests that the number is fairly high. At the heart of the trust-building dynamics appears to be a meeting of minds who possess a similar *weltanschauung*, which is probably the main reason why the networks actually work (this would be another research project in itself). The shared occupational values appear to sustain and culturally reproduce the Peelian policing paradigm, so that while the milieu of policing cybercrimes may be different, the public policing mandate remains much the same.

Conclusions: the challenge of cybercrime for the police–public mandate

This chapter has explored the challenges that cybercrimes pose for the police and their mandate from the public. It has examined the role played by the public police in policing the internet within the broader architecture of internet governance and its order-maintenance assemblage/compliance framework. It has illustrated how the internet, and the criminal behaviour it transforms, challenge the processes of order maintenance and law enforcement. Not only does internet-related offending take place within a global context while crime tends to be nationally defined, but the public police mandate prioritizes some offending over others, particularly where there is a dangerous 'other', as in the production of child pornographic images. Furthermore, policing the internet is a very complex affair by the very nature of policing and security being networked and nodal. It is also complex because within this framework the public police play only a small part in the overall policing process, yet the Peelian heritage of the police that has long defined their relationship with the state and the public has caused the police instinctively to assert ownership over the policing function.

Cyberspace thus places the public police in a rather contradictory position – on the one hand, the characteristics of cybercrimes contradict the basic Peelian principles of policing, yet those very same principles lead the public to rely upon the police for protection. This contradiction can be observed in most jurisdictions where policing takes place by consent, and even in some where the consent is less apparent. Cybercrimes generate many questions about whether the public police's cultural heritage and traditional constitutional position actually fits them organizationally for a role in policing cyberspace. However, the contradictions faced by 'the police', particularly the 'reassurance gap' between crimes experienced and those felt

(Innes, 2004: 151), has led to public concern about 'cybercrime'. This has subsequently shaped the demands made of the police for reassurance, which have been reconciled by the reconstitution of the Peelian principles of policing and the emergence of a neo-Peelian agenda across a global span. While this resituates the police as an authority within the networks of security it nevertheless creates a range of instrumental and normative challenges for them. One of those challenges is to temper the potentially dangerous drift towards the very edge of 'ubiquitous law enforcement' (Vinge, 2000) and excite a range of opposing debates. But there is also optimism in the potential for those same technologies to provide important opportunities for police reform (Chan et al., 2001). The surveillant characteristics that make technology a powerful policing tool also make it a natural tool for overseeing police practice and for increasing broader organizational and public accountability (see debate in Newburn and Hayman, 2001).

The future of the public police role in policing the internet is about more than simply acquiring new expert knowledge and capacity. It is about forging new types of working relationships with the other nodes within the networks of internet security. Relationships that require a range of new transformations to take place in order to enhance the effectiveness and legitimacy of the nodal architecture. Such transformations might include a flattening of policing structures, parity of legal definitions across boundaries, broadly accepted frameworks of accountability to the public, shared values, multi-agency and cross-sectoral dialogues and more. Without these new relationships there will be one less check on the danger of a drift towards 'ubiquitous law enforcement' and 'ubiquitous crime prevention'.

The long-standing myth that the internet is a lawless and disordered environment – a place where people go for a moral holiday (see Baron and Straus, 1989: 132) – continues to endure, but it is wholly mistaken. Rather, the evidence points to the contrary. In this chapter it was demonstrated that there exists an order-maintenance assemblage – almost a compliance framework – that intervenes in many different ways and for many different reasons to police behaviour on the internet. In this, law remains an important reference point, but it is not the sole driver of behaviour and in itself it is certainly not a sound basis for cybercrime prevention policy. Any policy needs to recognize not just law, but also social values, market forces and especially the extent to which the behaviour to be prevented has been mediated by technology. This latter point is important because many offences currently called 'cybercrimes' are actually traditional (or unmediated) crime. The true cybercrimes are only just beginning to emerge. Whereas this chapter has focused upon the present and the past, the next chapter looks to the future and focuses on the architecture of regulating and preventing cybercrimes.

9

Controlling and Preventing Cybercrime

How are cybercrimes to be regulated and prevented?

Chapter at a glance

- **Cybercrime control and prevention using technology**
- **The digital realism of cybercrime**
  Regulating spamming as a cybercrime
  Law and legal action
  Social values
  Market forces
- **Code and the public v. private interest**
- **Conclusions: technologies of control or the control of technology**

The 'digital' realism of cybercrime is quite simply that the networked technologies which cause crime can also be utilized to regulate, police, and prevent it. More specifically, the surveillant and 'dataveillant' (Clarke, 1994), panoptic and synoptic (Mathieson, 1997: 215) qualities of networked technologies that cause cybercrime also provide powerful new tools for policing the internet and collecting new sources of evidence by which to secure prosecutions and convictions. They also provide 'disciplinary' tools that can facilitate cybercrime control and prevention. But it does not stretch the libertarian imagination too much to see where this is going, because these 'tools' also take us to the very edge of 'ubiquitous law enforcement' to 'ubiquitous crime prevention' and the policing of pre-crime by anticipating intent. Not surprisingly, they excite a range of opposing debates about the nature of privacy and freedom in the information age. Is privacy and freedom as we know it now dead in an information age where it is almost impossible to evade the surveillant gaze? Do we need to get over it (Sprenger, 1999), protect it or rethink it? This chapter is not about privacy, rather it shifts the discussion towards how we regulate and prevent third-generation (true) cybercrimes. It explores whether or not true cybercrimes, which are wholly mediated by technology, should simply be regarded as a scientific technical problem to which a technical solution should be applied. Will, for example, the exercise of 'perfect control' (Post, 2000: 1450) be based upon scientific or commercial considerations that will override the influence of law, social values and market forces which normally combine with technology to form the architecture of environments that shape the behaviour that takes place within it? The answer to these questions will become progressively significant as cybercrimes become more and more automated.

The first part of the chapter looks briefly at the existing use of technology in cybercrime control and prevention. The second part explores the case study of spamming as an example of the new generation of cybercrime to identify the roles played by law, technological architecture, social values and the market in maintaining order and law on the internet. The third part looks at the issue of embedding law and policy into code and goes on to argue that while policy responses to online disorder need to reflect the 'digital' realism of the internet they also need to be based upon a multi-discourse approach in order to establish a balanced understanding of the governance of behaviour on the internet.

Cybercrime control and prevention using technology

The use of technology to effect crime control and prevention is long-standing, as illustrated earlier by the example of protecting the pyramids from grave robbers (chapter 1). Initiatives have tended to fall into one of two distinct strategies: designing crime out of systems or designing crime control into them. Each strategy finds a resonance in the broader literature on crime prevention (Clarke and Mayhew, 1980; Newman and Clarke, 2003; Clarke, 2004; and others). Situational crime prevention, as it is often known, draws upon the criminologies of everyday life (Garland, 2001: 127) to focus upon the reduction of opportunity by increasing the effort needed to commit a crime, increasing the risks to the offender, or reducing the reward of crime, but regardless of intent. At its heart is what Lessig has termed the 'old Chicago School' argument that if 'forces outside law regulate, and regulate better than law, the old school concludes that law should step aside' (Lessig, 1998b: 661; Mitchell, 1995).

Crucial to the success of crime control policies is the ability of the implementer not only to control the design process of the technology and its support systems, but also to be able to identify any vulnerabilities and then be able to modify designs accordingly prior to production. This is arguably more feasible with networked technologies (the internet) since the codes that make them work can easily be manipulated, which is a very appealing quality to crime scientists whose focus is on crimes rather than criminals and who take a multidisciplinary approach to understanding, preventing and detecting them (see Pease, 2001: 18). It is also attractive to governments who have made it part of their broader agenda for protecting trade development. In the UK, for example, though similar examples exist in other jurisdictions, the Department of Trade and Industry's 'Foresight' and 'Cyber-Trust' initiatives actively sought to identify the vulnerabilities in new technologies to encourage industry to modify designs and reduce the opportunities for crime without compromising usability (Pease, 2001; DTI, 2000; OST, 2004).

A useful example of designing crime out of an online payments system is the (policy) decision made by some online retailers not to accept direct credit card payments and only to allow escrowed payment services (such as PayPal). This decision effectively reduced some types of card-not-present frauds. Such decisions can be implemented by simply changing the software codes which operate the financial transactions aspect of the website. A particularly relevant example of designing out crime was the inclusion of security facilities into computer operating systems that keep the system automatically updated by the manufacturer. Another was the implementation of a further policy which changed the security default position in operating systems from 'off' to 'on'. But designing crime out of technologies or systems is not without its problems because it is very hard to ascertain how effective an intervention has been at the design stage, particularly when any means of measuring its success has also been designed out. This is especially the case in a networked virtual environment where functionality is primarily determined by software and its accompanying procedures rather than by the hardware itself. The strategy can also have undesirable knock-on effects which have to be taken into consideration. There is, for example, the ever-present conflict between the level of security provided and functionality of the product because security measures will always compete with the user's instinctive preference for ease of use. If security measures are too complicated, users will tend to switch them off. Similarly, if a system is too secure, displacement may take place to a less secure or even different part of the system, inadvertently creating new crime incentives. We saw in chapter 5, for example, how criminal attention focused upon the input or output stages of the transaction process as payment systems became more secure.

A more visible strategy is to design crime control into a system. Perhaps the most common, if not universal, experience of crime control is the use of usernames/ID and passwords to gain access to secure networks. Without these symbols of trust, the system will not allow access to individuals. Further crime control is also exercised through the retrieval and analysis of records of internet transactions. Although largely an afterthought in the original network design, the surveillant qualities of networked technologies can be utilized to effect crime control over individuals in a number of ways. *Data mining* is the analysis of collected and retained internet traffic data which records every internet transaction. The internet's 'fine-grained distributed systems' are linked to 'every part of social life' (Lessig, 1999: 1) and establish the potential for online monitoring and also the mining of the various databases of network traffic. Potentially analysed at speeds akin to real-time to identify specific deviant activities or patterns of behaviour (Gandy, 2003: 26), data mining is the key to unlocking the 'disciplinary' potential of networked technology. One of the great public misperceptions about the internet is the myth of anonymity. In fact, networked technology leans in the opposite direction, to the point that we are now in danger of experiencing what was described earlier as the 'disappearance of disappearance' (Haggerty and Ericson, 2000: 619). This adds further weight to Ericson and Haggerty's (1997) arguments that policing 'the risk society' is increasingly about information brokering and that relations between policing bodies are becoming largely concerned with negotiating the exchange of information. In this case, the information in question is internet traffic data, which can be used more broadly to gather intelligence about deviant, including terrorist, networks or to establish conclusive evidence of wrongdoing (Walker and Akdeniz, 2003). These negotiations lead to the emergence of formal and informal relationships that underpin the networks of security mentioned in the previous chapter. Nowhere is this information brokering more apparent than with the proposed Dragnet intelligence systems, which rely upon the data-mining principle to combine and analyse various databases created by converged digital technologies to identify a range of harmful and criminal intentions. The Terrorism (previously 'Total') Information Awareness (TIA), for example, was proposed in the US after September 11 specifically to join all key national databases together to 'drain the swamp to catch the snake' (Evans-Pritchard, 2001; Levi and Wall, 2004: 207). Another, the 'Nice' system, claims to analyse different multimedia intelligence sources to detect abnormal behavioural patterns that it identifies as a possible sign of illegal activity. In public spaces, the manufacturers of Nice claim that it 'can alert police when it detects loitering, crowd gathering, people running when they should be walking, tail-gating, parking in the wrong place, unauthorized entry, or any sort of behaviour the police want to track' (Ballard, 2006).

A second way of exerting crime control is to utilize the 'code' that controls networked technologies by actively designing in security/crime prevention without changing the hardware. Katyal argues that solutions to cybercrime must try to exploit the internet's potential for natural surveillance, territoriality (stewardship of a virtual area), and its capacity for building online communities without damaging its principal design innovation – its openness (Katyal, 2003: 2268). These characteristics can also be used to generate a range of automated active 'policing' tools that seek to identify wrongdoing of which 'honeynets' are an example. The 'honeynet' is a fake website with the outward appearance of the 'real thing' but constructed to display the 'key words' that offenders search for when trawling, say, for illegal images (The Honeynet Project, 2002). In effect, the honeynet socially engineers offenders to access the site and pass wilfully through various levels of security, agreeing at each stage that they are aware of the content and indicating their intent. They eventually find themselves facing a law enforcement message – a 'gotcha' – and a notice that their details will be recorded, or in cases where intent is clear, subsequently become the subject of investigation. Currently, honeynets exploit the discipline of the panopticon (Foucault, 1983: 206) to become the 'electronic' (Lyon, 1994: 69; Gordon, 1986: 483), 'virtual' (Engberg, 1996) or 'super panopticon' (Poster, 1995). Their purpose is to acquire intelligence about criminality, but also simultaneously to create a preventative 'chilling effect', which, through the awareness of being surveilled, tempers the actions of consumers of child pornography, fraudsters, spammers and hackers.

Designing in crime control, like designing out crime, is not without its problems and critics. The downside of using technological solutions to achieve crime prevention goals is that an acceptable balance has to be found between providing security and also maintaining fundamental rights such as privacy. While there often appears to be a 'common sense' security logic to crime control policies, they are not always desirable and may even conflict with the public interest, especially when they interfere with the free flow of information or invade individual privacy. It was precisely such concerns that undermined US government attempts in the mid-1990s to introduce devices into computer design to 'protect the interests of US industry' (Reno, 1996). The V-chip technology was designed to filter out violence and pornography and the 'clipper chip', was an 'escrowed encryption system' that would have provided government with codes to unscramble encrypted files (Akdeniz, 1996: 235; Post, 1995). A not dissimilar fate was experienced by the previously mentioned intrusive Dragnet intelligence gathering proposals for automated mass surveillance systems introduced in the US after the events of September 11. The TIA system failed largely because of the political and commercial backlash from challenges to the legality and efficacy of its objectives – as well as a funding shortfall because such systems are very expensive. Whether the likes of the 'clipper chip', V-chip and TIA programs would have delivered fully as intended is another matter; the crucial factor here is that the legal and political process intervened to protect the broader public interest.

The more vociferous critics of situational crime prevention and crime science argue that its major flaw is that while offending behaviour is the province of comparatively few individuals, *all* users are unfairly affected by what has been called an 'anti-social criminology of everyday life' (Hughes et al., 2001). Whereas the utilitarian argument may find some justification in the physical world, it begins to fall down in the online world. This is because the manipulation of software codes can have such an absolute impact on users' ability to exercise their rational choice, thus undermining the logic of the internet, which is to facilitate free communications between users. No longer is cyberspace the environment 'where everyone has the same level of access to the web and that all data moving around the web is treated equally' (Berners-Lee, cited by Fildes, 2006). The hope is rapidly being undermined that 'end-to-end' architecture will value free communication, while leaving the choice over what to receive and what not to receive to the user (Saltzer et al., 1984). Lessig (1998b) has argued in his 'new Chicago School' argument that the special characteristics of the internet are such that law cannot be rejected where alternative forms of regulation such as technology are found to be stronger; he also argues that state involvement cannot be avoided, indeed it can do more

(1998b: 661). The big question is 'how' with regard to alternative forms of regulation, and 'how' with regard to the role of the state.

The digital realism of cybercrime

In the shadow of technology, the law only has a limited direct impact upon online behaviour because software codes determine what can and cannot be done. Lessig, and others such as Greenleaf (1998), have stated, using a digital realist argument, that law does have the capacity to shape not only the environment that influences the formation of the code which forms the architecture of cyberspace, but also the social norms which internet users take with them online and the incentives and disincentives created by the market which shape the behaviour within. Of particular interest is the capacity of these four distinct, but interdependent, modalities of constraint, as Lessig calls them (1998a, 1999) to shape criminal or deviant behaviour positively or negatively – depending upon where one stands. At first glance, the broader themes are not so far removed from situational crime prevention theories that advocate the use of technological means to change the physical environment of criminal opportunity so as to reduce it. Indeed, there is also a resonance here with Foucault's analysis of Bentham's Panopticon prison design which shapes the physical and mental architecture of the prison and therefore the relationships within it, especially the power relationship between the observer (guard) and the observed (prisoner) (Foucault, 1983: 223). Where the digital realist argument departs from the more conventional crime prevention theories is in its consideration of the architecture of the internet as 'codes' which reactively create the online environment – and also the moral and economic framework within which it operates. In the next part of this chapter, the roles of, and indeed interplay between, law, architecture, social structure and economy are explored with regard to the regulation of spamming as a new form of automated offender–victim engagement.

Regulating spamming as a cybercrime

Spamming is the primary case study here because, as outlined in chapter 7, it is currently the main automated means by which online offenders engage with their victims, by eliciting a direct response infection or routing recipients to a website. If the malice is not in the message, then it is probably in the attachment. Not only are most spammed communications criminal in their intent, but the act of spamming itself is a criminal act in many jurisdictions. Furthermore, spamming is also a useful contemporary example of the impact of the dynamic evolution of the internet through the convergence of different networked communications. In spamming we find evidence of the true cybercrime: it is informational, networked and global. Of course, if the internet could be removed, then spamming and the cybercrimes it facilitates would disappear, but we cannot take it away and neither would there be any serious support for removing it. What, therefore, do we do about the spam problem and the range of harmful activities that fall under its umbrella?

Two major schools of thought currently dominate the debates over spamming: the legal determinists and the technological determinists (crime science if you like). The legal determinists believe that norms embodied in legislation condition social change whereas the technologists believe that technology can perform this role. The legal determinist solution to an undesirable behavioural problem is to introduce new laws to curtail it, and there has been no shortage of laws to deal with spamming. On 11 December 2003, the UK introduced compulsory opt-in legislation in the form of the Privacy and Electronic Communications (EC Directive) Regulations 2003 (SI/2003/2426). These regulations brought into effect Article 13 of EU Directive 2002/58/EC[1] on privacy and electronic communications, which had been passed in July of the previous year. Prior to December 2003, the UK had adopted a self-regulatory model in which spammers were supposed to provide those on their mail lists the facility to opt out. The new EU Directive outlawed spamming unless consent had previously been obtained from the recipient. The main problem for the UK, as table 9.1 illustrates, is that over 98 per cent of spam received originates outside the UK, with the bulk originating in the Far East and the US.[2]

In the US, federal legislation entitled 'Controlling the Assault of Non-Solicited Pornography and Marketing Act of 2003', or the 'CAN-SPAM Act of 2003' (S. 877) was passed by Congress in early December 2003 and came into effect on 1 January 2004. It imposed 'limitations and penalties on the transmission of unsolicited commercial electronic mail via the Internet'. The US legislation sits on top of a patchwork of state legislation, some of which is strong, as in California, and others either weak or non-existent. Unlike the EU legislation which requires recipients to have previously opted-in to spam lists, the CAN-SPAM Act made it a compulsory requirement that spammers provide an opt-out facility (the UK/EU's previous

Table 9.1   The 'dirty dozen': the top twelve spam-producing countries,
2004–2006 (% of all spam)

Country[a]	Feb. 2004	Aug. 2004	Apr. 2005	Sept. 2005	Apr. 2006	Jul. 2006
1 United States	56.7	42.5	35.7	26.4	23.1	23.2
2 China (incl. Hong Kong)	6.2	11.6	9.7	15.7	21.9	20
3 South Korea	5.8	15.4	25.0	19.7	9.8	7.5
4 France	1.5	1.2	3.2	3.5	4.3	5.2
5 Spain	1.1	1.2	2.7	2.2	3.3	4.8
6 Poland	n.a.	n.a.	1.2	n.a.	3.8	3.6
7 Brazil	2.0	6.2	2.0	2.7	2.9	3.1
8 Italy	n.a.	n.a.	n.a.	n.a.	n.a.	3.0
9 Germany	1.8	1.3	1.2	1.3	3.0	2.5
10 UK	1.3	1.2	1.6	1.6	1.9	1.8
11 Taiwan	n.a.	n.a.	n.a.	n.a.	1.6	1.7
12 Japan	n.a.	2.9	2.1	2.0	2.0	1.6
Others	12.2	11.8	11.7	18.9	20.6	22.0

[a] Listed in order of latest ranking (July 2006).
Source: Data from Sophos, 2004a, 2004b, 2005a, 2005e, 2006a, 2006b.

position). However, despite the discordance between the EU/UK and
US approaches and criticisms of their respective legal shortcomings,
the bodies of legislation were brought into effect from early 2004
where neither previously existed.

In comparing the above legal developments with the monthly spam
totals received by one email account from January 2000 until July
2004 in figure 9.1 (also described in chapter 7), it would be easy to
construct a case which shows the (delayed) positive impact of law in
reducing spamming.

A simple reading of line A in figure 9.1 appears to show that the legislative process did not have an immediate effect upon spamming; in
fact it increased exponentially from mid-2002 onwards, around the
same time that the EU Directive was passed and does not appear to
have been hindered by either the EU or US legislation. Indeed, the
cynical reader would be forgiven for thinking that law had actually
contributed to the spam problem. This dramatic increase in spamming also accurately reflects the data provided by the Distributed
Checksum Clearinghouse as reproduced in Race (2005: 3) – until
April/May 2004. It is also supported by the findings of research inde-

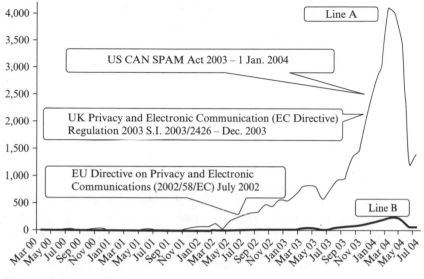

Line A: All spams received
Line B: All spams not identified by one or more spam filters

Figure 9.1 Monthly spam totals received by one email account, 2000–2004

pendently carried out by Commtouch Software Ltd., who found that the number of spams originating in the US increased by 43 per cent in the six months following the introduction of the US anti-spam legislation (Gaudin, 2004). More specifically, the increase is directly linked to the rise in the number of 'botnets' during this time period (Race, 2005). In their Global Internet Security Threat Report, Symantec found a huge increase in zombie PCs between January and June 2004, from under 2,000 to more than 30,000 per day – peaking at 75,000 on one day (Leyden, 2004i).

But after April/May 2004, line A departs from other contemporary sources of data on spams and shows that the number of spams received by the account reduced considerably. The sources cited in Race (2005), in contrast, illustrate that the number of spams in circulation remained more or less constant after April/May 2004. The explanation for the drop in spams shown by line A received after April/May 2004 was that the ISP holding the research email account restructured its service provision and moved the account to another server which automatically ran anti-spam software on all incoming emails. Many confirmed spams were then intercepted in transit before they reached the recipient's mailbox. Previously, the software had only flagged potential spams before placing them into the mailbox, thus giving the account owner the choice over what to do with them. So this 'technological' event, and not the emergence of new law, explains the dramatic fall in spams received by the test account after April 2004 and gives weight to the technological determinist argument that technology can be used to reduce opportunities for crime by suppressing, or 'designing out', the opportunities that encourage the offending behaviour. Without the intervention of anti-spam technology in April 2004 the number of spams received would have continued at the roughly the same level as the peak in April.

These observations demonstrate that code can trump the law (Edwards, 2004). They show the power of code to interrupt information flows (by up to 96 per cent – line B in figure 9.1) and therefore how technology can have a greater impact upon online behaviour than law in this context. They also appear to lend some support to Room's argument that the real weapons against spam may not actually be found in the law contained in Directive 2002/58 or SI2003/2426 or in the CAN-SPAM Act (Room, 2003: 1780), but by using 'code' in the form of anti-spam technology (also see Race, 2005). Similarly, Starr questions the use of law as a solution to spam: 'Trying to clamp down upon spammers with ever-more pedantic legislation could penalise email users while having a negligible effect on spam. If legislation consistently fails to meet the expectations of those seeking to suppress spam, then perhaps those expectations are being invested in the wrong thing' (Starr, 2004a: para. 25). Instead of law, Starr argues that the expectations should be invested in technology instead.

> Spam has been made into a moral issue, where those accused of sending it or apologising for it are automatically vilified, and those who oppose it are thought to occupy the moral high ground. This has left us without the perspective necessary to deal with spam effectively. The sooner we recognize that spam is nothing more than a thorny practical problem, the sooner we will develop technology that can solve that problem. (Starr, 2004b: para. 22)

The problem with the crime science/technological determinist position is, however, that while technology in the form of 'code' clearly disrupts the flow of spam, spams are not simply technological occurrences but the combined effect of a number of different variables. Simply to apply technological remedies does not solve the initial problem but addresses the effect rather than the cause. What is actually happening is not that spamming behaviour and its attendant dangers are necessarily being deterred, but that the spams are now being identified and deleted *en route* to the recipient. Although this interception brings internet users some respite from the seemingly never-ending spam tsunami, there is no reason to believe that purely 'technological' solutions can stem spamming behaviour – they have merely reduced the number of spams received. The solution to spamming is therefore much more complex than a technological fix. More worrying is that the decisions to impose policies to intercept spams appear to be based upon scientific considerations, often in the private interest, and made in the absence of any critical debate. Using technology to change the architecture in which the behaviour takes place wrongly assumes that spammers are heterogeneous, and act rationally and intentionally; it also contravenes the internet's established principle of openness and network neutrality.

As for the impact of legal or technological interventions upon spamming behaviour, the story is more complicated because law is clearly not rendered irrelevant by technology, as an analysis of table 9.1 and 9.2 illustrates. Table 9.2 aggregates the Sophos data in table 9.1 by continent of origin.

Table 9.2 shows a considerable decrease in spamming from North America during the two-and-a-half years from early 2004 until mid-2006 and a corresponding increase from elsewhere. The increase in spams from Asia, especially China (BBC, 2006j; Sophos, 2006a, 2006b) can be broadly explained by the recent take-up of networked technology and lower public awareness of the need for security, and therefore a corresponding increase in infected computers.

Table 9.2   The top twelve spam-producing countries by continent (% of all spam)

Continent	Feb. 2004	Aug. 2004	Apr. 2005	Sept. 2005	Apr. 2006	Jul. 2006
Asia	12	30.8	36.8	41.1	35.3	30.8
North America	63.5	45.4	38.4	28.9	23.1	23.2
Europe	7.8	4.9	9.9	8.5	18.1	20.8
South America	3.2	7.2	2.0	2.7	2.9	3.2
Australia	1.2	n.a.	1.2	n.a.	n.a.	n.a.
Unknown	12.2	11.8	11.7	18.9	20.6	22
Total	100	100	100	100	100	100

Source: As for table 9.1.

Additionally, for many of the reasons outlined in chapter 8, the law is imperfect and so is law enforcement, enabling entrepreneurial individuals to seize opportunities to make money/commit crimes, in much the same way as occurred in the West five or more years ago. Much less easy to explain, however, is the 10 per cent plus increase in spamming from Europe where the opt-in law, as opposed to the US opt-out, is stronger and arguably more enforceable. It is probable that this rise is mainly due to the presence of more insecure computers, especially in the new EU countries, which means a greater possibility of their being used as zombies. In addition, it is likely (though the evidence is not conclusive) that there may have been some displacement from the US because the number of spammers has not noticeably increased according to the Spamhaus ROKSO database (Register of Known Spam Operations). It still shows that 80 per cent of spams worldwide come from approximately 200 spammers (see www.Spamhaus.org). The decrease in spams from North America, on the other hand, appears to be related to an increase in security as users become more security conscious (and new computers come with stronger security), combined with the impact of US-based legal actions against known spammers which has put a few key spammers out of business and may have deterred others. We see, then, the influence of other variables, or modalities of constraint, at play here in addition to technology: namely law, social values and the market. Here they are explored in more detail.

Law and legal action

Law works in many ways. Soft law, in the form of the EU harmonizing directive, and hard laws in each EU country and other jurisdictions like the US remain a crucial source of authority. Law clarifies the formal state position on spamming and sends out a clear message to spammers, while, rightly or wrongly, also providing the ISPs with the authority to introduce anti-spam filters. Law also provides an authority for legal tactics which may be intended to fall short of formal prosecution, but which have a 'chilling effect' on behaviour. As stated earlier, this effect could also explain the decline in spamming from the US because it is widely regarded as a more litigious society than the UK and Europe. In 2005 and 2006, for example, the first prosecutions for spamming began to take place both in the US and also the UK (out-law.com, 2006) and it is arguable that they contributed to the decline in the US's production of spams from over half (57 per cent) in February 2004 to less than a quarter

(23 per cent) in July 2006 by removing major spammers and also maintaining the UK's low production of spams at less than 2 per cent. Evidence of the impact of out-of-court legal action is also to be found in the music industry where it has clearly reduced MP3 related breaches of copyright (Youngs, 2005; BBC, 2006c). However, there is some debate as to whether the actions have had the desired effect (Vance, 2005). Other forms of legal action range from 'cease and desist' tactics (letters before action in the UK) to private criminal actions. Alternatively, the Institute for Spam and Internet Public Policy (ISIPP) has proposed mass private legal action to 'chill' spamming behaviour through its 'death by 1000 paper cuts' strategy. ISIPP encourages victims of spam, mainly domain name owners, to 'sue a spoofer'. ISIPP wants domain owners to stand up for themselves shouting, '"[w]e're not going to take it", and fighting back, spammers will have to stop spoofing, if not stop spamming altogether' (ISIPP website). Taking forward the idea of consumer action against spam, Nigel Roberts was successful in suing an email marketing company for £300 for sending him unsolicited emails about contract car hire and their fax broadcasting service (*Roberts v. Media Logistics (UK) Ltd*, 2006). Fortified by his success, Roberts formed 'spam legal action' as a rallying call to victims of spam to bring their own actions against spammers. To assist them he provides a do-it-yourself spam suing kit containing sample documents through his Spam Legal Action website. So, in this sense, law is the authority and legal action can shape market demand by moulding social values about new types of activities.

Social values

The social values held by the individual are crucial in turning individual thoughts into social action and influencing the decision to act, not to act, or how to act. Two quite different tactics have been employed to reduce spamming by shaping values. In both examples, law provides both a reference point and also the means of empowerment. The first is by actively encouraging the building, or galvanizing, of online communities of users against the behaviour. A number of counter-spam communities already exist which individuals can consult to find out how they can remove their own addresses from existing spam lists. See, for example, Spamhaus.org, Junkbusters.com and Spambusters.com. Of course, these active groups also provide passive information which is educational. Alternatively, spam groups may go further and actively push the political process for change, for example, by lobbying politicians to bring about a more coordinated international response. The Parliamentary All Party Internet Group (apig.org.uk) has been very active in this endeavour, as has CAUCE (Coalition Against Unsolicited Commercial Email), resulting in legislative responses by the EU Parliament and US Congress.

The second way that social values are shaped is by providing information sources to educate spammers and users more generally as to what is, or is not, acceptable behaviour (i.e. what is and what is not spam) and also what the risks are. Education also equips users to make up their own minds and express their own choices by linking their own experiences with information made available to them by coalitions of interested parties, NGOs and government organizations. Especially informative are Spamhaus.org, CAUCE (cauce.org) and also David Sorkin's spamlaws.com site. Increased user awareness makes users begin to deal with their own spams, though with a sense of realism: '[d]on't think technology is ever going to be able to completely solve these problems because there is a human aspect . . . you need a lot of education to change behavior' (Timo Skytta, cited by Clarke, 2005). Increased user awareness, resulting from various educational sources, is a contributing factor to the overall drop in complaints to ISPs about unsolicited bulk emails (Wall, 2002b, 2003).

Market forces

In addition to the technological protection and the market disincentives created by legal action and the social values that law shapes, but which also shape law, the market can also determine the desirability of behaviour. Clearly, the high return on investment demonstrated in chapter 7 is the principal driver of spamming. Conversely, the negative impacts of spam on commerce have put pressure on ISPs and other organizations providing networked services to introduce increasingly robust policies against spamming. Aside from technological and legal actions, examples of such policies include giving recipients the choice over whether or not to accept attachments with their emails, thus reducing the risk of infection. Alternatively, it has been proposed to introduce a very small charge for each email transaction to make the cumulative cost of distribution expensive and reduce the return on investment, thereby reducing spamming by reducing incentives (BBC, 2006f, 2006g).

What the above analysis illustrates is that while technology can effect almost 'perfect control', law and legal action, social values and market demands also shape behaviour. It shows that the law plays a particularly important role in the governance of spamming (and cybercrime) by also indirectly moulding its physical and mental architecture. Under the 'shadow of law', technology is effective in shaping the architecture of spamming to prevent it from reaching its destination. But the shadow of law also strengthens social values against spammers by stating that spamming is wrong. It also mobilizes the market against spammers by reducing the return on investment and pressurising ISPs to protect their customers. However, faced with the choice, most would go for the technological fix. The fact that the receipt of spams in mailboxes can decline considerably, possibly by as much as 95 per cent, is certainly good news (Leyden, 2004a), but the problem is that the technological interventions have not been the product of a coherent policy formation process that has taken all implications into consideration. Technological interventions represent a marked shift away from the principle of network neutrality ('end-to-end') outlined earlier, towards the embedding of filtering and access policy into the very codes that facilitate communications. We therefore need to explore the governance of online behaviour as a multidisciplinary activity.

Code and the public v. private interest

While it is highly unlikely that any internet users would actually wish to receive more spams (other than perhaps spammers!), the uncritical adoption of technological interventions has much broader implications for the general flow of information across the internet. The fact that such interventions appear to be intuitive and logical belies the fact that they are policy decisions embedded in 'code'. Because of this, users can no longer exercise a free choice to mediate their own communications, and the big question is where does the restriction of free choice end? Which brings us back to Lessig, and his ideas on the role of government and law within the context of the origination and application of cybercrime prevention policy. Lessig shows us that the confluence of codes as regulators and codes as definers of architecture leaves the internet vulnerable because of a lack of acceptable mechanisms for providing oversight. Remember that Lessig's primary concern has been to 'build a world of liberty' into an internet whose future looks increasingly to be controlled by technologies of commerce and backed by the rule of law (Lessig, 1999: x), but also unnervingly controlled by distributed, rather than centralized, sources of authority:

> The challenge of our generation is to reconcile these two forces. How
> do we protect liberty when the architectures of control are managed as
> much by government as by the private sector? How do we assure privacy
> when the ether perpetually spies? How do we guarantee free thought
> when the push is to propertize every idea? How do we guarantee self-
> determination when the architectures of control are perpetually deter-
> mined elsewhere? (Lessig, 1999: x–xi)

In much the same way as Lessig, Sir Tim Berners-Lee, the originator
of the world wide web, has warned of the dangers of a two-tier internet in which broadband providers will become gatekeepers to the
web's content and companies or institutions that can pay will have priority over those that cannot. However, whereas Berners-Lee and the
net-libertarians are optimistic that the internet will resist attempts to
fragment it (Fildes, 2006), others (including Lessig) make convincing
arguments in support of third-party intervention to maintain the
public interest over the private – which begs the question: who should
intervene?

   Katyal (2003) seeks pragmatically to reconcile Lessig's concept of
digital architecture with ideas of crime prevention that employ the
manipulation of real-space architecture to show that the four digital
design principles of natural surveillance, territoriality, community
building and protecting targets can be employed to prevent cybercrime. Katyal argues that solutions to cybercrime must use the internet's distinctive qualities for control without damaging its principal
design innovation – its openness (2003: 2268). Yet he notes the merits
of balancing the advantages with the disadvantages, because this
'openness' can be 'both a blessing and a curse'. On the one hand, it
helps software, particularly open source code, adapt when vulnerabilities are found, but on the other hand, 'the ease with which architecture is changed can also facilitate exit and network fragmentation'
(Katyal, 2003: 2267). Similarly, closed or hidden code in the hands
of the private sector can lead to similar fragmentations, especially that
which creates the higher-end, structural, internet architecture.
Lessig, himself, has long argued that private ordering can 'pose
dangers as severe as those levied by the state' (Katyal, 2003: 2283;
Lessig, 1999: 208), which he similarly fears because of its lack of
transparency. But Katyal claims that since architecture is such an
important tool of control, then this lack of transparency is precisely
the reason why the government 'should regulate architecture, and
why such regulation is not as dire a solution as Lessig portrays'
(Katyal, 2003: 2283). Government regulation, for Katyal, is the lesser
of the two evils because it works within more transparent frameworks

of accountability. This view is also shared by Zittrain, who argues that government-mandated destination-based intervention 'stands the greatest chance of approximating the legal and practical frameworks by which sovereigns currently sanction illegal content apart from the Internet' (Zittrain, 2003: 688). Indeed, this interventionist position is really not so far removed from Lessig, who subsequently recognizes, like Katyal, that 'the invisible hand of cyberspace is building an architecture for cyberspace that is quite the opposite of what it was at cyberspace's birth' (Lessig, 1999: 5). He has therefore expressed concern that if governments cannot regulate conduct directly, then they will 'regulate the regulatability of cyberspace' (Lessig, 1999: 198; Post, 2000: 1450). Even worse is the inevitability that the forces of commerce will do it for them by constructing architectures of identity to effect 'perfect control' (Lessig, 1999: 30).

The above arguments bring us back to the issue of the uncritical application of anti-spam technology. In discussing 'Realtime Blackhole Listing' spam filtering, a process at the heart of many spam filtering systems which identifies emails that might be spams, Lessig argues that the decision to introduce it (pre the Spam laws) was not reasoned, deliberative or political. It was not a policy 'made by a collective process capable of expressing collective values' (Post, 2000: 1456). The argument here is that the 'invisible hand' of market forces is guided by the private rather than the public interest. Any dispute between Katyal and Lessig is whether or not the public interest should be represented respectively by government or a more broadly constituted democratic body. Although it is the case that government has since intervened in the case of spam since Lessig wrote in the late 1990s, the intervention did not include full consideration of the application of technological solutions. If anything, the position with regard to technological intervention is less clear now, because public law is, in effect, being used *de facto* to justify the inclusion of anti-spam filters to serve private interests.

Conclusions: technologies of control or the control of technology

The literature from Karl Marx through to Gary Marx (2001), via many others, illustrates quite conclusively that the application of technologies of control alone tends to inscribe distrust into the process. In so doing, it leads to the breakdown of trust relationships because they fail to reassure, create fresh demands for novel forms of trust, and then institutionalizes them (paraphrasing Crawford, 2000). In fact, history shows generally that technologies of control can often make much worse the very problems they were designed to solve, especially if, in the case of spam, they end up hardening the spammer's resolve, which is a possibility. Already there is evidence to show that the means of circumventing anti-spam measures is becoming more sophisticated (BBC, 2003d; McCusker, 2005: 3) and that there have been marked signs of resistance in the form of hacktivism, denial of service attacks and various forms of ethical and non-ethical hacking. This is in addition to the increasing convergence of the (cyber) criminal skill sets belonging to fraudsters, hackers, virus writers and spammers that led to the rise of the botnets.

This does not mean, however, that law has failed; rather, the preceding analysis reveals that the law works in a number of different ways and at a number of different levels to achieve its desired end. Basically, if law cannot shape behaviour directly then it can regulate the factors that shape behaviour. In many ways, the discussion over spamming is fairly unproblematic because of the overwhelming support for anti-spam measures, so it is therefore harder to make stick some of the arguments posed earlier. But what the discussion has exposed is the necessity to ensure that there is in place legal authority which justifies and legitimizes action, provides some transparency and allows recourse in cases where injustice occurs. This is because there is no agreed meaning as to what constitutes 'online order' which is common enough to render it simply and uncritically reducible to a set of formulae and algorithms that can be subsequently imposed (surreptitiously) by technological imperatives. The imposition of order online, as it is offline, needs to be subject to critical discussion and also checks and balances that have their origins in the authority of law, rather than technological capabilities.

When the discussion shifts to the contravention of the 'end-to-end' principle, using wholesale technological interventions, the importance of law becomes visible. Some measure of legal support for this principle might, interestingly, be found in the US case of *Metro-Goldwyn-Mayer Studios, Inc. v. Grokster, Ltd.* (2004) in which various facets of the music industry attempted to curtail use of peer-to-peer technology (in the distribution of MP3s). The 9th Circuit decided (and upheld on first appeal) against the plaintiffs on the basis that 'significant non-infringing uses' would be inconvenienced were the decision to be made in favour of MGM et al. That decision effectively begins to support generally the principle of 'end-to-end' because technological interventions also ensnare legitimate users of the technology. It will be interesting to see if a similar argument will be launched against the design of anti-spam filters, or any other form of intervention, at some point in the future.

All the indications suggest that spamming and new methods of offender-victim engagement are here to stay in one form or another. Not only does it continue to increase in volume, but spammers and their successors will continue to be inventive and reflexive in over-coming security measures (P. Wood, 2004: 31–2). Unfortunately, this enduring reflexivity means that we have some hard decisions to make if we are to maintain current internet freedoms and openness and not become strangled by security. Either we continue to allow decisions to be made on scientific grounds and allow the mission or 'control creep' (Innes, 2001) that is endemic to the present climate of post-September 11 security consciousness to continue (Levi and Wall, 2004), or we work towards developing workable, law-driven frameworks in which a range of considerations – including technology, but also social and market values – are employed to reduce harmful online behaviour. There is a hard message here: we need to take a much more holistic approach. Governments alone cannot tackle cybercrime, and neither should they; a multifaceted approach needs to be taken (McCusker, 2005). But it is an approach in which government can take a lead in establishing a framework for the different interventions.

Having argued for a governmental or democratic steer, we certainly need to counter the prevailing tendency towards over-regulation and also consider alternatives. To what extent, for example, can we learn from *laissez-faire* or deregulation approaches to the governance of behaviour? Could we, perhaps draw some lessons from the concept of 'safety through danger' which is a road safety policy currently being evaluated. Introduced to improve road safety (Hamilton-Baillie, 2004), the concept of 'safety through danger' removes all of the rules and their visible expression from an environment to make the space in which social activity takes place less predictable. The actors can no longer make any assumptions about each other because the absence of apparent rules removes any indications of the likely actions of others – or their relationship with their immediate physical environment. As a consequence, the actors have to interact with each other continually to negotiate a safe way through an environment and to ensure their own safety. They have to make hard decisions about their actions and in so doing take more responsibility for those same actions. After all, rules make the environment more predictable and the rights they create actually reduce the need for interaction between participants in transactions. In so doing, they also reduce individuals' decision-making abilities. But is this *laissez-faire* approach what was actually being originally proposed in the end-to-end principle and is it a position that cannot be sustained in the light of more powerful interests? What is certain is that retaining personal responsibility and online control is very important because of the constant threat of censorship and the need to retain the ability to determine truth.

> Citizens must do their best to guard against government censorship for political purposes. At the same time, they are responsible for trying to distinguish useful and truthful information from bad quality information and must therefore exercise critical thinking about what they see and hear. And that responsibility extends to all media, not only the internet. Moreover, where disinformation or misinformation exists, thoughtful citizens have a responsibility to draw attention to the problem, possibly even to provide information to counteract the bad data. (Cerf, 2003: 9)

This begs the ever-important question, raised at the beginning of this chapter, as to whether or not we should simply regard true cybercrimes as a scientific problem to which a technical solution should be applied. The answer is that if we regard it as a technical problem we lose too much in the process. There is a too strong a case against leaving decisions about whether or how to intervene to science or to the market. Rather they should be made in the public, rather than private, interest and should therefore rest with government (Katyal) or a responsible, democratically elected body (Lessig). These are important considerations; however, it is inevitable that in practice ideals will become moulded by the politics of compromise. If this means that we may have to tolerate spam and other incivilities to a small degree in order to preserve what is good about the internet, then it will arguably be a small price to pay.[3] Given that purely technological solutions are problematic for the reasons outlined earlier, a digital realist approach can inform (social) policy formation to constitute the most viable and effective attack upon what has quickly become 'the white noise' of the internet.

10

Conclusions: The Transformation of Crime in the Information Age

Chapter at a glance

- **A brief summary of the arguments so far**
  Generations of cybercrime
  Different types of substantive transformed behaviours
  Policing and regulating cybercrime
- **Conclusion**

In the pathway taken through this book it is clear that cybercrime means different things to different people. Contemporary debates encompass a range of legal/political, technological, social, and economic discourses that have led to some very different epistemological constructions of cybercrime. The *legal/administrative* discourse defines *what is supposed to happen* by establishing and clarifying the rules that identify boundaries of acceptable and unacceptable behaviour; the *criminological and general academic* discourse provides an informed analysis about *what has happened*, and why; *the expert* identifies *what is actually happening* and what, from their perspective, the tactical solutions might be; *the popular/lay* discourse reflects *what the person on the street thinks is happening*. So, while concerns about cybercrime are expressed by a range of voices they often look at the same thing from a different perspective and therefore do not always articulate a common understanding. Just about any offence that involves a computer nowadays seems to be regarded as a 'cybercrime', so not only is there a media shaping effect, but there is often the broader tendency to confuse crimes that *use* the internet with those *created by* the internet. It is the differences between the former and the latter which this book has sought to address – the ways in which crime has become, and is being transformed by, networked technologies. The first part of this short concluding chapter briefly retraces the steps of the book's journey. The second part draws some conclusions from the main themes and observations.

A brief summary of the arguments so far

Whatever its merits and demerits, the term 'cybercrime' has now entered the public parlance and we are now stuck with it. The term has a greater meaning if it is understood in terms of the *mediation* of criminal or harmful behaviour by networked technology, rather than an exhaustive listing of the acts themselves. If the hallmark of cyberspace is that it is informational, networked and global, then these qualities should also be characteristic of cybercrimes. So, by applying the simple 'transformation test' – thinking about what happens if the internet is removed from the activity – we can identify three progressive generations of cybercrime displaying different levels of (informational, networked and global) mediation by technology and three different groups of substantive cyber-criminal behaviours.

Generations of cybercrime

The first generation of cybercrimes are *traditional or ordinary crimes using computers* – usually as a method of communication or to gather precursor information to assist in the organization of a crime. Remove the internet and the behaviour persists because offenders will revert to other forms of available communication. The second generation of cybercrimes are *hybrid cybercrimes*, 'traditional' crimes for which network technology has created entirely new global opportunities. Take away the internet and the behaviour continues by other means, but not upon such a global scale or across such a wide span of jurisdictions and cultures. The third generation of cybercrimes are *true cybercrimes* that are solely the product of the internet. Take away the internet and they vanish – the problem goes away. This last generation includes spamming, 'phishing' and 'pharming', and variations of online intellectual property piracy.

An emerging characteristic of this third generation is the automation of offender–victim engagement, which, it can now be argued, is displacing the once feared act of 'hacking' by automating it. Offenders employ spammers who employ hackers who employ virus writers to write the scripts to do the spamming and hacking for them! The scripts (malicious software) they produce are automating the process of victimization. This is a new world of low-impact multiple victim crimes that creates *de minimis* problems for law enforcement and for the policing of offenders. On the one hand, the criminal justice system is not geared towards responding to such offences. On the other hand, the more behaviour is mediated by new technology, the more it can be governed by that technology. So, in addition to the prospect of being faced with 'ubiquitous' and automated victimization, we also face the uncomfortable prospect of being simultaneously exposed to 'ubiquitous law enforcement' and prevention. As a consequence, we need to begin rethinking the meaning of many concepts and values that we cherish and protect, such as security and privacy (but not in this book).

These 'generational' distinctions are important to identify for analytical and policy reasons because the first and second generations tend already to be the subject of existing laws, and existing professional experience can be applied to law enforcement practice. Any legal problems arising therefore relate more to legal procedures than substantive law. The greater challenge lies with the third generation.

Different types of substantive transformed behaviours

It is also important to look at common features in the transformation of substantive behaviours. Even though cybercrimes are increasingly being blended together as they become automated by malicious software, each facet of the blended attack still has a specific motivation which falls into one of the following categories. In this way they can be linked to existing bodies of law and associated experience in the justice processes. *Computer integrity crimes* assault the integrity of network access mechanisms (and include hacking and cracking, cyber-vandalism, spying, DDOS and viruses). *Computer-assisted crimes* use networked computers to engage with victims with the intention of dishonestly acquiring cash, goods or services ('phishing', advanced fee frauds, etc.). *Computer content crimes* relate to the illegal content on networked computer systems and include the trade and distribution of pornographic materials as well as the dissemination of hate crime materials.

Despite the existence of applicable bodies of national and international law, cybercrimes often conspire to impede the traditional investigative process. Particularly significant is the observation that the actual, rather than perceived, dangers posed by them are not always immediately evident to potential or actual victims. Either they are not individually regarded as serious, or they are genuinely not serious, but possess a latent danger in their aggregation or in being precursors to more serious crimes. Each of the substantive criminal behaviours (in addition to the main offence) illustrate this latency. Computer integrity cybercrimes, for example, often pave the way for other forms of more serious offending; identity theft from computers only becomes serious when the information is used against the owner. Similarly, zombie computers (infected by ratware) may be later used by 'bot herders' to facilitate other crimes. Computer-assisted cybercrimes, such as internet scams perpetrated by fraudsters in collusion with spammers, tend to be relatively minor in individual outcome, but serious by nature of their aggregate volume. Computer content crimes are informational; those that are not directly illegal may be extremely personal and/or politically offensive and may contribute to the incitement of violence or prejudicial actions against others.

So, an evolving picture of cybercrimes emerges which contrasts their informational, networked and globalized characteristics with the physical and local qualities of the more traditional and routine patterns of offending. Offending that is still defined by law, the criminal justice processes and crime debates which still underpin the criminal justice paradigm and therefore continue to shape expectations of it. Within the literature, cybercrimes may find some resonance with the study of white-collar crimes because they are both commonly regarded as soft or hidden crimes. However, they differ from white-collar crimes because they are not necessarily crimes of the powerful but of the 'knowledged' classes. As the third generation of true cybercrimes develops, they will be *sui generis*.

Policing and regulating cybercrime

The general public would be forgiven for their inability to square the apparent 'cybercrime' wave portrayed by the news media and cybersecurity sector with the relatively few arrests and prosecutions of so-called cyber-criminals. This shortfall can be explained partly because local police forces work within tightly prescribed budgetary parameters and often simply cannot cope with demands to investigate the crimes arising from globalized electronic networks. But the shortfall mainly arises because of the contrast between expectations and actuality because the public police only play a very small part in the overall policing and nodal network of the governance of cyberspace. Although now in the twenty-first century, the police still continue to work much along the lines of their 170-year-old Peelian public mandate to regulate the 'dangerous classes'. Hence, the understandable focus upon policing paedophiles, child pornographers, fraudsters and those who threaten the infrastructure, such as, but not solely, terrorists. However, this is not to say that cyberspace goes unpoliced, nor is it the case that police activity is either inefficient or ineffective. Rather the police role has to be understood within the broader and largely informal networked and nodal architecture of internet policing, comprised of internet users and user groups; network infrastructure providers; corporate security organizations; non-governmental, non-police organizations; governmental non-police organizations; and public police organizations. These not only enforce laws but also maintain order in very different ways.

Joining together these networks is a range of initiatives that are designed to make their governance function more effective: international coalitions of organizations; multi-agency, cross-sectoral partnerships and coalitions and also international coordination policies. Active public police participation in these partnerships and coalitions performs a number of functions. It enables 'the police' to extend their own reach at a symbolic and normative level by reconstituting the fundamental Peelian principles of policing across a global span and thereby resolving some of the contradictions they face. At a more practical level, it enables them to perform their emerging function as information brokers. The information in this sense relates to internet traffic data and its intelligence and evidential value.

While this neo-Peelian agenda enables police to resituate themselves as a lawful and legitimate authority within the broader networks of security, it nevertheless institutes a range of instrumental and normative challenges. A major challenge is to work effectively in partnership with the private sector to temper the latter's unreflective drift towards the routine use of the surveillant technologies to strengthen security by catching offenders and preventing crime by exclusion. The 'digital' realism of cyberspace is that the very technology which causes cybercrimes also has the potential to become part of the solution, but only partly because the solutions also have to be set in accepted legal, social, economic and technological frameworks, which frame the digital realist position. Unless checked, the 'ubiquitous policing' that follows this 'hard-wiring of society' (Haggerty and Gazso, 2005)[1] could contribute to the destruction of the democratic liberal values which currently bind most societies. For the time being, this adverse potential is tempered by the intervention of constitutional law, the imperfect human condition that results in inaccurate data entry and resistance against intrusion, and some theory failure in crime prevention caused by an inadequate conceptualization and understanding of cybercrime and its associated risks. However, if this tendency is contained within a supportive socio-legal context, for there is still time to achieve this, those same technologies could – optimistically – assist the process of police reform. This is because the same surveillant characteristics that make network technology a powerful policing tool also make it a natural tool for overseeing police and regulatory practice and also for creating broader organizational and public accountability.

Conclusion

We are gradually learning more about the impact of networked technologies on criminal behaviour, and therefore learning more effective and acceptable ways of dealing with them. Increasingly rigorous empirical research is now being conducted on internet victimization by a wide range of organizations, particularly the academic funding councils. The findings of this research will hopefully provide the means by which to verify or challenge trends outlined in the research findings of organizations that have a stake in the high prevalence of cybercrimes. Furthermore, the recent inclusion of relevant questions in the US National Crime Victimization Survey (NCVS) and the British Crime Survey (from 2003) will, in time, yield useful empirical data about victimization that will counter some of the misinformation that has accrued during the past decade. Within UK police organizations, the maturation of hi-tech crime capabilities, such as the National Hi-Tech Crime Unit (now absorbed into the Serious Organized Crime Agency) and various regional police units, has allowed the amassing of a wide corpus of policing experience in the field. This is also the case in the US and other jurisdictions. Laws are being revised and harmonized in many different ways, because of variations in the national debates and legislative procedures, in response to public and political concerns raised by the cybercrime debates. In the UK, for example, the Computer Misuse Act 1990 has been reviewed by the All Party Internet Group (APIG, 2004) and its scope expanded by sections 35–38 of the Police and Justice Act 2006 to make DDOS attacks and the distribution of hacking tools illegal. These new powers are in addition to the host of new state powers created in the UK, and also the US and beyond, by the anti-terrorism and domestic security legislation following the events of September 11, 2001. Of course, in the common law jurisdictions, the laws are also constantly being clarified by case law precedent.

Rather worryingly, however, it is apparent that while the actions of public police officers are framed by legislation and codes of practice, many of the other partners in policing the internet are not, other than to the broader confines of law. Also worrying is the lack of checks and balances on the noticeable shift towards the technological determinism of automated policing initiatives, driven largely by the influence of the cyber-security industry in the application of software solutions to cybercrime. There are, for example, a broad range of moral, ethical and legal concerns about the implications of the high degree of entrapment when employing 'honeypots' and 'honeynets', not least in the validity and strength of evidence presented to the court – assuming that this form of policing is in fact designed to capture offenders rather than simply to deter offending through the technological imposition of panoptic 'discipline' and its 'chilling effect'. Take, for example, something as seemingly innocuous as spamming, a true cybercrime in more ways than one, and one of a new legion of networked crimes. Many ISPs are in the process of introducing anti-spam software into the delivery process and in so doing contravene the long-standing end-to-end principle of the internet, which is freedom of movement across the network to its nodes while leaving choice and mode of receipt to the end users. No-one wants spam and few would be unhappy to see it disappear, yet – as outlined in chapter 9 – there has as yet been little critical discussion about the insertion of spam filters into the delivery mechanisms. The spam filters are one of many such technological solutions. Also currently emerging to deal with other true cybercrimes are software devices that identify and track the appropriation of various types of electronically conveyed intellectual property with increasing levels of efficiency. There is a danger that true cybercrime will generally come to be regarded as a 'technical problem' and that, as a consequence, important decisions are being made largely on scientific grounds – mainly because a filter can be made. In the case of spam there is understandably little objection, but since the technological solutions clearly work, what is to stop the application of filtering software to images or to certain words or combinations of words and thereby filter out everything that is deemed undesirable and against private interests? Are we witnessing the gradual embedding of private interpretations of law into code, into the technological fix?

What we do not want is for all users to be affected by the sins of a few. The technological fix is becoming easier and less contestable, especially when it is being carried out automatically on our behalf by technology. Although, our concerns may not warrant the dystopic hysteria invoked by George Orwell's *1984*, we may do well to heed Horkheimer and Adorno's warning in their *Dialectic of Enlightenment* about solving problems using technology:

> Once we assume that scientific methodology can solve all intellectual problems, *science becomes mythology, aware of everything but itself and its own blind spots and biases*. This results in authoritarianism, especially where science is harnessed to industrial-age technology and nature is conceptualised as a sheer utility for the human species. (see Agger, 2004: 147; my emphasis)

Put more simply, the simple application of 'policing software' to conduct sophisticated word searches that exclude everything undesirable is extremely problematic, because, as Cerf has observed, '[t]here are no electronic filters that separate truth from fiction' (Cerf, 2003: 10).

A delicate balance has therefore to be drawn between the need to maintain order and the enforcement of laws in order to provide a balance between the desires of law and the procedural protections it affords and the desires of law enforcement to catch offenders. The danger, as Scott Adams wittily proclaimed, is that 'new technology will allow the police to solve 100 percent of all crimes. The bad news is that we'll realize 100 percent of the population are criminals, including the police' (1998: 194). Without such a balance we will descend into a world of *de facto* strict liability and reverse burden of proof. Worse still, the practical realities of the transparent society may produce exactly the opposite effect (Brin, 1998) and '[a]s the Internet continues to become more transparent, the risk is that the stage may be set for a twenty-first century witch-hunt' (Campbell, 2005b). Let us hope that a balance can be achieved and that these dark predictions are unfounded and simply part of a societal reaction to the future shock of technology.

Notes

Chapter 2 Understanding Crime in the Information Age

1 There are a few exceptions, such as in Australia, where a Cybercrime Act was introduced in 2001, and in Nigeria, where a Draft Cybercrime Act has been proposed.

2 A separate debate exists about the methodological rigour of automated data collection systems, which I am not addressing here.

Chapter 3 Cyberspace and the Transformation of Criminal Activity

1 I am extending Braverman's (1976) deskilling hypothesis to social skills and the construction of virtual social life.

2 In previous literature I have referred to this as the 'elimination test'. Upon reflection, 'transformation' is a more useful concept.

3 The terms peer-to-peer and grid technologies are often used interchangeably.

4 For a very useful overview of the UK law in these three areas of behaviour, see Walden (2003: 295; 2007).

Chapter 4 Computer Integrity Crime

1 An example of computer spying was illustrated in the case of the Hanover Group (Hafner and Markoff, 1995; Young, 1995: 11).

2 The Offending, Crime and Justice Survey (OCJS) only asks respondents if they have committed an offence, and not why.

3 'All about PC, W97m/Michael-B' (www.all-about-pc.de/english/ Virus% 20Corner/Michael-B.asp).

4 They are new, but have a clue what they are talking about and are therefore referred to as cluebies.

Chapter 5　Computer-Assisted Crime

1 For further information about identity theft see Finch (2002).
2 Returns for input frauds are sent by the banks to the Chartered Institute of Public Finance and Accountancy (www.cipfa.org.uk/).
3 See Card Fraud Overviews at www.cardwatch.org.uk.
4 eBay provides a 'Trust & Safety (SafeHarbor) Answer Center!' for concerned clients at http://answercenter.ebay.com.
5 APWG is made up of over 1,500 members from the financial, communications and law enforcement sectors (www.antiphishing.org/index.html).
6 forum.carderplanet.net 'you can buy credit cards on www.carderplanet. net' (http://lists.debian.org/debian-hurd/2003/01/msg00074.html).
7 Interview conducted with convicted offender for this research. Note that credit card issuers now require information about the billing address.
8 Interview with banking official from an online banking operation.
9 See further PayPal's acceptable use policy with regard to gambling at www.paypal.com.
10 For full details of the criminal complaint see United States Attorney Northern District of California (2004) at www.usdoj.gov/usao/can/press/ assets/applets/2004_03_19_Bradley_complt.pdf.
11 See BBC advice for 'Safe Trading on eBay UK' (www.bbc.co.uk/ dna/h2g2/A2927388).
12 See 'Quick Reference Sheet of Felony Charges to Consider and Relevant Issues to Consider in Typical Intellectual Property Cases' at www.usdoj. gov/criminal/cybercrime/ipmanual/chart.htm.
13 Akdeniz describes the case of the Jet Report (on satanic abuse and witchcraft) which was released into the public domain on ethical grounds.
14 'Among warez users, there is often a distinction made between "gamez" (games), "appz" (applications), "crackz" (cracked applications), and "vidz" (movies).' (Wikipedia: http://en.wikipedia.org/wiki/Warez).

Chapter 6　Computer Content Crime

1 The original Jennicam pages at www.jennicam.com have now been removed. However, a history of the site along with some archives can be found at 'The Peeping Moe's JenniCAM Fan Page' at www.89.com/ d/?d=voyeur-jennicam.
2 The legal arrangements are slightly different in Scotland and are covered by section 51 (Obscene Material), section 52 (Indecent Photographs of Children) and section 52a (Possession of Indecent Photographs of Children) of the Civic Government (Scotland) Act 1982.
3 Statistics from the 'Operation Ore' pages of Survivors Swindon at www.survivorsswindon.com/ore.htm.
4 It must be noted here that there is some contention about Harding's claims. He states that 'snuff movies' are hard to find on the internet but

a 'user comment' from 2006 states that he/she had no problem in finding such sites.

5 See Mann and Sutton (1998) for a very useful description of the use of news groups for the distribution of information about the technologies used for committing offences.

6 See Schneier on 'Security': a weblog covering security and security technology at www.schneier.com/blog/archives/2005/08/london_bombing_1. html.

7 In the USA by the First Amendment to the US Constitution, and in Canada by the Canadian Charter of Rights, section 2.

8 http://protest.net/activists_handbook/economist_article.html – http:// protest.net/

9 Also see the 'Gangs or Us' pages on gangs and the internet at www.gang-sorus.com/Internet.html.

10 For a useful overview of the legislation applying to offensive emails, see Angus Hamilton's 'Awkward Customers' at www.hamiltons-solicitors.co. uk/archive-docs/awkward-customers 1.htm; also Neil Addison's web pages at www.harassment-law.co.uk.

11 See www.hamiltons-solicitors.co.uk/archive-docs/awkward-customers 1. htm.

Chapter 7   Cybercrime Futures

1 Brightmail's Probe Network Findings (Brightmail, 2002) used the following categories: Adult (8%), Financial (19%), Products (24%), Internet (14%), Other (35%).

2 See www.o-a.com/archive/1997/June/0197.html.

3 For up-to-date information on current spam legislation see the website of CAUCE (Coalition Against Unsolicited Commercial Email) at www. cauce.org.

4 To be distinguished from the parasitic computing that effectively 'steals' computing power from a network of individual computers (see Barabasi et al., 2001: 894; Barger and Crowell, 2004).

Chapter 8   Policing Online Behaviour

1 The research reported here took place after the National Hi-Tech Crime Unit had been announced, but before it formally came into operation.

2 A search using the key words 'reporting crimes to the police online' reveals many police-driven websites.

3 See further Donna M. Hughes' pages on 'Independent Tiplines and Vigilantes', at www.uri.edu/artsci/wms/hughes/ppitv.htm. This is a record of groups active in the late 1990s; some have since gone to ground or disbanded.

4 See further the 'Resolving Feedback Disputes' pages at http://pages. ebay.com/help/feedback/feedback-disputes.html. Note that the eBay system operates very differently to Amazon's book rating system.
5 I must thank Sophie Wall for enlightening me on the intricacies of the Habbo world.
6 See PayPal acceptable use policy with regard to gambling (18 May 2006) at www.paypal.com.
7 This is a hypothesis based upon observations and requires further research.

Chapter 9   Controlling and Preventing Cybercrime

1 See paragraphs 40, 41, 42, 43, 44, 45. The full text of the EU Directive on privacy and electronic communications (concerning the processing of personal data and the protection of privacy in the electronic communications sector) is available at europa.eu.int/eur-lex/pri/en/oj/dat/2002/ l_201/l_20120020731en00370047.pdf.
2 Others such as Kurt Einzinger, general secretary of Internet Service Providers Austria, have claimed that the percentage from the USA is even higher at around 80 per cent (Ermert, 2004).
3 I am referring here only to nuisance and minor infringements.

Chapter 10   Conclusions

1 Hard-wiring is a metaphor that signifies the construction of permanent structures of surveillance. Of course, the future structures will in fact be soft-wired through ambient technologies.

Glossary

advanced fee frauds are fraudulent tactics that deceive victims into paying fees in advance to facilitate a transaction which purportedly benefits them. Nigerian, or 419, frauds (after the Nigerian penal code which criminalizes them) deceive recipients into allowing the use of their bank account to help fraudsters allegedly to remove money out of their country. Once involved in the scam the victim is required to pay a series of advance fees to facilitate the transaction, which never takes place. Variations use internet auctions or online dating forums to obtain advance fees.

ambient technology joins devices together to create a wireless informational environment that links domestic household, business and leisure devices to assist the individual and improve their quality of life by automating many routine chores.

arbitrage/parallel imports is the exploitation of pricing differentials between different markets.

assemblage is a concept derived from Deleuze and Guattari (1987) which explains that phenomena may have an association with each other and even work together as a functional entity, but do not necessarily have any other unity.

asymmetry literally means the absence of symmetry. It is used in this book to describe the way that one individual can interact with many others simultaneously. Asymmetric relationships lead to *viral information flows*.

asynchronicity describes communications that take place outside conventional time-frames, for example in 'chosen-time', chosen by the end users in an email communication stream.

auction frauds is the use of internet auction sites to commit fraudulent acts, usually luring bidders into a transaction outside the auction site, or by selling fake or poor quality goods. Alternatively, the bank cheque clearance processes may be exploited.

black hat see *hacker*

blended threats are a type of *malicious software* that employs simultaneously, through multiple infection, a combination of attack techniques that make the viruses and worms even more potent and also much harder to detect.

blogs or **blogsites** are internet diaries or personal online journals shared with an online audience. They tend to be interlinked and the network of blogs forms an interconnected blog environment, a 'blogosphere', in which information and debate can escalate rapidly and virally, creating a frenzy of, sometimes heated, discussion known as a blogstorm.

bot herders see *botnets*

botnets comprise lists of the *internet protocol (IP) addresses* of 'zombie' computers that have been infected by *remote administration tools (malcode)* and which can subsequently be controlled remotely. Botnets are valuable commodities because of the power they can place in the hands of the remote administrators (bot herders) to deliver a range of harmful *malicious software*. For this purpose they can be hired out, sold, or traded.

bulletin board systems (BBS) are the forerunners to the *internet* and were popular from the mid-1980s to the mid-1990s. Located on locally situated individual computers fitted with remote dial-up software they allow users to connect to them and communicate with others who are also logged on to the same system.

cam girls see *web cams*

chat rooms are online forums that allow individuals to chat to fellow members in real time. They evolved from the usenet *newsgroups* (prefixed by 'alt.') into *internet relay chat* (IRC). The main difference between the two is that chat rooms operate in real-time, whereas newsgroups work in chosen time through the posting of messages and responses to those messages.

child pornography is the use of 'obscene' images of children by viewers to elicit sexual arousal.

chilling effect describes the way that a fear of legal or economic action encourages self-censorship.

click fraud/bogus click syndrome defrauds the internet advertising billing systems by bulk clicking advertisements either by low wage labour or automated scripts.

code can have two meanings. The first is with regard to codes that grant owners access to a secure environment. The second is a more colloquial term for software programming language.

computer is an electronic device that executes pre-determined instructions in the form of a program to manipulate data and, when networked, it becomes the platform from which networked activity takes place.

counterfeits are imitations of an object or virtual artefact constructed intentionally to deceive users into thinking that they possess the qualities and characteristics of the original.

cracker see *hacker*

crime harvest refers to the criminal gain made by offenders during the period between the opening of a window of criminal opportunity and its closure, by, for example, security 'patches' or public information.

cybercrime wave describes the very quick and almost 'viral' proliferation of cybercrimes across globalized networks. They are sometimes referred to as cyber-tsunamis.

cybercrimes are criminal or harmful activities that are informational, global and networked and are to be distinguished from crimes that simply use computers. They are the product of networked technologies that have transformed the division of criminal labour to provide entirely new opportunities for, and new forms of, crime which typically involve the acquisition or manipulation of information and its value across global networks for gain. They can be broken down into crimes which are related to the integrity of the system, crimes in which networked computers are used to assist the perpetration of crime, and crimes which relate to the content of computers. They tend to be individually small in impact though their harms are caused by their sheer volume.

cyberspace is the mentally constructed virtual environment within which networked computer activity takes place. The term was first used by novelist William Gibson in the early 1980s.

cyber-terrorism uses computers to attack the physical infrastructure to generate mass fear and anxiety and, in theory, manipulate the political agenda.

cyberworlds see *virtual environment*

darkside hackers evolve from script kiddies and are driven by financial or other types of gain. They are sometimes called crackers.

data doubling refers to the comparing of an individual's access codes (personal information) with data already held by the computer system to verify his or her access rights and identity.

data mining – see *dataveillance*

data trails are left by the informational transactions required to secure access to, and navigation around, the internet. They are also sometimes known as 'mouse droppings'.

dataveillance is the use of data trails, usually by mining databases, to provide evidence of transactions or to identify abnormal patterns of behaviour.

de minimism is from *de minimis non curat lex*, where it means the 'law does not deal with trifles'. It is used in this book to describe low-impact, bulk victimizations that cause large aggregated losses spread out globally across potentially all known jurisdictions.

deskilling describes the process of rationalizing and 'degrading' labour by breaking it down into essential tasks which are then automated to increase the efficiency and economy of the operation. The deskilling process is accompanied by a reskilling process whereby fewer people gain control over the whole automated process.

digital realism is a term used in this book to emphasize that the more a behaviour is mediated (shaped) by the architecture of networked technology, the more it can be governed by that same technology. The potential concerns arising from this *ubiquitous law enforcement* invokes debates about the role of technology and other forms of control (law, social values, market control) in tempering or legitimizing the use of technology as a means of governing online behaviour.

distributed denial of service (DDOS) attacks prevent legitimate users from gaining access to their web space (networks and computer systems) by bombarding access gateways with a barrage of data.

domain name systems (DNS) servers translate domain names into *IP (internet protocol)* addresses that facilitate access to, and navigation around, the world wide web.

drive-by downloads are a method of infection by *malicious software* disguised as images or software that are downloaded during the course of browsing the web.

end-to-end describes the internet's original principle of free communications online while leaving the end users the choice over what to, and what not to, receive.

escrow is an arrangement whereby two sides involved in a transaction supply a trusted third-party with finance, objects or access codes that are released once the conditions of the transaction have been fulfilled.

fraud is a deception perpetrated by one individual in order to obtain an advantage over another. The object of the fraud may be purely financial or informational. See *advanced fee frauds, click fraud, input fraud, output fraud, payment fraud, salami fraud, scams, short-firm fraud.*

gambling scams see *scams*

game cheats are virtual artefacts that enable players to map their way through computer games more quickly or gain access to hidden spaces within them. Some cheats exploit flaws in gaming programs, while others are strategically placed there by the game makers to sustain players' interest in the game.

gemeinschaft/gesellschaft are sociological terms used by Ferdinand Tönnies in 1887 to describe the transition from (gemeinschaft) organic communities based upon neighbourhood and familial bonds to (gesellschaft) communities of association defined by a common instrumental goal.

globalization is a social process that configures and reconfigures the relationships that exist between multiple entities from individuals to international agencies which are widely distributed in space.

glocalization describes the impact of globalized ideas upon a locality.

graphics user interface (GUI) uses graphical images in the form of pictures and words to represent information. GUI is associated with the advent of Windows and replaced the older text-based displays.

grid computing/technology see *peer-to-peer networks*

gullibility viruses use *social engineering* to trick individuals into deleting part of their computer's operating system.

gurus are expert 'white hat' *hackers*.

hacker is a term that has a history in the experimentation of often illicit access to communications systems. Computer hackers evolved to explore the boundaries of informational access and also the integrity of secure systems. 'White hat' hackers, *wizards* and *gurus* are allegedly driven by ethical motivations, whereas 'black hat' hackers, or crackers, are primarily motivated by the prospect of gain. See *samurai*, and 'black hat' *script kiddies* and *darkside hackers*. Also see *hacktivism*.

hacktivism is a fusion of ethical hacking and the use of computer technique to effect political protest.

hate speech seeks intentionally to degrade, exclude, intimidate, or incite violence or prejudicial action against someone based on their race, ethnicity, national origin, religion, sexual orientation, or disability.

honeynets are fake websites constructed to socially engineer offenders into accessing them and showing intent by wilfully passing through various levels of security, agreeing at each stage that they are aware of the content and indicating their intent. Offenders eventually find themselves facing a law enforcement message (a 'gotcha') and a notice that that their details will be recorded or that they will become subject to investigation in cases where intent is clear.

hotspot paranoia is the fear that free public *wi-fi* hotspots will create new opportunities for cybercrime.

identity theft/ID theft is the fraudulent acquisition of personal information that can be used to obtain credit facilities or take control of existing accounts online. It is often mistakenly used to describe credit card theft.

information society is a society in which the relationships of production/consumption, power and experience have been transformed by information technology. It is a product of the *network society*.

information warfare is commonly used today in a non-militaristic context to describe the use of information, misinformation or disinformation to shape public confidence with regard to patterns of consumption or participation in the democratic process. It is often confused with *cyber-terrorism*.

informational property is a term that refers to the rights of ownership over information. Although narrower in scope than *intellectual property*, the two are, however, often used coterminously.

input fraud refers to the illegal acquisition of credit facilities, typically credit cards.

intellectual property covers a range of claims and entitlements to the ways that ideas are expressed. The laws that establish and define intellectual property include copyright, trademarks, patents and designs.

internet is a global network of interconnected government, military, corporate, business and domestic computer networks. It is not a network but a network of networks. It is the platform upon which the *world wide web* operates.

internet protocol (IP) addresses are unique numerical identifiers that networked devices use to identify each other and then communicate once a route has been opened.

internet relay chat (IRC) see *chat rooms*

internet service providers (ISPs) are businesses that provide internet users access to internet and related services through a range of media that include dial-up, digital subscriber line (DSL) through telephone wires, Integrated Services Digital Network (ISDN) switched through telephone wires, broadband *wireless*, broadband through cable TV.

internet storms see *blogs* and *viral information flow*

internet year: Moore's Law states that hardware evolution is increasing desktop computing power by 2 to the n power. Calculations based upon this 1965 formula estimate that the rate of change is such that one internet year equals approximately three months or less in real-time.

java applets are small programs written in the Java programming language that can be included in an HTML webpage. They are used to provide interactive features to web applications that cannot be provided by the HTML (HyperText Markup Language), which is the main language used for creating web pages.

key-stroke loggers are diagnostic tools that record a user's keystrokes. Originally designed to identify errors in systems, they were subsequently put to use measuring employee's work output. More recently they have been incorporated in *spyware* to keep a log of the victim's keystrokes (including passwords, etc.) and return the information to a web address. They have also been used to spy upon offenders.

leet (l33t) comes from the phonetic form of 'elite' and was originally intended to signify communications between members of an elite group. Alternatively known as leetspeak, it uses non-alphabetical numbers that resemble syllables or sounds in words, for example, leet would become l33t or 1337. Many hackers reject it as they consider it to be an affectation.

local area networks (LAN) are local computer networks that serve small defined areas, such as an office, and usually link to WANs (wide area networks). Their advantage is to increase the speed of access in sharing files, plus they can be configured to suit particular office work practices.

logic bomb is a type of *malicious software* that activates once predetermined criteria are met, such as a specific date or after a system has been accessed a specified number of times. The best known of these is 'Michelangelo' which only activates on 6 March, Michelangelo's birthday.

lottery scams see *scams*

malicious software (**malware/malcode**) comprises software scripts that seek to disrupt, damage or steal information from computer systems. 'Worms' self-propagate themselves across networks by exploiting security flaws and are distinguished from 'viruses' which tend to infect static files and therefore require the actions of users to assist with their propagation. *Blended threats* are meta-trojans which can embody a combination of worms and viruses depending upon their intended purpose.

MP3 (full name MPEG-1 Audio Layer 3) is an audio compression format, which exploits the fallibility of the human ear by removing inaudible analogue sounds. By saving space, it enables sound files to be efficiently transmitted across the *internet*.

MP4 (MPEG-4) is a computer file compression format like *MP3* which allows video, audio and other information to be stored efficiently on one file and transmitted across the *internet*.

network society: Manuel Castells (2000a) (after Van Dijk, 1991) has argued that one of the hallmarks of the *information society*/age is the network society that emerged from the historical convergence of three independent processes during the late twentieth century: the information technology revolution in the 1970s; the restructuring of capitalism and of statism in the 1980s; the cultural social movements of the 1960s and their 1970s aftermath. Thus the network society, often attributed to the internet, actually predated it by a number of decades, but while the information technology revolution did not create the network society, it arguably would not exist in its present form without it.

networked technology is the various hard and software technologies plus protocols that enable computing devices to communicate with each other.

newsgroups see *chat rooms*

obscene materials are ideas and thoughts expressed in words, images and actions which offend the prevailing social morality. Most jurisdictions have laws which define where the boundaries of obscenity lie, but definitions are not always the same. Although the term 'obscene' can be applied broadly, legal and moral debates over 'obscene' materials tend to focus upon the depiction of sexual activities (extreme *pornography*).

output fraud refers to the use of credit facilities to obtain goods, services or money fraudulently.

panopticon: Bentham's panopticon prison design allowed prison officers to see prisoners without being seen. The disciplinary theory arising from Foucault's analysis (1983: 223) of the panopticon is that prisoners never knew when they being watched and therefore obeyed prison rules of conduct because they feared punishment. After a period of time under the panoptic gaze, prisoners eventually adhered to the regime and modified their behaviour to comply with the rules. The panopticon illustrates how prison architecture shapes the physical and mental architecture of the prison and therefore the relationships within it, especially the power relationship between the observer (guard) and the observed (prisoner). This theory lends itself to internet surveillance and to theorizing about the governance of online behaviour.

payment fraud is fraud that takes place in the payment phase of a transaction.

peer-to-peer networks (P2P) rely upon user participation to create networks to generate new forms of decentralized commercial and informational relationships between individuals. Variations of P2P are business to business (B2B) and business to consumer (B2C) and vice versa. The term is often confused with *grid computing* which connects distributed computers to create a virtual computer architecture that has a computing power that is greater than the sum of its parts.

people hacking see *social engineering*

personal digital assistants (PDAs) are small, but powerful, hand-held computers that can be connected to the internet by *wireless technologies*.

pharming is an automated version of *phishing* that does not rely upon *social engineering* to trick the recipient because it automatically redirects the recipient to the offending site.

phishing is the use of internet communications, e.g. emails, to *socially engineer* (trick people) out of personal financial information. Variations include 'spear phishing' where specific, rather than blanket, targets are chosen. Also *pharming, smishing, vishing*.

phlooding is a multiple *distributed denial of service (DDOS)* attack caused by a group of simultaneous, though geographically distributed, attacks which target the network log-in structure of a particular business to overload its central authentication server.

piracy is a term frequently used to describe the unauthorized reproduction and distribution of electronic and audio-visual media that are protected by *intellectual property* copyright laws. It is most commonly used with regard to the unauthorized distribution of *MP3* and *MP4* files.

policing is a term used broadly within this book to describe the act of regulating the behaviour of a population, usually to maintain order and enforce law. Although this function is commonly performed by the police (public police organizations), they are not the sole actors performing this function, indeed they arguably perform only a small part of 'policing'.

pornography describes the visual, textual or oral depiction of the human body with the intention of sexually arousing those who experience it. It is often linked to, but is distinguishable from, erotica which also has artistic merit. While pornography may be morally illicit, pornography is not necessarily illegal unless it is deemed to be *obscene*.

pseudo-photographs use new graphics technologies to 'morph' or graphically blend two photographic images together to make a new image with new meaning. The various laws relating to *pornographic* 'pseudo photographs' were amended in the early to mid-1990s to make possession of them illegal because they weakened the case for the prosecution which had long relied upon the fact that an individual (usually a child) had been abused in the construction of the picture.

pump and dump scams deceive stock market investors through the circulation of information on the internet that misrepresents the value and potential of real stock. This misinformation artificially drives up the price of the stock (the pump), which is then sold off at inflated prices (the dump).

pyramid selling scams have migrated online. They are elaborate confidence tricks which recruit punters with the promise of a good return on investment by introducing new recruits to the scheme. They are doomed to fail because they merely redistribute income towards the initiators and the many losers pay for the few winners. The schemes are fuelled by the fact that the very early investors often do get a good return on their money and their enthusiasm advertises their apparent authenticity.

ransom virus/ransomware is *malicious software* that hijacks a computer system until it is neutralized by a code provided by a blackmailer once a ransom has been paid.

ratware/remote administration trojans (RATs) are a form of *malicious software* that makes an infected 'zombie' computer become susceptible to remote administration and inclusion in a *botnet*.

reputation management systems: vendors build up profiles based upon customer feedback on their past sales performance which enables potential purchasers to vet them before making bids. Good reputations are highly valued and maintaining them discourages dishonest behaviour by vendors and bidders. See '*short-firm' fraud*.

reskilling see *deskilling*

reverse social engineering see *social engineering*

rogue dialler is a type of *malicious software* that automatically and discretely transfers users' existing telephone services from the normal domestic rate to a premium line service in order to defraud them.

salami fraud describes the perpetration of many small frauds from different sources or over a long time span, which are individually minor but large in aggregate.

samurai are *ethical hackers* who hire themselves out to undertake legal 'cracking' tasks and assist those who have legitimate reasons to use an electronic locksmith.

scams are confidence tricks, typically undertaken to engage and defraud a victim. Internet scams commonly originate in *spam* communications and include (a) health cure scams which seek to deceive victims by offering the promise of improvements to health, say, through performance enhancing drugs or surgery, or they may claim to cure ill health through various snake oil remedies; (b) finance scams, which seek to deceive victims by offering the promise of improvements to their finances, and include *phishing, pyramid selling, pump and dump*; (c) advertising scams which lure victims by offering free or discounted products, goods and services; (d) pornography scams which lure victims with offers of free access to sexual imagery; (e) others which include 'lottery scams', in which victims are lured by telling them that they have won a prize which they can claim once advance fees are paid or personal information is provided, and 'gambling scams' which entrap victims with a free line of gambling credit.

script kiddies are inexperienced and unskilled hackers who seek peer respect for their audacity by infiltrating or disrupting computer systems by using cracking scripts that they have designed.

short-firm fraud is a term used in this book to describe the fraudulent exploitation of online auction reputation management systems. Typically, once a good vendor 'trust' rating has been acquired then items are sold, usually offline to runners-up in the bidding war, and the vendor disappears without supplying the goods once the money has been received.

simulacra (simulacrum in singular) is a term used by Jean Baudrillard (1994) to describe a situation where one can have copies without originals. It introduces a useful language to describe the construction and dissemination of multi-media materials in computer file format.

simulation captures the essence of a real object in such a way that it can be used to observe and predict how that object may behave when subject to changing inputs.

situational crime prevention focuses upon the reduction of criminal opportunity by increasing the effort needed to commit a crime, increasing the risks to the offender, or reducing the reward of crime. It tends to ignore consideration of intent.

smishing is a form of *phishing* which uses bulk text messaging facilities to target mobile devices such as phones or PDAs (*personal digital assistants*) with urgent text requests for the recipient to call an alleged bank phone number or log onto a website and change their security information, thereby revealing it.

snake oil scams see *scams*

social engineering or 'people hacking' is the use of interpersonal deceptions to trick staff within organizations into giving out personal information such as passwords to secure systems by building up trust relationships with them and exploiting their personal weaknesses. 'Reverse social engineering' is where a hacker causes a technical problem within a system and then positions himself or herself to be commissioned to fix it, thereby gaining access.

social networking websites offer interactive, user-submitted networks of friends, personal profiles, blogs, groups, photos, music and videos. They connect people who possess different types of interests. Examples include MySpace, LiveJournal.com.

software defined radio see *wireless technology*

spam/spamming is the distribution of unsolicited bulk emails that deliver invitations to participate in schemes to earn money; obtain free products and services; win prizes; spy upon others; obtain improvements to health or well-being, replace lost hair, increase one's sexual prowess or cure cancer. They choke up bandwidth and present risks to the recipient should they respond.

spoofing is a term that describes an act where people, through software, falsify information in order to pretend to be someone or something else so as to deceive another to gain an illicit advantage over them.

spyware is software that covertly surveils the user's computer files to obtain and return personal information about the user.

surveillance is the act of monitoring the behaviour of another either in real-time using cameras, audio devices or key-stroke monitoring, or in chosen time by *data mining* records of internet transactions. Surveillance can be overt or covert. User awareness of being surveilled in real or chosen time can shape their online behaviour. See *panopticon*.

synopticon is the other end of the telescope to the panopticon in that 'the many watch the few' rather than 'the few watch the many'. As with the panopticon, knowledge of synoptic surveillance similarly has the potential to shape online behaviour.

TCP/IP (transmission control protocol/internet protocol): adopted in 1982 by the US Department of Defense and ratified in 1985 by the Internet Architecture Board, TCP/IP layered protocols enable internet communications to take place. They are the technical core of the internet.

technology is a term which describes the expression of ideas about methods that rationalize human activity. Usually such expression involves the use of tools – in this book, hardware and software – but it is the ideas and rationale behind the tools that are of primary interest.

trojans see *malicious software*

ubiquitous law enforcement arises from the *digital realism* that the same technologies which provide opportunities for cybercrime also provide opportunities for law enforcement and crime prevention. It creates a new agenda with regard to debate over the appropriate use of technologies in the policing function.

unsolicited bulk email see *spam*

URL (uniform resource locator) is simply another name for a web address (begins http://).

viral information flow is a term that describes how information proliferates across distributed networks by word of 'mouse' (rather than mouth). The information flows can be almost viral in the way that they are distributed exponentially from node to node across networks. The term 'viral' is now used colloquially to describe the internet video phenomenon; indeed they are actually called 'virals'.

virtual environment is a term often used synonymously with *cyberspace*, but virtual environments, such as Habbo Hotel or Second Life, to name but two, are actually the localities of cyberspace.

virus see *malicious software*

vishing is another form of *phishing* that uses *VoIP (voice over internet protocol)* to *spam* recorded messages to telephone numbers. The *VoIP* messages purport to be from banks, other financial institutions, online merchants such as Amazon or internet *auction* houses such as eBay, and warn that their credit card has been used for fraudulent transactions. As with *phishing* and its variations, recipients are asked to contact a phone number or logon to a website to verify and change their security information.

VoIP (voice over internet protocol) is a method of enabling telephone conversations to take place over the internet or through any other internet protocol (IP) based network.

web cams are cameras linked to networked computers via a website whose real-time images can be watched from afar by all who access the particular site. Their use ranges from closed circuit surveillance to video-conferencing. They were made popular in the mid-1990s by *cam girls*, such as JenniCAM, who broadcast voyeuristic images of themselves for a fee.

webmail is email that can be sent through a web browser, e.g. hotmail or Yahoo, rather than a dedicated email program such as Microsoft Outlook.

white-collar crime is a term that describes crimes of the powerful and crimes that are normally hidden from 'blue collar' criminologies of street crime. Cybercrime shares many of the characteristics of hidden crimes and can be informed by those debates; however, the fit with white-collar crime is not so easy since informational knowledge is power within *cyberspace*.

white hat see *hacker*

wi-fi is the form of *wireless technology* that enables wireless internet connections, but it is increasingly becoming the basis for connecting many other domestic electronic appliances.

wireless technology is a general term that describes the connectivity of a range of mobile IT equipment such as wireless networked computers, *personal digital assistants* (PDAs), mobile phones, and also wireless computer mice and keyboards, general positioning satellite units (GPS), even garage doors, satellite television and cordless telephones. New developments in 'software defined radio' (Tower of Babel technology) will radically change wireless technology by allowing devices supporting different protocols to talk to each other.

wizards are 'white hat' *hackers* who are renowned for their hacking knowledge.

world wide web (**www**) runs on the *internet* and is a network of interlinked and hypertext multimedia documents known as web pages.

worms see *malicious software*

zombies see *botnets* and *ratware*

Cases and References

Cases

ACLU et al. v. Reno (1997), 117 S. Ct. 2329.

Ashcroft v. Free Speech Coalition (2002) 535 U.S. 234 (2002) 198 F.3d 1083.

CompuServe Inc. V. Cyber Promotions, Inc. (1997) 962 F. Supp. 1015 (S.D. Ohio 1997).

Godfrey v. Demon Internet Ltd. (1999) 4 All E.R. 342.

In re Doubleclick Inc. (2001) 154 F. Supp.2d 497 – S.D.N.Y., March 28.

In re Verizon Internet Services, Inc. (2003); at http://news.findlaw.com/hdocs/docs/verizon/inreverizon12103opn.pdf.

Keith-Smith v. Williams (2006) EWHC 860.

League Against Racism and Anti-Semitism (LICRA) and The Union of French Jewish Students (UEJF) v. Yahoo Inc. and Yahoo France (2000), Interim Court Order, 20 November, The County Court of Paris, No. RG: 00/05308.

Metro-Goldwyn-Mayer Studios, Inc. v. Grokster, Ltd. (2004) 9th Circuit Court of Appeals, 19 August; at www.eff.org/IP/P2P/MGM_v_Grokster/20040819_mgm_v_grokster_decision.pdf.

Paris Adult Theater I v. Slaton (1973) 413 U.S. 49.

People v. Somm (1998), Amtsgericht Munich [Local Court], File No. 8340 Ds 465 Js 173158/95 (F.R.G.) (May), later overturned on appeal (173158/99).

Planned Parenthood v. ACLA (2001) *Planned Parenthood of the Columbia/Willamette, Inc. v. American Coalition of Life Activists*, No. 99–35320, 2001 U.S. App. LEXIS 4974 (9th Cir. Mar. 28, 2001).

Public Prosecutor v. Jon Lech Johansen (2003) Case No. 02-507 M/94, Oslo Court House, 7 January; at www.eff.org/IP/Video/Johansen_DeCSS_case/20030109_johansen_english_decision.rtf.

R. v. Jonathan Bowden (2000) 1 Cr. App. R. 438.

R. v. Brown (1993) 97 Cr. App. R. 44, (1994) 1 A.C. 212.

R. v. Fellows; R. v. Arnold (1997) 2 All ER 548.

R. v. Handyside v. United Kingdom (1976) 1 EHRR 737.

R. v. Wilson (1996) 2 Cr App Rep 241.

R. v. Zundel (1992) 95 D.L.R. (4th) 202 (1992) and (Can.Sup. Ct. Aug. 27, 1992, unreported).

Roberts v. Media Logistics (UK) Ltd (2006); http://spamlegalaction.pbwiki. com/.

United States v. Alkhabaz (1997); U.S. App. LEXIS 9060; (1996) 104 F.3d 1492; (1995) 48 F.3d 1220 and U.S. App. Lexis 11244.

United States v. Dost (1986) 636 F. Supp. 828.

United States of America v. Robert A. Thomas and Carleen Thomas (1996) 74 F.3d 701; 1996 U.S. App. Lexis 1069; 1996 Fed App. 0032P (6th Cir.).

References

AberdeenGroup, Inc. (2002) *Identity Management Systems: A Core Business Competence: An Executive White Paper*, Boston: Aberdeen Group, September, at www.aberdeen.com/summary/report/whitepaper/ 09022806.asp.

Abrams, P. (1982) *Historical Sociology*, Shepton Mallet: Open Books.

Adams, J. A. (1996) 'Controlling cyberspace: applying the computer fraud and abuse act to the internet', *Santa Clara Computer and High Technology Law Journal*, 12: 403–34.

Adams, S. (1998) *The Dilbert Future: Thriving on Business Stupidity in the 21st Century*, London: HarperBusiness.

Adler, A. (2001) 'The perverse law of child pornography', *Columbia Law Review*, 101: 209–73.

Agger, B. (2004) *The Virtual Self: A Contemporary Sociology*, Oxford: Blackwell.

AIN (2005) 'ASACP changes name: Association of Sites Advocating Child Protection', *Adult Industry News*, 2 March, at www.ainews.com/ story/8557/.

Akdeniz, Y. (1996) 'Computer pornography: a comparative study of US and UK obscenity laws and child pornography laws in relation to the internet', *International Review of Law, Computers and Technology*, 10 (2): 235–61.

Akdeniz, Y. (1997) 'The regulation of pornography and child pornography on the internet', *Journal of Information Law and Technology*, (1), at www2.warwick.ac.uk/fac/soc/law/elj/jilt/1997_1/akdeniz1/.

Akdeniz, Y. (2001) 'Controlling illegal and harmful content on the internet'. In D. S. Wall (ed.), *Crime and the Internet*, London: Routledge, 113–40.

Akdeniz, Y., Walker, C. P. and Wall. D. S. (eds) (2000) *The Internet, Law and Society*, London: Longman.

Allen, J., Forrest, S., Levi, M., Roy, H. and Sutton, M. (2005) 'Fraud and technology crimes: findings from the 2002/03 British Crime Survey and 2003 Offending, Crime and Justice Survey', *Home Office Online Report* 34/05, at www.homeoffice.gov.uk/rds/pdfs05/rdsolr 3405.pdf.

Anderson, A. (2000) *Snake Oil, Hustlers and Hambones: The American Medicine Show*, Jefferson, NC: McFarland.

APACS (2005a) *The UK Payments Industry: A Review of 2004*, London: APACS at www.apacs.org.uk/downloads/Annual Review 2004.pdf.

APACS (2005b) 'UK card fraud losses reach £504.8m: criminals increase their efforts as chip and PIN starts to make its mark', APACS press release, 8 March, London: APACS, at www.apacs.org.uk/downloads/cardfraudfigures%20national&regional%20-%208mar05.pdf.

APACS (2005c) *Card Fraud The Facts 2005*, APACS, at www.cardwatch.org.uk/pdf_files/cardfraudfacts 2005.pdf.

APACS (2006) *Fraud: The Facts 2006*, APACS, at www.apacs.org.uk/resources_publications/documents/FraudtheFacts 2006.pdf.

APIG, (2004) *Revision of the Computer Misuse Act: Report of an Inquiry by the All Party Internet Group*, June. at www.apig.org.uk/CMAReportFinal Version1.pdf.

APWG (2005) 'Phishing Activity Trends Report', April, at http://antiphishing.org/APWG_Phishing_Activity_Report_April_2005.pdf.

Appel, E. (2003) 'US cybercrime: model solutions', paper given to *Technologies for Public Safety in Critical Incident Response*, National Institute of Justice, Office of Science and Technology, 23 September, at www.nlectc.org/training/nij2003/Appel.pdf.

Arnott, S. (2003a) 'Strategies to defeat the terrorist threat: technology projects are at the heart of national security', *Computing*, 28 May, at www.computing.co.uk/News/1141224.

Arnott, S. (2003b) 'Security data project to combat terrorism: potential IT suppliers must apply for clearance for top-secret initiative' *Computing*, 28 May, at www.computing.co.uk/News/1141223.

Arthur, C. (2005) 'Interview with a link spammer', *The Register*, 31 January, at www.theregister.co.uk/2005/01/31/link_spamer_interview/.

Artòsi, A. (2002) 'On the notion of an empowered agent', paper to the 2002 workshop on the Law of Electronic Agents, Bologna, at www.cirfid.unibo.it/~lea-02/pp/Artosi.pdf.

Austin, J. (1962) *How to Do Things with Words*, Oxford: Clarendon Press.

Balkin, J. (2004) 'Virtual liberty: freedom to design and freedom to play in virtual worlds', *Virginia Law Review*, 90 (8): 2044–98, at www.yale.edu/lawweb/jbalkin/articles/virtual_liberty1.pdf.

Ballard, M. (2006) 'Police offered robot eye: Intelligence gets "intelligent"', *The Register*, 1 June, at www.theregister.co.uk/2006/06/01/police_eye/.

Barabasi, A.-L., Freeh, V. W., Jeong, H. and Brockman, J. B. (2001) 'Parasitic computing', *Nature*, 412: 894–7.

Barger, R. N. and Crowell, C. R. (2004) 'The ethics of parasitic computing: fair use or abuse of TCP/IP over the Internet?', in L. A. Freeman, and A. G. Peace (eds), *Information Ethics: Privacy and Intellectual Property*, Hershey, PA: Idea Group, ch. 9.

Barlow, J. P. (1994) 'The economy of ideas: a framework for rethinking patents and copyrights in the digital age (Everything you know about intellectual property is wrong)', *Wired*, 2 (3): 84.

Barlow, J. P. (1996) 'A declaration of the independence of Cyberspace', *John Perry Barlow Library*, at www.eff.org/Misc/Publications/John_Perry_Barlow/barlow_0296.declaration.txt.

Baron, L. and Straus, M. (1989) *Four Theories of Rape in American Society: A State-Level Analysis*, New Haven and London: Yale University Press.

Barone, M. (2004) 'The national interest: absence of evidence is not evidence of absence', *US News & World Report*, 24 March, at www.usnews.com/usnews/opinion/baroneweb/mb_040324.htm.

Barrett, N. (2004) *Traces of Guilt*, London: Bantam Press.

Bates, M. (2001) 'Emerging trends in information brokering', *Competitive Intelligence Review*, 8 (4): 48–53.

Baudrillard, J. (1988) 'Consumer society', in M. Poster (ed.), *Jean Baudrillard: Selected Writings*, Oxford: Blackwell.

Baudrillard, J. (1994) *Simulacra and Simulation*, Ann Arbor: University of Michigan Press.

Baudrillard, J. (1998) *The Consumer Society: Myths and Structures*, London: Sage.

Bauman, Z. (1998) *Globalization: The Human Consequences*, Cambridge: Polity.

BBC (1999a) 'Cyberstalking: pursued in cyber space', *BBC News Online*, 26 June, at http://news.bbc.co.uk/1/hi/uk/378373.stm.

BBC (1999b) 'Internet football hooligan probe', *BBC News Online*, 8 August, at http://news.bbc.co.uk/1/hi/uk/414634.stm.

BBC (2001a) 'US to close Echelon spy station', *BBC News Online*, 2 June, at http://news.bbc.co.uk/1/hi/world/europe/1365156.stm.

BBC (2001b) 'Warning over Nigerian mail scam', *BBC News Online*, 10 July, at http://news.bbc.co.uk/hi/english/uk/newsid_1431000/1431761.stm.

BBC (2002a) 'Shoe bomb suspect "did not act alone"', *BBC News Online*, 25 January, at http://news.bbc.co.uk/1/hi/world/americas/1783237.stm.

BBC (2002b) 'Asylum seekers given "smart" ID cards', *BBC News Online*, 31 January, at http://news.bbc.co.uk/1/hi/uk_politics/1793151.stm.

BBC (2003a) 'In defence of "net naming and shaming"', *BBC News Online*, 6 January, at http://news.bbc.co.uk/1/hi/technology/2631143.stm.

BBC (2003b) 'Net "naming and shaming" wins support', *BBC News Online*, 7 January, at http://news.bbc.co.uk/1/hi/technology/2634809.stm.

BBC (2003c) 'Tax records "for sale" scandal', *BBC News Online*, 16 January, at http://news.bbc.co.uk/1/hi/business/2662491.stm.

BBC (2003d) 'Spammers and virus writers unite', *BBC News Online*, 30 April, 2003, at http://news.bbc.co.uk/1/hi/technology/2988209.stm.

BBC (2003e) 'Public oppose ID card scheme', *BBC News Online*, 19 June, at http://news.bbc.co.uk/1/hi/technology/3004376.stm.

BBC (2003f) 'Plans for "£40 ID cards"', *BBC News Online*, 6 July, at http://news.bbc.co.uk/1/hi/uk_politics/3048386.stm.

BBC (2003g) 'US snooping plan blocked', *BBC News Online*, 18 July, at http://news.bbc.co.uk/1/hi/technology/3076849.stm.

BBC (2003h) 'Extortionists target technology', *BBC News Online*, 12 November, at http://news.bbc.co.uk/1/hi/business/3265423.stm.

BBC (2003i) 'E-commerce targeted by blackmailers', *BBC News Online*, 26 November, at http://news.bbc.co.uk/1/hi/technology/3238230.stm.

BBC (2004a) 'R.I.P. Jennicam: LET THE CREDITS roll, Jennicam is dead', *BBC News Online*, 1 January, at http://news.bbc.co.uk/1/hi/magazine/3360063.stm.

BBC (2004b) 'Hefty fine for X-rated spam scam', *BBC News Online*, 17 February, at http://news.bbc.co.uk/1/hi/technology/3497061.stm.

BBC (2004c) 'Hacker threats to bookies probed', *BBC News Online*, 23 February, at http://news.bbc.co.uk/1/hi/technology/3513849.stm.

BBC (2004d) 'Ex-marine jailed for abduction', *BBC News Online*, 2 April, at http://news.bbc.co.uk/1/hi/england/manchester/3594235.stm.

BBC (2004e) 'Teen "confesses" to Sasser worm', *BBC News Online*, 8 May, at http://news.bbc.co.uk/1/hi/world/europe/3695857.stm.

BBC (2004f) 'Iraqis seek a voice via blogs', *BBC News Online*, 8 September, at http://news.bbc.co.uk/1/hi/technology/3632614.stm.

BBC (2004g) 'London "call girl" gives up blog', *BBC News Online*, 17 September, at http://news.bbc.co.uk/1/hi/technology/3665440.stm.

BBC (2004h) 'Poison porn pics show up online: viewing jpegs could soon be a risky business', *BBC News Online*, 30 September, at http://news.bbc.co.uk/1/hi/technology/3701640.stm.

BBC (2005a) 'Rich pickings for hi-tech thieves', *BBC News Online*, 25 January, at http://news.bbc.co.uk/1/hi/technology/4203601.stm.

BBC (2005b) 'Net regulation "still possible" ', *BBC News Online*, 27 January, at http://news.bbc.co.uk/1/hi/technology/4211415.stm.

BBC (2005c) 'Warnings about junk mail deluge', *BBC News Online*, 4 February, at http://news.bbc.co.uk/1/hi/technology/4236709.stm.

BBC (2005d) 'Internet piracy pair facing jail', *BBC News Online*, 6 May, at http://news.bbc.co.uk/1/hi/technology/4518771.stm.

BBC (2005e) 'Phishing pair jailed for ID fraud', *BBC News Online*, 29 June, at http://news.bbc.co.uk/1/hi/uk/4628213.stm.

BBC (2005f) 'No more "Hot Coffee" sex for GTA', *BBC News Online*, 11 August, at http://news.bbc.co.uk/1/hi/technology/4142184.stm.

BBC (2005g) 'Web trade threat to rare species', *BBC News Online*, 15 August, at http://news.bbc.co.uk/1/hi/sci/tech/4153726.stm.

BBC (2005h) 'Tools drive point-and-click crime', *BBC News Online*, 15 August, at http://news.bbc.co.uk/1/hi/technology/4152626.stm.

BBC (2005i) 'Ex-AOL man jailed for e-mail scam', *BBC News Online*, 18 August, at http://news.bbc.co.uk/1/hi/technology/4162320.stm.

BBC (2005j) 'Student held over online mugging', *BBC News Online*, 20 August, at http://news.bbc.co.uk/1/hi/technology/4165880.stm.

BBC (2005k) 'Shoppers "still wary of the web" ', *BBC News Online*, 24 August, at http://news.bbc.co.uk/1/hi/wales/4178586.stm.

BBC (2005l) 'Hollywood pursues fake film sites', *BBC News Online*, 14 October, at http://news.bbc.co.uk/1/hi/technology/4342910.stm.

BBC (2005m) 'TV download sites hit by lawsuits', *BBC News Online*, 13 May, at http://news.bbc.co.uk/1/hi/technology/4545519.stm.

BBC (2005n) 'How eBay fraudsters stole £300k', *BBC News Online*, 28 October, at http://news.bbc.co.uk/1/hi/uk/4386952.stm.

BBC (2005o) 'US internet use rises as do fears', *BBC News Online*, 28 October, at http://news.bbc.co.uk/1/hi/technology/4384482.stm.

BBC (2005p) 'Virtual club to rock pop culture', *BBC News Online*, 2 November, at http://news.bbc.co.uk/1/hi/technology/4385048.stm.

BBC (2005q) 'US "winning war" on e-mail spam', *BBC News Online*, 20 December, at http://news.bbc.co.uk/1/hi/technology/4547474.stm.

BBC (2006a) 'Sites selling child porn targeted', *BBC News Online*, 16 March, at http://news.bbc.co.uk/1/hi/technology/4812962.stm.

BBC (2006b) 'Tougher hacking laws get support', *BBC News Online*, 7 March, at http://news.bbc.co.uk/1/hi/technology/4781608.stm.

BBC (2006c) '29 held in "biggest" piracy raids', *BBC News Online*, 16 March, at http://news.bbc.co.uk/1/hi/entertainment/4812658.stm.

BBC (2006d) 'Cyber bullies haunt young online', *BBC News Online*, 14 March, at http://news.bbc.co.uk/1/hi/technology/4805760.stm.

BBC (2006e) 'Extortion virus code gets cracked', *BBC News Online*, 1 June, at http://news.bbc.co.uk/1/hi/technology/5038330.stm.

BBC (2006f) 'E-mail charging plan to beat spam', *BBC News Online*, 6 February, at http://news.bbc.co.uk/1/hi/technology/4684942.stm.

BBC (2006g) 'E-mail delivery "tax" criticised: Protests about the plan have come from many non-profit groups', *BBC News Online*, 6 March, at http://news.bbc.co.uk/1/hi/technology/4778136.stm.

BBC (2006h) 'Paedophiles face cancelled cards', *BBC News Online*, 19 July, at http://news.bbc.co.uk/1/hi/business/5194150.stm.

BBC (2006i) 'Web users to "patrol" US border', *BBC News Online*, 2 June, at http://news.bbc.co.uk/1/hi/world/americas/5040372.stm.

BBC (2006j) 'China close to being top spammer', *BBC News Online*, 21 April, at http://news.bbc.co.uk/1/hi/technology/4929716.stm.

BBC (2006k) 'UK hackers condemn McKinnon trial', *BBC News Online*, 8 May, at http://news.bbc.co.uk/1/hi/technology/4984132.stm.

BBC (2006l) 'McKinnon's extradition condemned', *BBC News Online*, 7 July, at http://news.bbc.co.uk/1/hi/technology/5157674.stm.

BBC (2006m) 'Spammers manipulate money markets', *BBC News Online*, 25 August, at http://news.bbc.co.uk/1/hi/technology/5284618.stm.

BBC (2006n) 'Hackers are now targeting mobile phones', *BBC News Online*, 19 September, at http://news.bbc.co.uk/1/hi/technology/4849402.stm.

BBC (2006o) '"Tower of Babel" technology nears', *BBC News Online*, 27 September, at http://news.bbc.co.uk/1/hi/technology/5382086.stm.

Beck, U. (1992) *Risk Society*, London: Sage.

Beck, U. (1999) *World Risk Society*, Cambridge: Polity.

Bell, D. (2001) *An Introduction to Cybercultures*, London: Routledge.

Bennett, M. (2006) 'British FBI drops Confidentiality Charter for IT crime victims', *IT Week*, 7 April, at www.itweek.co.uk/itweek/news/2153704/british-fbi-drops.

Berger, A. (1996) 'The low-tech side of information warfare', *Air & Space Power Chronicles – Chronicles Online Journal*, at www.airpower.maxwell.af.mil/airchronicles/cc/berger.html.

Berinato, S. (2006) 'Attack of the bots', *Wired*, 14:1, at www.wired.com/wired/archive/14.11/botnet_pr.html.

Berkowitz, B., and Hahn, R. W. (2003) 'Cybersecurity: who's watching the store?', *Issues in Science & Technology*, 19(3): 55–63, at www.issues.org/issues/19.3/berkowitz.htm.

Bevan, M. (2001) 'Confessions of a hacker', *Sunday Business Post Online*, 1 April, at www.kujimedia.com/modules.php?op=modload&name=News&file=article&sid=60.

Biever. C. (2004) 'How zombie networks fuel cybercrime', *New Scientist.Com*, 3 November, at www.newscientist.com/news/news.jsp?id=ns99996616.

Bottoms, A. and Wiles, P. (1996) 'Understanding crime prevention in late modern societies', in T. Bennett (ed.), *Preventing Crime and Disorder: Targeting Strategies and Responsibilities*, Cambridge: University of Cambridge, Institute of Criminology.

Bourdieu, P. (1977) *Outline of a Theory of Practice*, Cambridge: Cambridge University Press.

Bowden, C. and Akdeniz, Y. (1999) 'Cryptography and democracy: dilemmas of freedom', in Liberty (ed.), *Liberating Cyberspace: Civil Liberties, Human Rights, and the Internet*, London: Pluto Press, 81–125.

Boyle, J. (1996) *Shamans, Software and Spleens: Law and the Construction of the Information Society*, Cambridge, MA: Harvard University Press.

Bradbury, J. S, Shell, J. S. and Knowles, C. B. (2003) 'Hands on cooking: towards an attentive kitchen', published as an extended abstract in *Proceedings of the Conference on Human Factors in Computing Systems*, Fort Lauderdale, Florida, April.

Braithwaite, J. (1992) *Crime, Shame and Reintegration*, Cambridge: Cambridge University Press.

Braithwaite, J. and Drahos, P. (2000) *Global Business Regulation*, Cambridge: Cambridge University Press.

Brandt, A. (2001) 'Hacking Hollywood', *PCWorld.com*, 4 April, at www.pcworld.com/reviews/article/0,aid,45804,pg,2,00.asp.

Braverman, H. (1976) *Labour and Monopoly Capital*, New York: Monthly Review Press.

Brenner, S. (2001) 'Is there such a thing as "virtual crime"?', *California Criminal Law Review*, 4 (1): 11.

Brenner, S. (2002) 'Organized cybercrime? How cyberspace may affect the structure of criminal relationships', *North Carolina Journal of Law & Technology*, 4(1): 1–41.

Brightmail (2002) *Slamming Spam*, San Francisco: Brightmail.

Brin, D. (1998) *The Transparent Society: Will Technology Force us to Choose between Privacy and Freedom?*, London: Addison-Wesley.

Brin, D. (2002) 'Citizen Gain', *Telephony*, February 4, at http:// telephonyonline.com/ar/telecom_citizen_gain/index.htm.

Britz, M. T. (2003) *Computer Forensics and Computer Crime*, New Jersey: Pearson Prentice Hall.

Broadhurst, R. and Grabosky, P. (eds) (2005) *Cyber-Crime: The Challenge in Asia*, Hong Kong: Hong Kong University Press.

Brodeur, J.-P. (1983) 'High policing and low policing: remarks about the policing of political activities', *Social Problems*, 30 (5): 507–20.

Broersma, M. (2004) 'Boost UK govt cybercrime resources', *ComputerWeekly*, 17 May, at www.computerweekly.com/articles/article. asp?liArticleID=130607&liArticleTypeID=1&liCategoryID=6&liChann elID=22&liFlavourID=1&sSearch=&nPage=1.

Butterfield, F. (2005) 'U.S. limits on internet gambling are backed', *New York Times*, 8 April: 14.

C'T (2004) 'Uncovered: trojans as spam robots', *C'T Magazine*, 23 February, at www.heise.de/english/newsticker/news/44879.

Caden, M. L. and Lucas, S. E. (1996) 'Accidents on the information superhighway: on-line liability and regulation', *Richmond Journal of Law & Technology*, 2: 1.

Cain, M. (2002) 'International crime and globalisation', *Criminal Justice Matters*, 46: 34–5.

Campbell, D. (1997) 'More Naked Gun than Top Gun', *The Guardian*, 27 November: 2.

Campbell, D. (2005a) 'A flaw in the child porn witch-hunt', *Sunday Times*, 26 June, at www.timesonline.co.uk/article/0,,2092-1669131,00.html.

Campbell, D. (2005b) 'Operation Ore exposed', *PC Pro*, 1 July, at www.pcpro.co.uk/features/74690/operation-ore-exposed.html.

CAPA (2001) *Controlling Fraud on the Internet: A CAPA Perspective*, Kuala Lumpur: Confederation of Asian and Pacific Accountants/ Australian Institute of Criminology.

Cards International (2003) 'Europe "needs mag-stripe until US adopts chip"', *epaynews.com*, 28 July, at www.epaynews. com/ index.cgi? survey=&ref=browse&f=view&id=1059392963622215212&block=.

Carey, M. and Wall, D. S. (2001) 'MP3: more beats to the byte', *International Review of Law, Computers and Technology*, 15 (1): 35–58.

Carr, J. H. (2004) *Child Abuse, Child Pornography and the Internet*, London: NCH.

Carter, D. (1995) 'Computer crime categories: how techno-criminals operate', *FBI Law Enforcement Bulletin*, 64 (7): 21–26, at www.fbi.gov/ publications/leb/1989-1995/leb89-95.htm#1995issues and at www. lectlaw.com/files/cri14.htm.

Cashell, B., Jackson, W. D., Jickling, M. and Webel, B. (2004) *The Economic Impact of Cyber-Attacks*, Order Code RL32331, Government and Finance Division, Congressional Research Service, Library of Congress.

Castells, M. (1997a) 'An introduction to the Information Age', *City*, 7: 6–16.

Castells, M. (1997b) *The Information Age: Economy, Society, and Culture, Volume 2: The Power of Identity*, Oxford: Blackwell.

Castells, M. (2000a) 'Materials for an explanatory theory of the network society', *British Journal of Sociology*, 51 (1): 5–24.

Castells, M. (2000b) *The Information Age: Economy, Society, and Culture, Volume 1: The Rise of the Network Society*, 2nd edn, Oxford: Blackwell.

Castells, M. (2000c) *The Information Age: Economy, Society, and Culture, Volume 3: End of Millennium*, 2nd edn, Oxford: Blackwell.

CBI (2001) *Cybercrime Survey 2001: Making the Information Superhighway Safe for Business*, London: Confederation of British Industries.

Center for Democracy and Technology (1998), *Regardless of Frontiers: Protecting the Human Right to Freedom of Expression on the Global Internet*, Washington: Global Internet Liberty Campaign.

Cerf, V. (2003) 'The internet under surveillance: obstacles to the free flow of information online', *Reporters Without Borders*, at www.rsf.org/IMG/pdf/doc-2236.pdf.

Chan, J. (2001) 'The technological game: how information technology is transforming police practice', *Criminal Justice*, 1 (2): 139–60.

Chan, J., Brereton, D. Legosz, M. and Doran, S. (2001) *E-Policing: The Impact of Information Technology on Police Practices*, Brisbane: Queensland Criminal Justice Commission.

Chandler, A. (1996) 'The changing definition and image of hackers in popular discourse', *International Journal of the Sociology of Law*, 24: 229–51.

Chatterjee, B. (2001) 'Last of the Rainmacs? Thinking about pornography in Cyberspace', in D. S. Wall (ed.), *Crime and the Internet*, London: Routledge, 74–99.

Chicago Crime Commission (2000) 'Internet gang sites', Chicago Crime Commission press release, 28 November, at http://ccc.dr-technology.com/gangsites.html.

Clarke, G. (2005a) 'Liberty goes after phishers', *The Register*, 15 June, at www.theregister.co.uk/2005/06/15/_liberty_phishing/.

Clarke, G. (2005b) 'US postpones biometric passport plan – again', *The Register*, 16 June, at www.theregister.co.uk/2005/06/16/_bio_delay/.

Clarke, R. (1994) 'Dataveillance: delivering 1984', in L. Green and R. Guinery (eds), *Framing Technology: Society, Choice and Change*, Sydney: Allen & Unwin, 117–30.

Clarke, R. (2004) 'Technology, criminology and crime science', *European Journal on Criminal Policy and Research*, 10 (1): 55–63.

Clarke, R. and Felson, M. (eds) (1993) *Routine Activity and Rational Choice*, London: Transaction Press.

Clarke, R. and Mayhew, P. (eds) (1980) *Designing Out Crime*, London: HMSO.

CNN (2005) 'Video shows executions, life inside North Korea', *CNN.Com*, 14 November, at www.cnn.com/2005/WORLD/asiapcf/11/13/nkorea.hiddenvideo/index.html.

Computing (2005) 'Sentences should deter virus writers', *Computing*, 13 July, at www.computing.co.uk/computing/comment/2139739/sentences-should-deter-virus.

COE (2001) *Convention on Cybercrime*, Council of Europe, Budapest, 23 November (ETS No. 185), at http://conventions.coe.int/Treaty/EN/Treaties/Html/185.htm.

COE (2003) *Additional Protocol to the Convention on Cybercrime, Concerning the Criminalisation of Acts of a Racist and Xenophobic Nature Committed through Computer Systems*, Council of Europe, Strasbourg, 28 January (ETS No. 189), at http://conventions.coe.int/Treaty/en/Treaties/Html/189.htm.

Cowan, R. (2005) 'Arrests of internet paedophiles quadruple over two years', *The Guardian*, 5 March, at http://society.guardian.co.uk/children/story/0,1074,1430881,00.html.

Cracknell, D. (2003) 'ID cards for all to cost £40', *Sunday Times*, 6 July, at www.timesonline.co.uk/article/0,,2087-736390,00.html.

Crawford, A. (2000) 'Situational crime prevention, urban governance and trust relations', in A. von Hirsch, D. Garland and A. Wakefield (eds), *Ethical and Social Perspectives on Situational Crime Prevention*, Oxford: Hart, 193–213.

Crawford, A. (2003) 'Contractual governance of deviant behaviour', *Journal of Law and Society*, 30 (4): 479–505.

Crawford, A. and Lister, S. (2004) 'The patchwork future of reassurance policing in England & Wales: integrated local security quilts or frayed, fragmented and fragile tangled webs?', *Policing: An International Journal of Police Strategies & Management*, 27 (3): 413–30.

Creighton, S. (2003) 'Child pornography: images of the abuse of children', *NSPCC Information Briefings*, NSPCC Research Department, November, at www.nspcc.org.uk/inform/Info_Briefing/ChildPornography.pdf.

Critchley, T. A. (1978) *A History of the Police in England and Wales*, London: Constable.

CSI/FBI (2005) *CSI/FBI Computer Crime and Security Survey 2005*, San Francisco: Computer Security Institute.

CSI/FBI (2006) *CSI/FBI Computer Crime and Security Survey 2006*, San Francisco: Computer Security Institute.

Cullen, D. (2001) 'Doubleclick squares privacy suit', *The Register*, 30 March, at www.theregister.co.uk/2002/03/30/doubleclick_squares_privacy_suit/.

Cullen, D. (2004) 'Norway throws in the towel in DVD Jon case', *The Register*, 5 January, at www.theregister.co.uk/content/6/34706.html.

Davies, P., Francis, P. and Jupp, V. (eds) (1999) *Invisible Crimes: Their Victims and their Regulation*, London: Macmillan.

Day, J., Janus, A. and Davis, J. (2005) *Computer and Internet Use in the United States: 2003*, Washington: US Census Bureau, at www.census.gov/prod/2005pubs/p 23-208.pdf.

Deflem, M. (1997) 'The globalization of heartland terror: reflections on the Oklahoma City bombing', *The Critical Criminologist*, Newsletter of the ASC Critical Criminology Division, Fall: 5.

Deleuze, G. and Guattari, F. (1987) *A Thousand Plateaus: Capitalism and Schizophrenia*, Minneapolis: University of Minnesota Press.

Denning, D. (2000) 'Cyberterrorism', *Testimony before the Special Oversight Panel of Terrorism Committee on Armed Services*, US House of Representatives, 23 May, at www.cs.georgetown.edu/~denning/infosec/ cyberterror.html.

Diamond, J. (1997) 'Teletubbies: the truth at last', *New Statesman*, 19 December, at www.findarticles.com/p/articles/mi_m0FQP/is_n4365_v126/ai_20329788.

Diamond, M. and Uchiyama, A. (1999) 'Pornography, rape and sex crimes in Japan', *International Journal of Law and Psychiatry*, 22 (1): 1–22, at www.hawaii.edu/PCSS/online_artcls/pornography/prngrphy_rape_jp.html.

Dibbell, J. (1999) *My Tiny Life: Crime and Passion in a Virtual World*, New York: Henry Holt.

Ditzion, R., Geddes, E. and Rhodes, M. (2003) 'Computer crimes', *American Criminal Law Review*, 40: 285.

Dolinar, L. (1998) 'Hackers hit Pentagon system: organised attack highlights flaws', *Newsday*, 26 February, A03.

Downey R. (2002) 'Victims of wonderland', *Community Care*, 1412: 30–1.

DTI (2000) *Turning the Corner*, London: Department of Trade and Industry.

DTI (2002) *Information Security Breaches Survey 2002*, London: Department of Trade and Industry.

DTI (2004) *Information Security Breaches Survey 2004*, London: Department of Trade and Industry.

Duff, L. and Gardiner, S. (1996) 'Computer crime in the global village: strategies for control and regulation – in defence of the hacker', *International Journal of the Sociology of Law*, 24: 211–28.

Dupont, B. (2004) 'Security in the age of networks', *Policing and Society*, 14 (1): 76–91.

EC (1997) *Action Plan on Promoting Safe Use of the Internet*, COM (97) 582 final, 26 November at http://aei.pitt.edu/5894/01/001336_1.pdf.

Edwards, L. (2000) 'Canning the spam: is there a case for the legal control of junk electronic mail?', in L. Edwards and C. Wealde (eds), *Law and the Internet: A Framework for Electronic Commerce*, 2nd edn, Oxford: Hart.

Edwards, L. (2004) 'Code and the law: the next generation', paper given at the LEFIS workshop 'Lessig's Code: lessons for legal education from the frontiers of IT law', Queen's University, Belfast.

Edwards, L. and Wealde, C. (eds) (2000) *Law and the Internet: A Framework for Electronic Commerce*, 2nd edn, Oxford: Hart.

Edwards, S. (2000) 'Prosecuting "child pornography": possession and taking of indecent photographs of children', *The Journal of Social Welfare & Family Law*, 22 (1): 1–21.

EFF (2001), *Marin Co. Superior Court Ruling against DoubleClick Demurrer*, Electronic Frontier Foundation, 6 June, at www.eff.org/Legal/Cases/DoubleClick_cases/20010606_marin_rulinjg.html.

electricnews.net (2004) 'Click here to become infected (Part 2)', *The Register*,

5 October, at www.theregister.co.uk/2004/10/05/messagelabs_spam_warning/.

electricnews (2005) '13 EU countries link up to fight spam', *The Register*, 7 February, at www.theregister.co.uk/2005/02/07/ec_antispam_campaign/.

Engberg, D. (1996) 'The virtual panopticon', *Impact of New Media Technologies*, Fall, at http://is.gseis.ucla.edu/impact/f96/Projects/dengberg/.

Ericson, R. and Haggerty, K. (1997) *Policing the Risk Society*, Oxford: Oxford University Press.

Erickson, J. (2003) *Hacking: The Art of Exploitation*, San Francisco: No Starch Press.

Ermert, M. (2004) 'Good spam: bad spam', *The Register*, 5 February, at www.theregister.co.uk/content/55/35353.html.

European Commission Select Committee (1996) *Green Paper on the Protection of Minors and Human Dignity in Audio-visual and Information Services*, Brussels: European Commission.

European Commission (1997) *Green Paper on the Convergence of the Telecommunications, Media and Information Technology Sectors, and the Implications for Regulation. Towards an Information Society Approach*, Brussels: European Commission, COM (97) 623, 3 December, at http://aei.pitt.edu/archive/00001160/01/telecom_convergence_gp_COM_97_623.pdf.

European Commission (2005) 'European countries launch joint drive to combat "spam" ', Press release, IP/05/146, Brussels, 7 February.

Evans-Pritchard, A. (2001) 'US asks Nato for help in "draining the swamp" of global terrorism', *The Daily Telegraph*, 27 September, at www.telegraph.co.uk/news/main.jhtml?xml=/news/2001/09/27/wusa27.xml.

Experian (2001) *Internet Fraud: A Growing Threat to Online Retailers*, Nottingham: Experian, at www.uk.experian.com (last accessed 15 March 2002).

Fay, J. (2005a) 'WTO rules in online gambling dispute', *The Register*, 8 April, at www.theregister.co.uk/2005/04/08/wto_online_gambling/.

Fay, J. (2005b) 'Biometrics won't deter passport fraudsters, chief admits', *The Register*, 1 July, at www.theregister.co.uk/2005/07/01/bio_passport_fraud/.

Felson, M. (2000) 'The routine activity approach as a general social theory', in S. Simpson (ed.), *Of Crime and Criminality: The Use of Theory in Everyday Life*, Thousand Oaks, CA: Sage.

Fildes, J. (2006) 'Web inventor warns of "dark" net', *BBC News Online*, 23 May, at http://news.bbc.co.uk/1/hi/technology/5009250.stm.

Finch, E. (2001) *The Criminalisation of Stalking: Constructing the Problem and Evaluating the Solution*: London: Cavendish.

Finch, E. (2002) 'What a tangled web we weave: identify theft and the internet', in Y. Jewkes (ed.), *dot.cons: Crime, Deviance and Identity on the Internet*, Cullompton: Willan, 86–104.

Findlay, M. (1999) *The Globalisation of Crime: Understanding Transitional Relationships in Context*, Cambridge: Cambridge University Press.

Finnemann, N. (2002) 'Perspectives on the internet and modernity: late modernity, postmodernity or modernity modernized?', in N. Brügger and H. Bødker (eds), *The Internet and Society?*, papers from Centre for Internet Research, University of Aarhus, Denmark, 29–39.

Fleming, M. (2005) *UK Law Enforcement Agency Use and Management of Suspicious Activity Reports: Towards Determining the Value of the Regime*, Jill Dando Institute of Crime Science, University College London, 30 June, at www.jdi.ucl.ac.uk/downloads/pdf/Fleming_LEA_Use_and_Mgmt_of_SA Rs_June2005.pdf.

Foucault, M. (1978) *The History of Sexuality, Volume I: An Introduction*, London: Penguin.

Foucault, M. (1979) *Discipline and Punish: The Birth of the Prison*, London: Peregrine.

Foucault, M. (1983) 'Afterword: the subject and power', in H. Dreyfus and P. Rainbow (eds), *Michel Foucault: Beyond Structuralism and Hermeneutics*, 2nd edn, Chicago: University of Chicago Press, 208–26.

Fowles, A. J. (1983) 'Order and the law', in K. Jones, J. Brown and J. Bradshaw (eds), *Issues in Social Policy*, London: Routledge & Keegan Paul.

Francisco, J. (2003) 'Defensive information warfare: a review of selected literature', Eller College Working Paper No. 1004-04, December, at http://ssrn.com/abstract=607443.

Frieder, L. and Zittrain, J. (2006) 'Spam works: evidence from stock touts and corresponding market activity', Working Paper, Krannert School of Management and Oxford Internet Institute, 25 July, at http://ssrn.com/abstract=920553.

Friedewald, M., Vildjiounaite, E. and Wright, D. (eds) (2006) *The Brave New World of Ambient Intelligence: A State-Of-The-Art Review*, Safeguards in a World of Ambient Intelligence (SWAMI), European Commission, January, at http://swami.jrc.es/pages/documents/SWAMI_D1_Final_ 000 .pdf.

Furedi, F. (2002) *Culture of Fear*, London: Continuum.

Furedi, F. (2006) 'What is distinct about our rules of fear?', Leeds Social Sciences Institute Public Guest Lecture, Leeds, 23 October.

Gandy, O. (2003) 'Data mining and surveillance in the post-9.11 environment', in F. Webster and K. Ball (eds), *The Intensification of Surveillance: Crime Terrorism and Warfare in the Information Age*, London: Pluto Press, 26–41.

Garland, D. (2000) 'The culture of high crime societies: some preconditions of recent "law and order" policies', *British Journal of Criminology*, 40 (3): 347–75.

Garland, D. (2001) *The Culture of Control*, Oxford: Oxford University Press.

Garland, D. and Sparks, R. (2000) 'Criminology, social theory and the challenge of our times', *British Journal of Criminology*, 40 (2): 189–204.

GartnerG2 (2002) 'GartnerG2 says 2001 online fraud losses were 19 times as high as offline fraud', Press release, at www.gartnerg2.com/press/ pr 2002-03-04a.asp (checked 16 March 2002).

Gaudin, S. (2004) 'U.S. sending more than half of all spam', *Internetnews.com*, 1 July, at www.internetnews.com/stats/article.php/3376331.

Geer, D. (2004) 'The physics of digital law', Plenary Speech at the Digital Cops in a Virtual Environment Conference, Information Society Project, Yale Law School, 26–28 March 2004.

Geist, M. (2006) 'Video and the net an explosive mix', *BBC News Online*, 17 July, at http://news.bbc.co.uk/1/hi/technology/5188482.stm.

Gey, S.G. (2000) 'The Nuremberg Files and the First Amendment Value of Threats', *Texas Law Review*, 78: 541.

Gibson, O. (2005) 'Online file sharers "buy more music" ', *Guardian Online*, 27 July, at www.guardian.co.uk/arts/news/story/0,11711,1536886,00. html.

Gibson, O. (2006) 'Warning to chatroom users after libel award for man labelled a Nazi', *Guardian Online*, 23 March, at www.guardian.co.uk/law/ story/0,,1737445,00.html.

Gibson, W. (1982) 'Burning chrome', *Omni Magazine*, July.

Gibson, W. (1984) *Neuromancer*, London: HarperCollins.

Giddens, A. (1990) *The Consequences of Modernity*, Cambridge: Polity.

Glasner, J. (2005) 'RFID: the future is in the chips', *Wired News*, at www.wired.com/news/print/0,1294,68500,00.html.

Goodman, M. (1997) 'Why the police don't care about computer crime', *Harvard Journal of Law and Technology*, 10: 645–94.

Goodman, M. and Brenner, S. (2002) 'The emerging consensus on criminal conduct in cyberspace', *UCLA Journal of Law and Technology*, 3, at www.lawtechjournal.com/articles/2002/03_020625_goodmanbrenner.pdf.

Goodrich, P. (1998) 'Social sciences and the displacement of law', *Law and Society Review*, 32 (2), 473.

Gordon, D. (1986) 'The electronic panopticon: a case study of the development of the National Criminal Records System', *Politics and Society*, 15: 483–51.

Gordon, S. and Chess, D. (1999) 'Attitude adjustment: trojans and malware on the internet: an update', proceedings of the 22nd National Information Systems Security Conference, 18–21 October, Crystal City, Virginia, at http://csrc.nist.gov/nissc/1999/proceeding/papers/p 6.pdf.

Gorman, S. (2003) 'FBI, CIA remain worlds apart', *The National Journal*, 1 August, reproduced at http://198.65.138.161/org/news/2003/030801-fbi-cia01.htm.

Goss, A. (2001) 'Jay Cohen's brave new world: the liability of offshore operators of licensed internet casinos for breach of United States' anti-gambling laws', *Richmond Journal of Law & Technology*, 7 (4): 32, at www.richmond.edu/jolt/v7i4/article2.html.

Gostev, A., Shevchenko, A. and Nazarov, D. (2006) *Malware Evolution: January–March 2006*, Kaspersky Labs, at www.viruslist.com/en/ analysis? pubid=184012401.

Gottfredson, G. and Hirschi, T. (1990) *A General Theory of Crime*, Stanford: Stanford University Press.

Grabosky, P. N. and Smith, R. G. (1998) *Crime in the Digital Age: Controlling communications and cyberspace illegalities*. New Jersey: Transaction.

Grabosky, P.N., Smith, R.G. and Dempsey, G. (2001), *Electronic Theft, Unlawful Acquisition in Cyberspace*, Cambridge: Cambridge University Press.

Granovsky, Y. (2002) 'Yevroset tainted by gray imports', *The Moscow Times*, 9 July: 8, at www.themoscowtimes.com/stories/2002/07/09/045.html.

Green, E. (1999) *FUD 101 v1.0*, November 15, at http://badtux.org/home/eric/editorial/fud101-1.0.0.html.

Greenberg, S. (1997) 'Threats, harassment and hate on-line: recent developments', *The Boston Public Interest Law Journal*, 6: 673.

Greene, T. (2004) 'US lubes passports with RFID snake oil', *The Register*, 20 May, at www.theregister.co.uk/2004/05/20/us_passports/.

Greene, T. (2006) 'Piracy losses fabricated – Aussie study', *The Register*, 9 November, at www.theregister.co.uk/2006/11/09/my_study_beats_your_study/

Greenleaf, G. (1998) 'An endnote on regulating cyberspace: architecture vs. law?', *University of New South Wales Law Journal*, 21 (2). Reproduced in D. S. Wall (ed.), *Cyberspace Crime*, Aldershot: Dartmouth, 2003, 89–120.

Gurulé, J. (2003) 'The global effort to stop terrorist financing', *U.S. Foreign Policy Agenda*, 8 (1), at http://usinfo.state.gov/journals/itps/0803/ijpe/pj81gurule.htm.

Hafner, K. and Markoff, J. (1995) *Cyberpunk: Outlaws and Hackers on the Computer Frontier*, London: Simon & Schuster.

Haggerty, K. and Ericson, R. (2000) 'The surveillant assemblage', *British Journal of Sociology*, 51 (4): 605–22.

Haggerty, K. and Ericson, R. (eds) (2006) *The New Politics of Surveillance and Visibility*, Toronto: University of Toronto Press.

Haggerty, K. and Gazso, A. (2005) 'Seeing beyond the ruins: surveillance as a response to terrorist threats', *The Canadian Journal of Sociology*, 30 (2): 169–87.

Hall, C. (2005) 'Internet fuels boom in counterfeit drugs', *Sunday Telegraph*, 16 August, at www.telegraph.co.uk/news/main.jhtml?xml=/news/2005/08/16/ndrugs 16.xml.

Hamilton-Baillie, B. (2004) 'Urban design: why don't we do it in the road? Modifying traffic behaviour through legible urban design', *Journal of Urban Technology*, 11 (1): 43–62 at www.hamilton-baillie.co.uk/papers/urban_design.pdf.

Hamin, Z. (2003) 'Hacking through the Malaysian Computer Crimes Act 1997: a potent tool or an investor booster?', paper given to the APEC Cybercrime Legislation and Enforcement Capacity Building Conference of Experts and Training, Bangkok, Thailand, 21–25 July, at www.apectelwg. org/apec/comple/clecb/Zai's.doc.

Harding, K. (2001) 'Snuff films', *Planet Papers*, at www.planetpapers.com/Assets/2136.php.

Harris, J. (2001) (ed.) *Tönnies: Community and Civil Society*, Cambridge: Cambridge University Press.

Haux, R. and Kulikowski, C. (eds) (2005) *Ubiquitous Health Care Systems, Yearbook of Medical Informatics 2005*, Stuttgart: Schattauer.

Hayes, P. (2005) 'No "sorry" from Love Bug author', *The Register*, 11 May, at www.theregister.co.uk/2005/05/11/love_bug_author/.

Hayward, D. (1997) 'Censorship coming to the Continent', *TechWeb*, 13 March, at www.techweb.com/wire/news/mar/0314porn1.html.

Heins, M. (2001a) *Not in Front of the Children: Indecency, Censorship and the Innocence of Youth*, New York: Hill and Wang.

Heins, M. (2001b) 'Criminalising online speech to "protect" the young: what are the benefits and costs?', in D. S. Wall (ed.), *Crime and the Internet*, London: Routledge, 100–12.

Hermer, J. and Hunt, A. (1996) 'Official graffiti of the everyday', *Law and Society Review*, 30 (3), 455–80.

Hewson, B. (2003) 'Fetishising images', *Spiked Online*, 23 January, at www.spiked-online.com/Printable/00000006DC06.htm.

Hier, S.P. (2003) 'Probing the surveillant assemblage: on the dialectics of surveillance practices as processes of social control', *Surveillance & Society*, 1 (3): 399–411. Available at www.surveillance-and-society.org/articles1(3)/probing.pdf.

High Tech Magazine (2003) 'Cybercrime wave stretches resources', *High Tech Magazine*, 21 July, at http://hightechmagazine.com/managearticle.asp?C=290&A=124.

Hindelang, M., Gottfredson, M., and Garofalo, J. (1978) *Victims of Personal Crime: An Empirical Foundation for a Theory of Personal Victimization*, Cambridge, MA: Ballinger.

Hof, R. (2005) 'PayPal spreads its wings: the web service is going beyond parent eBay. Will the next foray be offline?', *Business Week Online*, 23 May, at www.businessweek.com/magazine/content/05_21/b3934111_mz063.htm?chan=tc.

Home Office (2003) *Identity Cards: The Next Steps*, at www.homeoffice.gov.uk/docs 2/identity_cards_nextsteps_031111.pdf.

Home Office (2005) 'Crackdown on violent pornography', Home Office press release, Ref: 125/2005, 31 August, at http://press.homeoffice.gov.uk/press-releases/Crackdown_On_Violent_Pornography?version=1.

Home Office (2006) *Consultation on the Possession of Extreme Pornographic Material: Summary of responses and next steps*, Home Office, August, at www.homeoffice.gov.uk/documents/cons-extreme-porn-3008051/Gvt-response-extreme-porn2.pdf?view=Binary.

Honeynet Project (2002) *Know Your Enemy: Revealing the Security Tools, Tactics, and Motives of the Blackhat Community*, Essex: Addison Wesley.

Howie, M. (2006) 'Accused in child porn inquiry to sue police', *The Scotsman*, 15 September, at http://news.scotsman.com/uk.cfm?id=1362272006.

Hughes, G., McLaughlin, E. and Muncie, J. (2001) 'Teetering on the edge: the futures of crime control and community safety', in G. Hughes,

E. McLaughlin and J. Muncie (eds), *Crime Prevention and Community Safety: Future Directions*, London: Sage.

Humble, C. (2005) 'Inside the fake Viagra factory', *Sunday Telegraph*, 21 August, at www.telegraph.co.uk/news/main.jhtml?xml=/news/2005/08/21/nviag21.xml.

Huntington, S. (1998) *The Clash of Civilizations and the Remaking of the World Order*, London: Simon & Schuster.

IFAW (2005) *Born to be Wild: Primates are Not Pets*, London: International Fund for Animal Welfare, at www.ifaw.org/ifaw/dfiles/file_553.pdf.

Illuminati News (2004) 'What's wrong with the "execution videos"?', *Illuminati News*, 10 October, at www.illuminati-news.com/execution-videos.htm.

Ingle, A. (2004) 'The new breed of cracker, verse the next generation of defenses', *SANS Institute GIAC Papers*, April, at www.giac.org/certified_professionals/practicals/gsec/3799.php.

Innes, M. (2001) 'Control creep', *Sociological Research Online*, 6 (3), at www.socresonline.org.uk/6/3/innes.html.

Innes, M. (2004) 'Reinventing tradition? Reassurance, neighbourhood security and policing', *Criminal Justice*, 4 (2): 151–71.

Innes, M. (2005) 'Why disorder matters? Antisocial behaviour and incivility as signals of risk', paper given to the Social Contexts and Responses to Risk (SCARR) Conference, Kent, UK, 28–29 January, at www.kent.ac.uk/scarr/papers/papers.htm.

Intelligence and Security Committee (2005) *Annual Report 2004–2005*, Cm 6510, April, at www.cabinetoffice.gov.uk/publications/reports/intelligence/iscannualreport.pdf.

Internet Freedom (1997) 'Will the Net become an Oasis-free zone?', *Internet Freedom*, 19 May, at www.netfreedom.org/news.asp?item=36.

IPTS (2003) *Security and Privacy for the Citizen in the Post-September 11 Digital Age: A Prospective Overview*. Report by the Institute for Prospective Technological Studies, Joint Research Committee, Seville, to the European Parliament Committee on Citizens' Freedoms and Rights, Justice and Home Affairs., European Commission, July. (EUR 20823 EN – ISBN: 92-894-6133-0).

Jackson, W. (2005) 'Is a new ID theft scam in the wings?', *Government Computer News*, 14 January, at www.gcn.com/vol1_no1/security/34815-1.html.

Jewkes, Y. (ed.) (2003) *Dot.Cons: Crime, Deviance and Identity on the Internet*, Cullompton: Willan.

Jewkes, Y. and Andrews, C. (2005) 'Policing the filth: the problems of investigating online child pornography in England and Wales', *Policing & Society*, 15 (1): 42–62.

Johnson, D. R. and Post, D. (1996) 'Law and borders: the rise of law in cyberspace', *Stanford Law Review*, 48: 1367.

Johnson, P. (1996) 'Pornography drives technology: why not to censor the internet', *Federal Communications Law Journal*, 49 (1): 217–26.

Johnston, L. (1993) 'Privatisation and protection: spatial and sectoral ideologies in British policing and crime prevention', *Modern Law Review*, 56: 771.

Johnston, L. and Shearing, C. (2003) *Governing Security: Explorations in Policing and Justice*, London: Routledge.

Jones, G. and Levi, M. (2000) *The Value of Identity and the Need for Authenticity*, London: DTI Crime Foresight Panel.

Jones, R. (2003) ' "Review of Crime in The Digital Age" by P. Grabosky and R. Smith', *International Journal of Law and Information Technology*, 11: 98.

Jones, T. and Newburn, T. (2002) 'The transformation of policing? Understanding current trends in policing systems', *British Journal of Criminology*, 42: 129–46.

Jordan, T. (1999) *Cyberpower: The Culture and Politics of Cyberspace and the Internet*, London: Routledge.

Kabay, M. E. (2002) 'Salami fraud', *Network World Security Newsletter*, 24 July, at www.networkworld.com/newsletters/sec/2002/01467137.html.

Katyal, N. K. (2001) 'Criminal Law in Cyberspace', *University of Pennsylvania Law Review*, 149: 1003.

Katyal, N. K. (2003) 'Digital architecture as crime control', *Yale Law Journal*, 112: 2261–89.

Kerr, Orin S. (2003) 'Cybercrime's scope: interpreting "access" and "authorization" in computer misuse statutes', *New York University Law Review*, 78 (5): 1596–668.

Kewney, G, (2005) 'Hotspot paranoia: try to stay calm', *The Register*, 24 January, at www.theregister.co.uk/2005/01/24/wi_fi_hotspot_security/.

Khong, W. K. (2001) 'Spam law for the internet', *Journal of Information, Law and Technology*, 3, at http://elj.warwick.ac.uk/jilt/01-3/khong.html/.

Knight, P. (2000) *Conspiracy Culture: from Kennedy to the X-Files*, London: Routledge.

Kozlovski, N. (2004) 'Designing accountable online policing', paper give to the Digital Cops in a Virtual Environment Conference, Information Society Project, Yale Law School, 26–28 March, at http://islandia. law.yale.edu/isp/digital%20cops/papers/kozlovski_paper.pdf.

KPMG (2001) Global E.fraud Survey, at www.kpmg.ca/english/services/ docs/fas/efraud2000e.pdf (checked 23 March 2002).

Kravetz, A. (2002) 'Qatari national taken into federal custody in wake of terrorist attacks allegedly committed credit card fraud', *Peoria Journal Star*, 29 January, at www.collegefreedom.org/AMpsj02.htm.

Krebs, B. (2006a) 'Shadowboxing with a bot herder', *Washington Post* (washingtonpost.com), 9 March, at http://blog.washingtonpost.com/ securityfix/2006/03/post.html.

Krebs, B. (2006b) 'Hacked ad seen on MySpace served spyware to a million', *Washington Post.com*, 19 July, at http://blog.washingtonpost.com/security-fix/2006/07/myspace_ad_served_adware_to_mo.html.

Krone, T. (2004) 'A typology of online child pornography offending', *Trends and Issues in Crime and Criminal Justice*, No. 279, Canberra: Australian Institute of Criminology. at www.aic.gov.au/publications/tandi2/ tandi279.pdf.

Laeken European Council (2001) 'EUROJUST – Helping the EU's legal systems to combat cross-border crime', *EU Justice and Home Affairs Council*, 6 December, at http://europa.eu.int/comm/justice_home/news/laecken_council/en/eurojust_en.htm.

Landau, M. (2002) 'The First Amendment and "virtual" child pornography', *Gigalaw*, at www.gigalaw.com/articles/2002-all/landau-2002-07-all.html.

Langdon, R. (1993) 'Speech acts and unspeakable acts', *Philosophy and Public Affairs*, 22 (4): 293–330.

Lastowka, G. and Hunter, D. (2005) 'Virtual crime', *New York Law School Law Review*, 49 (1), 293–316.

Law Commission (1997) *Legislating the Criminal Code: Misuse of Trade Secrets* (Consultation Paper 150), at www.lawcom.gov.uk/library/lccp150/summary.htm.

Leading Question (2005) 'Music pirates spend four-and-a-half times more on legitimate music downloads than average fans', *The Leading Question*, 27 July, at www.musically.com/theleadingquestion/files/theleadingquestion_piracy.doc.

Legat, K. and Hofmann-Wellenhof, B. (2000) 'Galileo or for whom the bell tolls', at www.teleconsult-austria.at/download/galileo_or_forwhomthebelltolls_tsukuba2000.pdf.

Lemos, R. (2005a) 'Phishers look to net small fry', *The Register*, 20 June, at www.theregister.co.uk/2005/06/20/phishers_target_us_credit_unions/.

Lemos, R. (2005b) 'DNS attacks attempt to mislead consumers', *The Register*, 8 April, at http://news.bbc.co.uk/1/hi/technology/4420325.stm.

Lemos, R. (2005c) 'Fingerprint payments taking off despite security concerns', *The Register*, 8 Oct., at www.theregister.co.uk/2005/10/08/fingerprint_payments/.

Lemos, R. (2006) 'Bot nets likely behind jump in spam', *The Register*, 31 Oct., at www.theregister.co.uk/2006/10/31/botnet_spam_surge/page2.html.

Leong, G. (1998) 'Computer child pornography – the liability of distributors?', special edition: 'Crime, Criminal Justice, and the Internet', *Criminal Law Review* (December) 19–28.

Leppard, D. (2005) 'Child porn suspects set to be cleared in evidence "shambles" ', *Sunday Times*, 3 July, at www.timesonline.co.uk/printFriendly/0,,1-523-1678810-523,00.html.

Lessig, L. (1998a) 'The laws of cyberspace', paper presented at the *Taiwan Net '98 conference*, Taipei, March.

Lessig, L. (1998b) 'The New Chicago School', *Journal of Legal Studies*, 27 (2): 661–91.

Lessig, L. (1999) *Code and Other Laws of Cyberspace*, New York: Basic Books.

Lettice, J. (2005) 'Study reveals gaps in UK system to track criminal and terror finance: lots of data, but police can't or won't use it fully', *The Register*, 13 October, at www.theregister.co.uk/2005/10/13/uk_sars_ report/.

Levene, T. (2003) 'The artful dodgers', *Guardian*, 29 November, at http://money.guardian.co.uk/scamsandfraud/story/0,13802,1095616, 00.html.

Levi, M. (2001) ' "Between the risk and the reality falls the shadow": evidence and urban legends in computer fraud', in D. S. Wall (ed.), *Crime and the Internet*, London: Routledge, 44–58.

Levi, M. and Gilmore, B. (2002) 'Terrorist finance, money laundering and the rise and rise of mutual evaluation: a new paradigm for crime control?', *European Journal of Law Reform*, 4 (2): 337–64.

Levi, M. and Maguire, M. (2004) 'Reducing and preventing organised crime: an evidence-based critique', *Crime, Law and Social Change*, 41: 397–469.

Levi, M. and Wall, D. S. (2003) 'Crime and security in the aftermath of September 11: security, privacy and law enforcement issues relating to emerging information communication technologies', in *Security and Privacy for the Citizen in the Post-September 11 Digital Age: A Prospective Overview* (EUR 20823) Seville: Institute for Prospective Technological Studies, Joint Research Committee, European Commission, 92-100; 163–86.

Levi, M. and Wall, D. S. (2004) 'Technologies, Security and Privacy in the post-9/11 European Information Society', *Journal of Law and Society*, 31 (2): 194–220.

Leyden, J. (2002a) 'Lies, damned lies and anti-virus statistics', *The Register*, 16 January, at www.theregister.co.uk/2002/01/16/lies_damned_lies_ and_antivirus/.

Leyden, J. (2002b) 'Online gambling tops Internet card fraud league', *The Register*, 28 March, at www.theregister.co.uk/content/23/24633.html.

Leyden, J. (2003a) 'Spam epidemic gets worse', *The Register*, 3 December, at www.theregister.co.uk/content/55/34331.html.

Leyden, J. (2003b) 'DVD Jon is free – official', *The Register*, 7 January, at www.theregister.co.uk/2003/01/07/dvd_jon_is_free_official/.

Leyden, J. (2004a) 'IBM dissects the DNA of spam', *The Register*, 23 August, at www.theregister.co.uk/2004/08/23/spam_or_ham/.

Leyden, J. (2004b) 'The rise of the white collar hacker', *The Register*, 30 March, at www.theregister.co.uk/content/55/36663.html.

Leyden, J. (2004c) 'Phatbot arrest throws open trade in zombie PCs', *The Register*, 12 May, at www.theregister.co.uk/2004/05/12/phatbot_zombie_ trade/.

Leyden, J. (2004d) 'Probably the simplest phishing trick in the world', *The Register*, 9 December, at www.theregister.co.uk/2004/12/09/secunia_ browser_exploit_warning/.

Leyden, J. (2004e) 'UK banks launch anti-phishing website', *The Register*, 1 October, at www.theregister.co.uk/2004/10/01/bank_safe_online/.

Leyden, J. (2004f) 'Phishing losses overestimated – survey', *The Register*, 3 December, at www.theregister.co.uk/2004/12/03/phishing_survey_tower- group/.

Leyden, J. (2004g) 'WTO rules against US gambling laws', *The Register*, 11 November., at www.theregister.co.uk/2004/11/11/us_gambling_wto_ rumble/.

Leyden, J. (2004h) 'Gizza job, virus writers ask AV industry', *The Register*, 10 September, at www.theregister.co.uk/2004/09/10/mydoom_job_plea/.

Leyden, J. (2004i) 'Rise of the botnets', *The Register*, 20 September, at www.theregister.co.uk/2004/09/20/rise_of_the_botnets/.

Leyden, J. (2005a) 'Phishing morphs into pharming', *The Register*, 31 January, at www.theregister.co.uk/2005/01/31/pharming/.

Leyden, J. (2005b) 'Adware-infected PCs net slimeware firms $3 a pop', *The Register*, 2 February, at www.theregister.co.uk/2005/02/02/adware_market_estimate/.

Leyden, J. (2005c) 'MCI makes $5m a year from spam gangs', *The Register*, 7 February, at www.theregister.co.uk/2005/02/07/spamhaus_mci/.

Leyden, J. (2005d) 'Beware of toxic blogs', *The Register*, 14 April, at www.theregister.co.uk/2005/04/14/toxic_blogs/.

Leyden, J. (2005e) 'Fight fraud not ID theft', *The Register*, 28 April, at www.theregister.co.uk/2005/04/28/id_fraud/.

Leyden, J. (2005f) 'UK under cyber blitz', *The Register*, 16 June, at www.theregister.co.uk/2005/06/16/uk_cyber-blitz/.

Leyden, J. (2005g) 'World is safe from mobile viruses for a few years longer', *The Register*, 23 June, at www.theregister.co.uk/2005/06/23/mobile_malware_forecast_gartner/.

Leyden, J. (2005h) 'Aussie crooks recruit teen phishing mules', *The Register*, 6 January, at www.theregister.co.uk/2005/01/06/phisherman_fagins/.

Leyden, J. (2005i) 'Hacker magazine shuts up shop', *The Register*, 11 July, at www.theregister.co.uk/2005/07/11/phrack_shuts/.

Leyden, J. (2005j) 'Webroot guesstimates inflate UK spyware problem', *The Register*, 20 October, at www.theregister.co.uk/2005/10/20/webroot_uk_spyware_guesstimates/.

Leyden, J. (2005k) 'Spyware blizzard shows no sign of let up', *The Register*, 29 June,at www.theregister.co.uk/2005/06/29/stealth_trojan/.

Leyden, J. (2005l) 'Virus writers craft PnP botnet client', *The Register*, 24 October, at www.theregister.co.uk/2005/10/24/pnp_botnet_encore/.

Leyden, J. (2005m) 'Victims coughing up to online extortionists', *The Register*, 6 October, at www.theregister.co.uk/2005/10/06/ibm_botnet_vb/.

Leyden, J. (2006a) 'Spear phishers target eBay', *The Register*, 5 January, at www.theregister.co.uk/2006/01/05/ebay_spear_phishing/.

Leyden, J. (2006b) 'Phishing fraudsters offer cash reward', *The Register*, 14 March, at www.theregister.co.uk/2006/03/14/chase_phishing_scam/.

Leyden, J. (2006c) 'Zombie PCs menace mankind: script-kiddies make way for Mr Big', *The Register*, 7 March, at www.theregister.co.uk/2006/03/07/symantec_net_threat_report_2h2005/.

Leyden, J. (2006d) 'Slobodan Trojan poses as murder pics', *The Register*, 15 March, at www.theregister.co.uk/2006/03/15/slobodan_trojan/.

Leyden, J. (2006e) 'Online fraudsters love webmail – true: easier to block accounts linked to spamming than fraud', *The Register*, 19 July, at www.theregister.co.uk/2006/07/19/online_fraud_survey/.

Leyden, J. (2006f) 'VXers add rootkit tech to MyDoom and Bagle', *The*

Register, 30 March, at www.theregister.co.uk/2006/03/30/mainstream_rootkit/.

Leyden, J. (2006g) 'MySpace adware attack hits hard', *The Register*, 21 July, at www.theregister.co.uk/2006/07/21/myspace_adware_attack/.

Leyden, J. (2006h) 'Ohio child hospital hack exposes 230,000 files', *The Register*, 30 October, at www.theregister.co.uk/2006/10/30/ohio_hospital_hack/.

Leyden, J. (2006i) 'US ID thieves target kids: . . . as UK banks give crooks a helping hand', *The Register*, 31 October, at www.theregister.co.uk/2006/10/31/id_theft_trends/.

Libbenga, J. (2004) 'Trojans as spam robots: the evidence', *The Register*, 22 February, at www.theregister.co.uk/2004/02/22/trojans_as_spam_robots/.

Licklider, J. and Taylor, R. (1990) 'The computer as a communication device', in R. Taylor (ed.), *In Memoriam: J.C.R. Licklider 1915–1990*, Palo Alto, California: Digital Research Center, 21–41 (reprinted from *Science and Technology*, April 1968).

Liedtke, M. (2005) 'Click fraud' threatens online advertising boom, *Legal Technology*, 14 February, at www.law.com/jsp/ltn/pubArticleLTN.jsp?id=1107783347883.

Lloyd, I. J. (2000) *Information Technology Law*, London: Butterworths.

Loader, Brian D. (ed.) (1998) *Cyberspace Divide: Equality, Agency and Policy in the Information Society*, London: Routledge.

Loader, B. and Thomas, D. (eds) (2000) *Cybercrime: Security and Surveillance in the Information Age*, London: Routledge.

Loader, I. and Walker, N. (2001) 'Policing as a public good: Reconstituting the connections between policing and the state', *Theoretical Criminology*, 5 (1): 9–35.

Lorek, L. A. (1997) 'Outwitting cybercrime: no, you're not paranoid. Computer villains really are out to get you', *Sun-Sentinel of South Florida*, 14 September, 1.

Lueck, M. (2005) 'UK in grip of hi-tech crime wave', *BBC News Online*, 17 June, at http://news.bbc.co.uk/1/hi/business/4102480.stm.

Lyon, D. (1994) *The Electronic Eye: The Rise of Surveillance Society*, Minneapolis: University of Minnesota Press.

Lyon, D. (2001) *Surveillance Society*, Buckingham: Open University Press.

Lyon, D. (2003) 'Surveillance after September 11', in F. Webster and K. Ball (eds), *The Intensification of Surveillance: Crime Terrorism and Warfare in the Information Age*, London: Pluto Press, 16–25.

MacKinnon, C. (1993) *Only Words*, Cambridge, MA: Harvard University Press.

MacKinnon, R. (1997) 'Virtual rape', *Journal of Computer Mediated Communication*, 2 (4), at www.ascusc.org/jcmc/vol2/issue4/mackinnon.html.

McBarnet, D. (1979) 'Arrest: the legal context of policing', in S. Holdaway (ed.), *The British Police*, Arnold, London.

McConnell International (2000) *Cyber Crime . . . and Punishment? Archaic*

Laws Threaten Global Information, Washington: McConnell International, at www.witsa.org/papers/McConnell-cybercrime.pdf.

McCullagh, D. (2003) 'RFID tags: Big Brother in small packages', *CNET News.com*, 13 January, at http://news.com.com/2010-1069-980325. html?tag=fd_nc_1.

McCusker, R. (2005) 'Spam: nuisance or menace, prevention or cure?', *Trends and Issues in Criminal Justice*, No. 294, Canberra: Australian Institute of Criminology, March, at www.aic.gov.au/publications/tandi2/tandi294.pdf.

McDowell, R. (1994) 'Do snuff films really exist, or are they merely popular myth?', *San Francisco Chronicle*, 7 August.

McKenzie, S. (2006) 'Partnership policing of electronic crime: an evaluation of public and private police investigative relationships', PhD thesis, University of Melbourne.

McQuade, S. (2006a) 'Technology-enabled crime, policing and security, *Journal of Technology Studies*, 32 (1).

McQuade, S. (2006b) *Understanding and Managing Cybercrime*, Boston: Allyn & Bacon.

McQuade, S. and Berg, S. (2004) 'Computer-related crime theories tested: self-report survey findings', paper given to the American Society of Criminology 2004 Annual Meeting, Nashville, 17 November.

McWilliams, B. (2001) 'Stealing MS passport's wallet', *Wired News*, 2 November, at www.wired.com/news/technology/0,1282,48105,00.html.

Madow, M. (1993) 'Private ownership of public image: popular culture and publicity rights', *California Law Review*, 81: 125–240.

Maguire, E. R. and King, W. R. (2004) 'Trends in the policing industry', *Annals of the American Academy of Political and Social Science*, 593 (1): 15–41.

Makowski, F. (2002) 'Vehicular vision: your car may be tracking the way you drive', *ABCNEWS.com*, 16 July, at http://abcnews.go.com/sections/wnt/DailyNews/blackboxes020716.html.

Mann, D. and Sutton, M. (1998) 'Netcrime: more change in the organisation of thieving', *British Journal of Criminology*, 38 (2): 210–29.

Manners, I. (2002) 'European [security] Union: from existential threat to ontological security', *Copenhagen Peace Research Institute Papers*, at www.ciaonet.org/wps/mai04/mai04.pdf.

Manning, P. K. (1978) 'The Police: mandate, strategies, and appearances', in P. Manning and J. Van Maanen (eds), *Policing: A View from the Street*, New York: Random House, 7–32.

Manning, P. (2001) 'Technology's ways: information technology, crime analysis and the rationalizing of policing', *Criminal Justice*, 1 (1): 83–103.

Manning, P. (2004) 'Some observations concerning a theory of democratic policing', *Proceedings of the Conference on Police Violence*, Bochom, Germany, April.

Marshall, L. (2002) 'Metallica and morality: the rhetorical battleground of the Napster Wars', *Entertainment Law*, 1 (1): 1.

Marx, G. T. (1991) 'Critique: no soul in the new machine: technofallacies in the electronic monitoring movement', *Justice Quarterly*, 8 (3).

Marx, G. T. (2001) 'Technology and social control: the search for the illusive silver bullet', *International Encyclopaedia of the Social and Behavioral Sciences*, Amsterdam: Elsevier.

Mathieson, T. (1997) 'The viewer society: Foucault's Panopticon revisited', *Theoretical Criminology*, 1: 215–34.

Matsuda, M. J., Lawrence, C.R., Delgado, R. and Crenshaw, K. W. (1993) *Words That Wound: Critical Race Theory, Assaultive Speech, and the First Amendment*, Boulder: Westview Press.

Matza, D. (1964) *Delinquency and Drift*, New York: John Wiley & Sons.

Maynard, D. (2001) 'Circuit Court case notes: violence in the media', *Communications Lawyer*, Spring: 41–2.

Meier, G. (2003) *Curious to Criminal: Sophisticated White Collar Crime of the Future*, GIAC papers, SANS Institute, at www.giac.org/certified_professionals/practicals/gsec/2823.php.

Melossi, D. (1994) 'Normal crimes, élites and social control', in D. Nelken (ed.), *The Futures of Criminology*, London: Sage, pp. 202–19.

Mendelson, H. and Pillai, R. (1999) 'Information Age organisation, dynamics and performance', *Journal of Economic Behaviour and Organization*, 38 (3): 253–81.

Miller, P. and Rose, N. (1990) 'Governing economic life', *Economy and Society*, 1 (1): 1.

Mitchell, W. (1990) *The Logic of Architecture: Design, Computation, and Cognition*, Cambridge, MA: MIT Press.

Mitchell, W. (1995) *City of Bits: Space, Place, and the Infobahn*, Cambridge, MA: MIT Press.

Mitnick, K. and Simon, W. L. (2002) *The Art of Deception: Controlling the Human Element of Security*, New York: John Wiley and Sons.

Moitra, S. (2003) *Analysis and Modelling of Cybercrime: Prospects and Potential*, Freiburg: Max-Planck Institute for Foreign and International Criminal Law.

Moore, G. E. (1965) 'Cramming more components onto integrated circuits', *Electronics*, 38 (8): 114–17.

Morgan, G. (2003) 'Government to press on with ID cards: but experts still warn that biometric technologies are not yet mature enough', *VNUNET.COM*, 26 November, at www.vnunet.com/News/1150506.

Morris, M. and Ogan, C. (1996) 'The Internet as mass medium', *Journal of Communication*, 46 (1), 39–49.

Morris, S. (2004) 'The future of netcrime now: part 1 – threats and challenges', Home Office Online Report 62/04, at http://www.homeoffice.gov.uk/rds/pdfs04/rdsolr 6204.pdf.

Morse, M. (1999) 'Teletubby, televangelist, tell a bad joke', *San Francisco Examiner*, 11 February.

Mosnews (2005) 'Ukrainian busted in CarderPlanet online fraud ring', *Mosnews (The Moscow News)*, 21 July, at www.mosnews.com/news/2005/07/21/ukronlinefraud.shtml.

Muncie, J. (1999) *Youth and Crime: A Critical Introduction*, London: Sage.

Naraine, R. (2005) 'Triple-barrelled trojan attack builds botnets', *eweek.com*, 4 June, at www.eweek.com/article2/0,1759,1823690,00.asp.

Nasheri, H. (2004) *Economic Espionage and Industrial Spying*, Cambridge: Cambridge University Press.

Natsui, T. (2003) 'Recent cybercrime legislations in Japan', *Meiji Law Journal*, 10: 1–34.

NCIS (1999) *Project Trawler: Crime On The Information Highways*, London: National Criminal Intelligence Service.

NCIS (2000) *The National Intelligence Model*, London: National Criminal Intelligence Service.

NCIS (2003) *United Kingdom Threat Assessment of Serious and Organised Crime 2003*, London: National Criminal Intelligence Service.

Newburn, T. (2002) 'Atlantic crossings: policy transfer and crime control in England and Wales', *Punishment and Society*, 4 (2): 165–94.

Newburn, T. and Hayman, S. (2001) *Policing, CCTV and Social Control: Police Surveillance of Suspects in Custody*, Cullompton: Willan.

Newman, G. R. and Clarke, R. V. (2003) *Superhighway Robbery: Preventing e-commerce crime*, Cullompton: Willan.

NFIC (2006) *Internet Scams, Fraud Trends, January–December 2005*, National Fraud Information Center, at www.fraud.org/2005_Internet_Fraud_Report.pdf.

NHTCU (2002a) *Confidentiality Charter: The NHTCU working with Business*, London: National Hi-Tech Crime Unit.

NHTCU (2002b) *Hi-Tech Crime: The impact on UK Business*, London, National Hi-Tech Crime Unit.

NISCC (2005) 'Targeted trojan email attacks', *NISCC Briefing 08/2005*, 16 June, at www.niscc.gov.uk/niscc/docs/ttea.pdf.

Oates, J. (2004a) 'Email fraud soars', *The Register*, 18 February, at www.theregister.co.uk/content/55/35635.html.

Oates, J. (2004b) 'Queen of the Sky gets marching orders', *The Register*, 3 November, at www.theregister.co.uk/2004/11/03/airline_blogger_sacked/.

Oates, J. (2005) 'AOL man pleads guilty to selling 92m email addies', *The Register*, 7 February at www.theregister.co.uk/2005/02/07/aol_ email_ theft/.

Oates, J. (2006) 'Online attack holds files to ransom: Rochdale nurse hit by ransomware', *The Register*, 31 May, at www.theregister.co.uk/2006/05/31/virus_ransoms_files/.

O'Connor, P. (2003) *Oppression and Responsibility: A Wittgensteinian Approach to Social Practices and Moral Theory*, University Park: Penn State Press.

Ofcom (2005a) 'More broadband, more digital, more mobile – a common picture of accelerating take-up of new products and services', Press release, 13 July, at www.ofcom.org.uk/media/news/2005/07/nr_20050713.

Ofcom (2005b) 'The communications market 2005, 3: Telecommunications', at www.ofcom.org.uk/research/cm/cm05/telecommunications.pdf.

O'Harrow, R. (2001) 'Identity thieves thrive in information age: rise of online data brokers makes criminal impersonation easier', *Washington Post*, 31 May, at www.washingtonpost.com/ac2/wp-dyn?pagename=article& node=&contentId=A77996-2001May25.

O'Malley, P. (1999) 'Governmentality and the risk society', *Economy and Society*, 28: 138–48.

Oliver, C. (2006) 'All sides of the story?', *BBC Editor's Blog*, 31 Aug., at www.bbc.co.uk/blogs/theeditors/index.html#a003979.

OST (2004) *Cybertrust and Crime Prevention Project: Executive Summary*, Office of Science and Technology, at www.foresight.gov.uk/Previous_ Projects/Cyber_Trust_and_Crime_Prevention/Reports_and_Publication/ Executive%20Summary.pdf.

Ottawa Citizen (2002) 'Hacker gurus' recruit unsuspecting youth: RCMP report, *Ottawa Citizen*, 6 June, at www.fpinfomart.ca/ar/ar_result. php? page=1.

OUT-LAW (2006) 'How to sue a British spammer', *The Register*, 6 January, at www.theregister.co.uk/2006/01/06/spam_court_media_logistics/.

Pattavina, A. (ed.) (2005) *Information Technology and the Criminal Justice System*, Thousand Oaks, CA: Sage.

PDD (1998) 'The Clinton Administration's policy on critical infrastructure protection', Presidential Decision Directive (PDD) no. 63, 22 May, at www.cybercrime.gov/white_pr.htm.

Pease, K. (2001) 'Crime futures and foresight: challenging criminal behaviour in the information age', in D. S. Wall (ed.), *Crime and the Internet*, London: Routledge, 18–28.

Perry, W. J. (1998) 'Information technology as a force multiplier', *Hoover Digest*, 4, at www.hooverdigest.org/984/perry.html.

Pew (2004) 'The Can-Spam Act has not helped most email users so far', *Pew Internet Project Data memo*, March, at www.pewinternet.org/pdfs/PIP_ Data_Memo_on_Spam.pdf.

Pocar, F. (2004) 'New challenges for international rules against cyber-crime', *European Journal on Criminal Policy and Research*, 10 (1): 27–37.

Post, D. (1995) 'Encryption vs. The Alligator Clip: the Feds worry that encoded messages are immune to wiretaps', *American Lawyer*, January/ February: 111.

Post, D. (2000) 'What Larry doesn't get: code, law, and liberty in cyberspace', *Stanford Law Review*, 52: 1439–59.

Poster, M. (1995) *Second Media Age*, Cambridge: Polity.

Poster, M. (2001) *What's the Matter with the Internet?*, Minneapolis: University of Minnesota Press.

Potier, B. (2004) 'File sharing may boost CD sales: study defies traditional beliefs about Internet use', *Harvard University Gazette*, 15 April, at www.news.harvard.edu/gazette/2004/04.15/09-filesharing.html.

Power, R. (2000) *Tangled Web: Tales of Digital Crime from the Shadows of Cyberspace*, Indianapolis: Que.

Powers, T. (2003) 'Real wrongs in virtual communities', *Ethics and Information Technology*, 5 (4): 191–8.

PRAI (Princeton Research Associates International) (2005) *Leap of Faith: Using the Internet despite the Dangers*, Yonkers, NY: Consumer Reports WebWatch, 26 October, at www.consumerwebwatch.org/pdfs/princeton.pdf.

Presdee, M. (2000) *Cultural Criminology and the Carnival of Crime*, London: Routledge.

Race, J. (2005) 'You needn't eat spam (or worms): The real reasons why spam still exists today – and what to do about it', *Free Software Magazine*, 6 (July), at www.ftc.gov/os/comments/canspam3/516736-00048.pdf.

Rathmell, A. (1998) 'The world of open sources (2): Information warfare and hacking', paper to 1998 International Conference for Criminal Intelligence Analysts: Meeting the Challenge from Serious Criminality, Manchester, UK.

Rathmell, A. (2001) 'Controlling computer network operations', *Information & Security*, 7: 121–44.

Rauterberg, M. (2004) 'Positive effects of entertainment technology on human behaviour', in R. Jacquart (ed.), *Building the Information Society*, London: Kluwer, 51–8.

Reed, C. and Angel, J. (eds) (2003) *Computer Law*, Oxford: Oxford University Press.

Reiner, R. (1992) 'Policing a postmodern society', *Modern Law Review*, 55: 761.

Reiner, R. (2000) *The Politics of the Police*, 3rd edn, Oxford: Oxford University Press.

Reno, J. (1996) 'Law enforcement in cyberspace', address to the Commonwealth Club of California, San Francisco Hilton Hotel, 14 June.

Reuters (2005) 'Microsoft, Nigeria fight e-mail scammers', *e-week.com*, 14 October, at www.eweek.com/article2/0,1895,1871565,00.asp.

Rheingold, H. (1994) *The Virtual Community: Homesteading the Electronic Frontier*, New York: Harper Perennial.

Rhodes, R. (1996) 'The new governance: governing without government', *Political Studies*, 44: 652–67.

Richards, S. (2005) *Internet Shopping: The Consumer Perspective*, Cardiff: Welsh Consumer Council, at www.wales-consumer.org.uk/Research%20and%20policy/pdfs/WCC_Shopping_on_the_Internet_(English)pdf.

Richardson, T. (2005a) 'Online fraud could dent economies', *The Register*, 18 February, at www.theregister.co.uk/2005/02/18/fraud_threat_warning/.

Richardson, T. (2005b) 'Brits fall prey to phishing', *The Register*, 3 May, at www.theregister.co.uk/2005/05/03/aol_phishing/.

Richardson, T. (2005c) 'BT cracks down on rogue diallers', *The Register*, 27 May, at www.theregister.co.uk/2005/05/27/rogue_bt_diallers/.

Rimm, M. (1995) 'Marketing pornography on the information superhighway: a survey of 917,410 images, descriptions, short stories, and animations downloaded 8.5 million times by consumers in over 2000 cities in forty countries, provinces, and territories', *Georgetown Law Review*, 83: 1849–934.

Robertson, R. (1995) 'Globalisation', in M. Featherstone, S. Lash and R. Robertson (eds), *Global Modernities*, London: Sage, 40–65.

Rowland, D. and Macdonald, E. (1997) *Information Technology Law*, London: Cavendish.

Room, S. (2003) 'Hard-core spammers beware?', *New Law Journal*, 28 November: 1780.

Rosenberger, R. (2003) 'Computer viruses and "false authority syndrome"', *Vmyths.com* at http://vmyths.com/fas/fas 1.cfm - fas 8.cfm.

Rosenbluth, W. (2001) *Investigation and Interpretation of Black Box Data in Automobiles: A Guide to the Concepts and Formats of Computer Data in Vehicle Safety and Control Systems*, Monograph 4, West Conshohocken, PA: ASTM/SAE.

Ross, A. (1990) 'Hacking away at the counterculture', *Postmodern Culture*, 1/1: at http://jefferson.village.virginia.edu/pmc/issue.990/contents.990.html.

Rotenberg, R. (2001) 'What Larry doesn't get: fair information practices and the architecture of privacy', *Stanford Technology Law Review*, February, at http://stlr.stanford.edu/STLR/Symposia/Cyberspace/00_rotenberg_1/article.htm.

Rothman, J. E. (2001) 'Freedom of speech and true threats', *Harvard Journal of Law & Public Policy*, 25 (1): 1.

Rupnow, C. (2003) 'Not "made of money"', *Wisconsin Leader-Telegram*, 23 April, at www.xpressmart.com/thebikernetwork/scam.html.

Rushkoff, D. (1998) 'E-mail of the species is deadlier than the mail', *Electronic Mail and Guardian*, 8 July, at www.chico.mweb.co.za/pc/rushkoff/980708-rushkoff.htm.

Ryan, J. and Jefferson, T. (2003) 'The use, misuse and abuse of statistics in information security research', *Proceedings of the 2003 ASEM National Conference*, St. Louis, MO, at www.attrition.org/archive/misc/use_misuse_abuse_stats_infosec_research.pdf.

Saltzer, J., Reed, D. and Clark, D. (1984) 'End-to-end arguments in system design', *ACM Transactions in Computer Systems*, 2 (4): 277–88.

Sambrook, R. (2006) 'How the net is transforming news', *BBC News Online*, 20 January, at http://news.bbc.co.uk/1/hi/technology/4630890.stm.

Sandars, N. K. (1972) *The Epic of Gilgamesh: An English Version With an Introduction*, Harmondsworth: Penguin Classics.

Sanders, T. (2005) 'Botnet operation controlled 1.5m PCs: largest zombie army ever created', *vnunet.com*, 21 October, at www.vnunet.com/vnunet/news/2144375/botnet-operation-ruled-million.

Satchwell, G. (2004) *A Sick Business: Counterfeit medicines and organised crime*, Lyon: Interpol, at www.interpol.int/Public/FinancialCrime/Intellectual Property/Publications/SickBusiness.pdf.

Saunders, K. M. and Zucker, B. (1999) 'Counteracting identity fraud in the information age: the Identity Theft and Assumption Deterrence Act', *International Review of Law Computers and Technology*, 13 (2).

Savona, E. and Mignone, M. (2004) 'The fox and the hunters: how IC technologies change the crime race', *European Journal on Criminal Policy and Research*, 10 (1): 3–26.

Schechter, S. and Smith, M. (2003) 'Access for sale: a new class of worm', paper given at the workshop on Rapid Malcode (WORM), at the *Tenth ACM Conference on Computer and Communications Security*, Washington DC, USA, 27 October, at www.cs.berkeley.edu/~nweaver/papers/taxonomy.pdf.

Scheeres, J. (2002) 'They want their ID chips now', *Wired News*, 6 February.

Schneider, J. L. (2003) 'Hiding in plain sight: an exploration of the illegal(?) activities of a drugs newsgroup', *The Howard Journal of Criminal Justice*, 42 (4): 374–89.

Schneier, B. (2003) *Beyond Fear: Thinking Sensibly about Security in an Uncertain World*, New York: Springer-Verlag.

Schwartz, J. (2004) 'A heretical view of file sharing', *New York Times*, 5 April, at www.umsl.edu/~sauter/DSS/05music.html.

Searle, J. (1969) *Speech Acts: An Essay in the Philosophy of Language*, Cambridge: Cambridge University Press.

Seife, C. (1997) 'Model explains Internet "storms"', *Science*, 277: 477.

Senior Mag.com (2003) 'Are you riding on a black box?' *Senior Mag.com*.

Sennett, R. (1992) *The Fall of Public Man*, New York: W. W. Norton.

Sentencing Advisory Panel (2002) *The Panel's Advice to the Court of Appeal on Offences Involving Child Pornography*, London: Sentencing Guidelines Council, 15 August, at www.sentencing-guidelines.gov.uk/docs/advice_child_porn.pdf.

Sentencing Guidelines Council (2006) *Sexual Offences Act 2003: Consultation Guideline*, London: Sentencing Guidelines Council.

Shapiro, A. L. (1999) *The Control Revolution: How the Internet is Putting Individuals in Charge and Changing the World We Know*, New York: Century Foundation.

Shearing, C. (2004) 'Thoughts on sovereignty', *Policing and Society*, 14 (1): 5–12.

Shearing, C. and Ericson, R. (1991) 'Culture as figurative action', *British Journal of Sociology*, 42 (4): 481–506.

Shell, J. S. (2002) 'Taking control of the panopticon: privacy considerations in the design of attentive user interfaces' at http://smg.media.mit.edu/cscw2002-privacy/submissions/jeff.pdf.

Shenon, P. (2001) 'Internet piracy is suspected as U.S. agents raid campuses', *New York Times*, 12 December, at www.criminology.fsu.edu/transcrime/articles/Internet%20Piracy%20Is%20Suspected%20as%20_S_%20Agents%20Raid%20Campuses.htm.

Sheptycki, J. (2000) 'Introduction', in J. E. Sheptycki (ed.), *Issues in Transnational Policing*, London: Routledge, 1–20.

Sheptycki, J. (2002) *In Search of Transnational Policing : Towards a Sociology of Global Policing*, Aldershot: Ashgate.

Sherman, B. and Bently, L. (1999) *The Making of Modern Intellectual Property Law*, Cambridge: Cambridge University Press.

Sherriff, L. (2004) 'Child porn suspect suicide tally hits 32', *The Register*, 21 December, at www.theregister.co.uk/2004/12/21/child_porn_suicide_shame/.

Shinder, D. and Tittel, E. (2002) *Scene of the Cybercrime*, Rockland, MA: Syngress Media.

Sieber, U. (2004) 'The threat of cybercrimes', in Council of Europe, *Organised Crime in Europe: The Threat of Cybercrime*, Strasbourg: Council of Europe, 81–218.

Singleton, T. (2002) 'Stop fraud cold with powerful internal controls', *Journal of Corporate Accounting & Finance*, 13 (4): 29–39.

Smith, G. (1998) 'Electronic Pearl Harbor? Not likely', *Issues in Science and Technology*, 15 (3): 68–73, at www.nap.edu/issues/15.1/smith.htm.

Smith, R. G., Grabosky, P. N. and Urbas, G. (2004) *Cyber Criminals on Trial*, Cambridge: Cambridge University Press.

Sommer, P. (2004) 'The future for the policing of cybercrime', *Computer Fraud & Security*, 1: 8–12.

Sophos (2004a) 'Sophos outs "dirty dozen" spam producing countries: anti-spam specialist maps the spam world', Sophos press release, 26 February, at www.sophos.com/spaminfo/articles/dirtydozen.html.

Sophos (2004b) 'Sophos reveals latest "Dirty Dozen" spam producing countries. Anti-spam specialist reveals the biggest exporters of junk email', Sophos press release, 24 August, at www.sophos.com/spaminfo/articles/dirtydozenaug04.html.

Sophos (2005a) 'Sophos reveals latest "Dirty Dozen" spam producing countries', Sophos press release, 7 April, at www.sophos.com/pressoffice/pressrel/us/20050407dirtydozen.html.

Sophos (2005b) 'Spam is no laughing matter, Sophos reports on apologetic joke trend', *Sophos Articles*, 4 May, at www.sophos.com/spaminfo/articles/spamjoke.html.

Sophos (2005c) *Field Guide to Spam* (A compendium of the various types of tricks that spammers use to subvert anti-spam filtering software), at www.sophos.com/spaminfo/explained/fieldguide.html.

Sophos (2005d) 'Virus writing on the up as average time to infection spirals down', *Sophos News*, 1 July, at www.sophos.com/pressoffice/pressrel/uk/midyearroundup 2005.html.

Sophos (2005e) 'Sophos reveals latest "Dirty Dozen" spam producing countries', Sophos press release, 13 October, at www.sophos.com/pressoffice/pressrel/us/dirtydozoct05.html.

Sophos (2006a) 'Sophos report reveals latest "Dirty Dozen" spam relaying countries: Asia named worst spam relaying continent', Sophos press release, 20 April, at www.sophos.com/pressoffice/news/articles/2006/04/dirtydozapr06.html.

Sophos (2006b) 'Sophos reveals "Dirty Dozen" spam relaying countries',

Sophos press release, 24 July, at www.sophos.com/pressoffice/news/articles/2006/07/dirtydozjul06.html.

Sprenger, P. (1999) 'Sun on privacy: "Get Over It"', *Wired News.com*, 26 Jan., at www.wired.com/news/politics/0,1283,17538,00.html.

Standage, T. (1998) *The Victorian Internet: The Remarkable Story of the Telegraph and the Nineteenth Century's Online Pioneers*, London: Phoenix.

Stark, C. (1997) 'Is pornography an action? The causal vs. the conceptual view of pornography's harm', *Social Theory and Practice*, 10 (2): 277–305.

Starr, S. (2004a) 'Can the law can spam? Legislation is a blunt instrument with which to beat junk email', *Spiked*, 7 April, at www.spiked-online.com/articles/0000000CA4BF.htm.

Starr, S. (2004b) 'Can technology can spam? IT companies do battle with bulk email', *Spiked*, 5 May, at www.spiked-online.com/Articles/0000000CA50F.htm.

Stenning, P. (2000) 'Powers and accountability of private police', *European Journal on Criminal Policy and Research*, 8 (3): 325–52.

Stenning, P. and Shearing, C. (2005) 'Reforming police: opportunities, drivers and challenges', *Australian and New Zealand Journal of Criminology*, 38 (2): 167–80.

Stenson, K. and Edwards, A. (2003) 'Crime control and local governance: the struggle for sovereignty in advanced liberal polities', *Contemporary Politics*, 9 (2): 203–17.

Stephenson, N. (1992) *Snowcrash*, London: ROC/Penguin.

Sterling, B. (1994) *The Hacker Crackdown: Law and Disorder on the Electronic Frontier*, London: Penguin.

Stiennon, R. (2005) 'Spyware: 2004 was only the beginning', *CIO Update*, 26 January, at www.cioupdate.com/trends/article.php/3464551.

Stoll, C. (2000) *The Cuckoo's Egg: Tracking a Spy Through the Maze of Computer Espionage*, London: Simon & Schuster.

Sturcke, J. (2006) 'Expert warns of more chatroom libel awards', *Guardian Online*, 22 March, at www.guardian.co.uk/uk_news/story/0,,1737000,00.html.

Surman, D. (2003) 'CGI animation: pseudorealism, perception and possible worlds', MA thesis, Warwick University, UK.

Sussman, V. (1995) 'Policing cyberspace', *U.S. News & World Rep.*, 23 January: 54–61.

Swift, R. (2002) 'Rush to nowhere', *New Internationalist*, 343, March, at www.newint.org/issue343/keynote.htm (Turbo Capitalism) also see 'Rush to nowhere: the facts', at www.newint.org/issue343/facts.htm.

Symantec (2006) 'Symantec Internet Security Threat Report: trends for January 06–June 06, Volume X', Symantec, September, at www.symantec.com/specprog/threatreport/ent-whitepaper_symantec_internet_security_threat_report_x_09_2006.en-us.pdf.

Szafranski, R. (1995) 'A theory of information warfare: preparing for 2020',

Airpower Journal, Spring, at www.airpower.maxwell.af.mil/airchronicles/apj/szfran.html.

Taipale, K. A. (2003) 'Data mining and domestic security: connecting the dots to make sense of data', *Columbia Science and Technology Law Review*, 5: 2.

Taylor, M. (1999) 'The nature and dimensions of child pornography on the Internet', paper given to the Combating Child Pornography on the Internet conference, Vienna, September.

Taylor, M. and Quayle, E. (2003) *Child Pornography: An Internet Crime*, London: Brunner-Routledge.

Taylor, P. (1999) *Hackers: Crime in the Digital Sublime*, London: Routledge.

Taylor, P. (2001) 'Hacktivism: in search of lost ethics?', in D. S. Wall (ed.), *Crime and the Internet*, London: Routledge, 59–73.

The Mentor, (1986) 'The conscience of a hacker (Hacker's Manifesto)', *Phrack*, 1 (7): phile 3 at www.phrack.org/show.php?p=07.

Thomson, I. (2002) 'Police unveil e-crime Confidentiality Charter' *vnunet.com*, 10 December, at www.vnunet.com/vnunet/news/2121007/police-unveil-crime-confidentiality-charter?vnu_lt=vnu_art_related_articles.

Thurley, P. (2005) 'Pornography as performative utterance', paper given to the Northwest Student Philosophy Conference, Washington State, 29 May, at http://artsweb.uwaterloo.ca/~pthurley/index/Pornography.htm.

Toffler, A. (1970) *Future Shock*, New York: Bantam Books.

Toyne, S. (2003) 'Scam targets NatWest customers', *BBC News Online*, 24 October, at http://news.bbc.co.uk/1/hi/business/3211635.stm.

Trubek, D. and Trubek, L. (2005) 'Hard and soft law in the construction of social Europe: the role of the open method of co-ordination', *European Law Journal*, 11 (3): 343–64.

Turner, G. (2004) *Celebrity*, London: Sage.

Twist, J. (2004) 'Facing a biometric future', *BBC News Online*, 13 January, at http://news.bbc.co.uk/1/hi/technology/3389209.stm.

Uhlig, R. (1996) 'Hunt is on for Internet dealer in child porn', *Electronic Telegraph*, issue 518, 23 October, at www.telegraph.co.uk/htmlContent.jhtml?html=/archive/1996/10/23/nporn23.html.

Uhlig, R. (1997) 'Oasis threatens fans over Internet piracy', *Electronic Telegraph*, 16 May, issue 721.

Ungoed-Thomas, J. (1998) 'The schoolboy spy', *Sunday Times*, 29 March, 1–2.

USDOJ (2002) 'Warez leader sentenced to 46 months', US Department of Justice press release, 17 May, at www.cybercrime.gov/sankusSent.htm.

USDOJ (2004) 'Computer programmer arrested for extortion and mail fraud scheme targeting Google, Inc.', US Department of Justice press release, 18 March, at www.usdoj.gov/usao/can/press/html/ 2004_03_ 19_ bradley.html.

Van de Linde, E., O'Brien, K, Lindstrom, G., Spiegeleire, S., Vayrynen, M. and Vries, H. (2002) *Quick Scan of Post 9/11 National Counter-terrorism Policy Making and Implementation in Selected European Countries: Research Project for the Netherlands Ministry of Justice*, MR-1590, May, Leiden: Rand Europe.

Van Dijk, J. (1999) 'The one-dimensional network society of Manuel

Castells: a review essay', *The Chronicle* at www.thechronicle.demon.co.uk/ archive/castells.htm.

Vance, A. (2005) 'Music sales slide despite RIAA's crushing blows against piracy', *The Register*, 31 December, at www.theregister.co.uk/2005/12/31/ riaa_2005_piracy/.

Vincent-Jones, P. (2000) 'Contractual governance: institutional and organisational analysis', *Oxford Journal of Legal Studies*, 20: 317–51.

Vinge, V. (2000) 'The digital Gaia: as computing power accelerates, the network knows all – and it's everywhere', *Wired*, 8 (1), at www.wired.com/ wired/archive/8.01/forward.html.

Wakefield, J. (2005) 'Online service foils ransom plot', *BBC News Online*, 31 May, at http://news.bbc.co.uk/1/hi/technology/4579623.stm.

Walden, I. (2003) 'Computer crime', in C. Reed and J. Angel (eds), *Computer Law*, Oxford: Oxford University Press, 295–329.

Walden, I. (2007) *Computer Crimes and Digital Investigations*, Oxford: Oxford University Press.

Walker, C. and Akdeniz, Y. (1998) 'The governance of the Internet in Europe with special reference to illegal and harmful content', *Criminal Law Review*, Special Issue on Crime, Criminal Justice and the Internet, 5–18.

Walker, C. P. and Akdeniz, Y. (2003) 'Anti-terrorism laws and data retention: war is over?', *Northern Ireland Legal Quarterly*, 50 (2): 159–82.

Walker, C. P. and McGuinness, M. (2002) 'Commercial risk, political violence and policing the City of London', in A. Crawford (ed.), *Crime and Insecurity*, Cullompton: Willan, 234–59.

Walker, C. P., Wall. D. S. and Akdeniz, Y. (2000) 'The Internet, law and society', in Y. Akdeniz, C. P. Walker and D. S. Wall (eds), *The Internet, Law and Society*, London: Longman, 3–24.

Walker, D. (2004) 'Who watches murder videos?', *BBC News Online*, 12 October, at http://news.bbc.co.uk/1/hi/magazine/3733996.stm.

Walker, R. and Bakopoulos, B. (2005) 'Conversations in the dark: how young people manage chatroom relationships', *First Monday*, 10 (4) at http:// firstmonday.org/issues/issue10_4/walker/index.html.

Wall, D. S. (1997) 'Policing the virtual community: the internet, cybercrimes and the policing of cyberspace', in P. Francis, P. Davies and V. Jupp (eds), *Policing Futures*, London: Macmillan, 208–36.

Wall, D. S. (1998) *The Chief Constables of England and Wales: The Socio-Legal History of a Criminal Justice Elite*, Aldershot: Dartmouth.

Wall, D. S. (1999) 'Cybercrimes: new wine, no bottles?', in P. Davies, P. Francis and V. Jupp (eds), *Invisible Crimes: Their Victims and their Regulation*, London: Macmillan, 105–39; reproduced in D. S. Wall (ed.), *Cyberspace Crime*, Aldershot: Dartmouth, 2003, 3–37.

Wall, D. S. (2000) 'The theft of electronic services: telecommunications and teleservices', Essay 1 on the CD-ROM annex to DTI, *Turning the Corner*, London: Department of Trade and Industry, 2000.

Wall, D. S. (ed.) (2001a) *Crime and the Internet*, London: Routledge.

Wall, D. S. (2001b) 'Maintaining order and law on the internet', in D. S. Wall (ed.), *Crime and the Internet*, London: Routledge, 1–17.

Wall, D. S. (2002a) 'Insecurity and the policing of cyberspace', in A. Crawford (ed.), *Crime and Insecurity*, Cullompton: Willan, 186–210.

Wall, D. S. (2002b) *DOT.CONS: Internet Related Frauds and Deceptions upon Individuals within the UK*, Final Report to the Home Office, March (unpublished).

Wall, D. S. (2003) 'Mapping out cybercrimes in a cyberspatial surveillant assemblage', in F. Webster and K. Ball (eds), *The Intensification of Surveillance: Crime Terrorism and Warfare in the Information Age*, London: Pluto Press, 112–36.

Wall, D. S. (2004) 'Policing Elvis: legal action and the shaping of post-mortem celebrity culture as contested space', *Entertainment Law*, 2 (3): 35–69 (published in 2004, journal dated 2003).

Wall, D. S. (2005a) 'The Internet as a conduit for criminals', in A. Pattavina (ed.), *Information Technology and The Criminal Justice System*, Thousand Oaks, CA: Sage, 77–98.

Wall, D. S. (2005b) 'Digital realism and the governance of spam as cyber-crime', *European Journal on Criminal Policy and Research*, 10 (4): 309–35.

Wall, D. S. (2006) 'Surveillant Internet technologies and the growth in infor-mation capitalism: spams and public trust in the information society', in K. Haggerty and R. Ericson (eds), *The New Politics of Surveillance and Visibility*, University of Toronto Press/ Oxford University Press.

Wall, D. S. (2007) 'Policing cybercrime: situating the public police in net-works of security in cyberspace', *Police Practice and Research: An International Journal*, 8 (1).

Wallace, J. and Mangan, M. (1996) *Sex, Laws and Cyberspace*, New York: Henry Holt.

Ward, M. (2005a) 'Key hacker magazine faces closure', *BBC News Online*, 9 July, at http://news.bbc.co.uk/1/hi/technology/4657265.stm.

Ward, M. (2005b) 'Home PC face security onslaught', *BBC News Online*, 12 August, at http://news.bbc.co.uk/1/hi/technology/4745053.stm.

Ward, M. (2006) 'Criminals exploit net phone calls', *BBC News Online*, 18 July, at http://news.bbc.co.uk/1/hi/technology/5187518.stm.

Warren, P. (2005) 'UK trojan siege has been running over a year', *The Register*, 17 June, at www.theregister.co.uk/2005/06/17/niscc_warning/.

Wasik, M. (2000) 'Hacking, viruses and fraud', in Y. Akdeniz, C. P. Walker and D. S. Wall (eds), *The Internet, Law and Society*, London: Longman, 272–93.

Weaver, N., Paxson, V., Staniford, S. and Cunningham, R. (2003) 'A taxon-omy of computer worms', paper given at the workshop on Rapid Malcode (WORM), at the Tenth ACM Conference on Computer and Communications Security, Washington DC, 27 October, at www.cs.berkeley.edu/~nweaver/papers/taxonomy.pdf.

Webroot (2005) *The State of Spyware, Q2*, Webroot Software Inc., October, at www.webroot.com/pdf/2005-q2-sos.pdf.

Webster, F. (2002) *Theories of the Information Society*, 2nd edn, London: Routledge.

Welsh, I. (2002) *Porno*, London: Vintage.

WHO (2004) *Report of Pre-eleventh ICDRA Satellite Workshop on Counterfeit Drugs*, Madrid, Spain, 13–14 February, at www.who.int/medicines/organization/qsm/activities/qualityassurance/cft/Pre-ICDRA_Counterfeit_report.pdf.

Wible, B. (2003) 'A site where hackers are welcome: using hack-in contests to shape preferences and deter computer crime', *Yale Law Journal*, 112: 1577.

Williams, K. (2004) 'Child pornography law: does it protect children?', *Journal of Social Welfare and Family Law*, 26 (3): 245–61.

Williams, M. (2001) 'The language of cybercrime', in D. S. Wall (ed.), *Crime and the Internet*, London: Routledge, 152–66.

Williams, M. (2003) 'Virtually criminal: deviance, harm and regulation within an online community', PhD thesis, University of Cardiff, UK.

Wilson, D., Patterson, A., Powell, G. and Hembury, R. (2006) 'Fraud and technology crimes: findings from the 2003/04 British Crime Survey, the 2004 Offending, Crime and Justice Survey and administrative sources', *Home Office Online Report 09/06*, at www.homeoffice.gov.uk/rds/pdfs06/rdsolr0906.pdf.

Wilson, J. Q. and Kelling, G. (1982) 'Broken windows', *Atlantic Monthly*, 249 (3): 29–38.

Wired (2003) 'Verizon must reveal song swappers', *Wired News*, 24 April, at www.wired.com/news/digiwood/0,1412,58620,00.html.

Wolfowitz, P. (2002) 'Prepared testimony to the Inquiry into 9/11', Joint House and Senate Select Intelligence Committee, 19 September.

Wood, J. (2004) 'Cultural change in the governance of security', *Policing and Society*, 14 (1): 31–48.

Wood, P. (2003) 'The convergence of viruses and spam: lessons learned from the SoBig.F experience', *MessageLabs White Paper*, at www.nframe.com/PDF/VirusSpam.pdf.

Wood, P. (2004) 'Spammer in the works: everything you need to know about protecting yourself and your business from the rising tide of unsolicited "spam" email', *A MessageLabs White Paper*, April 2004, at www.security.iia.net.au/downloads/spammer%20in%20works%20-%20an%20update%2014.5.pdf.

Wordtracker (2005) 'Top 500 search engine keywords of the week', *Wordtracker*, 3 May, at www.searchengineguide.com/wt/2005/0503_wt1.html.

WTO (2005) *United States — Measures affecting the cross-border supply of gambling and betting services, World Trade Organization*, AB-2005-1, Report of the Appellate Body, 7 April, at http://docsonline.wto.org/ DDF Documents/t/WT/DS/285ABR.doc.

Yar, M. (2005a) 'Computer hacking: just another case of juvenile delinquency?', *Howard Journal of Criminal Justice*, 44 (4): 387–99.

Yar, M. (2005b) 'The novelty of "cybercrime": an assessment in light of routine activity theory', *European Journal of Criminology*, 2: 407–27.

Yar, M. (2006) *Cybercrime and Society*, London: Sage.

Yaukey, J. (2001) 'Common sense can help you cope with spam', *USA Today*, 19 December, at www.usatoday.com/life/cyber/ccarch/2001/12/19/yaukey .htm.

Young, J. (1997), 'Left realism: the basics', in B. MacLean and D. Milovanovic (eds), *Thinking Critically About Crime*, Vancouver: Collective Press.

Young, L. F. (1995) 'United States computer crime laws, criminals and deterrence', *International Yearbook of Law, Computers and Technology*, 9: 1–16.

Youngs, I. (2005) 'Song sites face legal crackdown', *BBC News Online*, 9 December, at http://news.bbc.co.uk/1/hi/entertainment/4508158.stm.

Zittrain, J. (2003) 'Internet points of control', *Boston College Law Review*, 44 (2): 653–88.

Index